POSTMODERN SCHOOL LEADERSHIP

POSTMODERN SCHOOL LEADERSHIP

Meeting the Crisis in Educational Administration

Edited by **SPENCER J. MAXCY**

Westport, Connecticut
London

Library of Congress Cataloging-in-Publication Data

Postmodern school leadership : meeting the crisis in educational administration / edited by Spencer J. Maxcy.
    p. cm.
Includes bibliographical references (p.) and index.
ISBN 0-275-94565-0 (alk. paper)
1. Educational leadership—Social aspects—United States.
2. School management and organization—Social aspects—United States. 3. Educational change—United States. I. Maxcy, Spencer J.
LB2805.P733 1994
371.2'00973—dc20   93-2868

British Library Cataloguing in Publication Data is available.

Copyright © 1994 by Spencer J. Maxcy

All rights reserved. No portion of this book may be reproduced, by any process or technique, without the express written consent of the publisher.

Library of Congress Catalog Card Number: 93-2868
ISBN: 0-275-94565-0

First published in 1994

Praeger Publishers, 88 Post Road West, Westport, CT 06881
An imprint of Greenwood Publishing Group, Inc.

Printed in the United States of America

The paper used in this book complies with the Permanent Paper Standard issued by the National Information Standards Organization (Z39.48-1984).

10 9 8 7 6 5 4 3 2 1

This Book Is Dedicated in Memory of My Father,
Spencer Thomas Maxcy (1903-1993)
—Tool Maker and Machine Designer—

Contents

Acknowledgments ix

1. Introduction 1
   Spencer J. Maxcy

Part I: Postmodern Knowing

2. Social Relativism: A Postmodernist Epistemology for Educational Administration 17
   James Joseph Scheurich

3. One Postmodern Feminist Perspective on Educational Leadership: And Ain't I a Leader? 47
   Jackie M. Blount

4. A Postmodernist Analysis of Educational Administration 61
   Jon S. Davies and William Foster

Part II: Postmodern Processes

5. Postmodernism and Educational Leadership: The New and Improved Panopticon 71
   Joseph R. McKinney and James W. Garrison

6. Education Administration in a Postmodern Society: Implications for Moral Practice 85
   Charles J. Fazzaro, James E. Walter, and K. Kelly McKerrow

7. Qualitative Criticism 97
   James D. Swartz

Part III: Postmodern Organization

8. Educational Administration in the Postmodern Age 115
   Bill J. Johnston

9. Moral Leadership in a Poststructural Era 133
   Louis F. Miron and Richard J. Elliott

10. Reconceptualizing Higher Education Organizations 141
    Barbara Curry

    Afterword: Postmodern Directions in Educational Leadership 153
    Spencer J. Maxcy

    References 163

    Index 179

    Contributors 185

Acknowledgments

Edited books require the pooled resources of a broad range of people and organizations to be successful.

To each of the authors who have contributed to this book, I give an expression of thanks. I have come to respect the plural voices of this postmodern community of scholars more than they shall ever know.

Suggestions for the project were tested out with colleagues at several universities: Abbas Tashakkori, Wen-song Hwu, Bill Doll, and Bill Pinar at LSU; Jim Van Patten of the University of Arkansas; Sheryl Boutte at USL; Bob Slater of Texas A&M; Fenwick English of the University of Kentucky; Joseph Claudet of Texas Tech; and George Noblit at UNC-Chapel Hill. Talks with friends at meetings of the Southwest Philosophy of Education Society, Philosophy of Education Society, and American Educational Research Association provided additional focus and direction for the book. Thanks to Bill Stanley, Bob Donmoyer, Anthony Rud, Ron Reed, Nelda Cambron-McCabe, Jim Garrison, and Phil Smith for helpful suggestions and recommendations that enhanced the contributions to the present effort.

For careful reading of drafts and for long hours of inspiring dialogue at Highland Coffees, I wish to thank Doreen Maxcy.

My graduate students have tested much of what is in this book in "postmodern seminars." To Sue Roy, Gloria Nye, Sylvette Gunigundo, Marla Hudson, and Lynds Barr, I give my particular appreciation. I have been fortunate to have an ex-librarian, Sharon Roberts, as a graduate assistant.

Additionally, a debt of gratitude to Kofi Lomotey, Chairman of the Educational Administrative & Foundational Services Department at LSU, for his encouragement and support. I also wish to thank Ellen Albarado for her word processing,

Carol Eubanks for duplication, and Cyn D. Reynaud for smoothing the overall effort.

Finally, an expression of deep appreciation to Lynn Flint and Penny Sippel, my editors, for their patient encouragement and steady hands.

POSTMODERN
SCHOOL
LEADERSHIP

1

Introduction

Spencer J. Maxcy

Today, the leadership of American schools has collapsed in the face of crises on several fronts: Drugs, AIDS, delinquency and crime, parental disinterest, dropouts, interracial, cultural, and gender conflicts, and so on form a pattern of almost insurmountable problems. Efforts to use traditional rational and technical methods to solve these problems have failed. While these substantive problems resist solution, the *old roles and ways of thinking* beg for replacement. This book introduces a collection of chapters by scholars who suggest new "postmodern" and "poststructural" intellectual strategies for dealing with the social and cultural crises taking place in America as we approach the end of the twentieth century.

First, the role of administration in educational institutions in the United States has become suspect as the school leadership itself fails year after year to deliver on its promise of improving test scores, graduation rates, and access to the good society. Failure to satisfy its own norms of efficient and effective management of schools viewed as organizations, educational administration confronts the prospect of leaving the determination of the aims and goals and their successful accomplishment to outside forces such as business and industry. The school norms of Americans have been collapsed into the production-consciousness Americans have come to embrace on the heels of the rhetoric of competition with Japan, fostered first by government and political interests and then taken up into school management philosophy itself. The irony rests in the educational administrators valorizing the standards of competition and excellence, while repeatedly failing to achieve goals set by their own normative standards.

Next, educational administration theory is in turmoil. Structuralist/positivist theorists who had dominated the research and writing on organizational theory, educational management, and "leadership science" since World War II, reached a cul de sac in which the orgy of data gathering (under the rubric of "The Theory Movement") that was to generate more precise and sophisticated theories of how schools worked and would thus predict that practice fell fallow on a barren ground (Foster, 1986).

It is not surprising that educational administration has sought to "reach out and touch someone" for help. The first major acknowledgment that things were not going well for the rank and file school directors occurred in the fuller embrace of competition among themselves. School effectiveness thrusts pitted school manager against school manager in a battle that eroded the mystique of unlimited progress and generated the breakdown in the public perception that schools, at least in their administration, were fine.

Third, the field of educational administration faced a spate of criticism that sought to reunite the theoretically oriented field with actual school practice. Universities rewarding increasingly more rarified research had effectively cordoned off their best minds from real-life public schools with the result that the practical problems in such schools went understudied. The solution to the end of confidence in school administration was the admonition, coming from such significant groups as the Carnegie Foundation and University Council on Educational Administration (UCEA), for the reform of school administrator preparation programs. The rationale for these new administrator-training programs on the university level was built from a perception that leaders-to-be required emersion in the real world of public school administration. Hence, the programs provided more internships and clinical experiences, problem-centered course work, school-based administrator research projects, and, in some instances, programmatic shifts from Ph.D. to Ed.D. formats to increase the practical nature of their intent.

Standard scholarship in the field of school administration (governance of elementary and secondary schools, community colleges, and universities), since at least World War II, has depicted educational leadership through discourses reflecting a positivist and cultural conservative mindset that has largely defied critique. The scholarly literature, controlled by key groups in the field of educational administration, has persisted in telling the rank and file school managers how schools are to be run. The structuralist/modernist mentality has taken for granted the virtues of a structured, nondemocratic school site, as well as stressing the value of control and bureaucratic manipulations of children, teachers, and parents. It has followed from the acceptance of this structuralist/modernist metanarrative, with its assumptions regarding the nature of school culture and the superiority of a narrow band of so-called "scientific" methods of inquiry, that depictions of school administration have overemphasized the rational/technical and machine-like workings of the educational system, as well as the derivative and powerless status of teachers, parents, and children within its boundaries.

The research establishment in educational administration has also engaged in self-doubt. Qualitative research, not a home-grown reform, confronted educational administration researchers with new assumptions about the role of values and presuppositions regarding rational techniques, structures of schooling, and conclusion-oriented study. As varieties of positivism fell under critical scrutiny by social scientists and humanistic scholars, the "old guard" research establishment sought to circle the wagons.

These three breakdowns have set the stage for the large-scale rethinking of the role of leadership in education at all levels from preschool to university. One interesting platform that has emerged from which reformers are viewing the crises in educational administration is that of postmodernism. We may argue that schools, like other areas of our cultural life, are caught on the cusp of a new era, one between a modernist paradigm (characterized by professional values such as responsibility, mediative role, and concern for bottom-line results) and the postmodern pattern (with swift currents of institutional change marked by decentralization, pluralist demands from multiple voices, and school system redesign). While not solely derived from the emerging critique that is labeled "postmodernism" and/or "poststructuralism," these educational reform themes have come to dominate the research and popular literature in education. The chapters assembled in the present text seek to introduce the question: What does postmodern/poststructuralist theory have to say about educational leadership and the solution to school problems as America enters this new reform period?

Postmodernist thinkers have sought to challenge the modernist and structuralist characterizations of social institutions like schools. In this book a representative group of these scholars take on the topic of educational leadership with the goal of providing revealing avant garde perspectives on the nature of organizations, inquiry and knowledge, stability and change, and so forth as these bear on the administration of schools at all levels.

A HISTORY OF MODERNITY AND STRUCTURALISM

It is virtually impossible to understand the new postmodern views without understanding "structural" and "modern" as these relate to institutions. And, a grasp of the contemporary educational scene is required if we are to see how such poststructural/postmodern theorizing connects with these newer shifts in institutional configuration and purpose. Fortunately, there appears to be some consensus as to what "modernity" may mean. Emerging as a part of nation-building, modernist thinking aimed at extending the tasks of the Enlightenment (and in particular the philosophic agenda of Rene Descartes). Modernity entailed a penchant for rational and scientific method and stressed dichotomous characterizations of mind and body, thought and action, and observer and phenomenon. Modernity came to equal a deep faith in progress.

Cahoone (1988) defines modernism as "the ideas, principles and patterns of interpretation, of diverse kinds ranging from the philosophic to the economic, on which western and central European and American society and culture, from the sixteenth through the twentieth centuries, increasingly found itself based" (p. 1). The key concepts attached to modernity were democracy, the nation-state, science and the devotion to the scientific method, secularism, rationality, and humanism.

There is less agreement regarding the precise starting date for this modern era for all aspects of culture. Not all dimensions of culture embraced modernity at the same time in history. When we look at the art world, and in particular in the field of architecture for example, modernity erupted quite recently — some time in the twentieth century. However, in the realm of political economy, modernity started somewhere between 1600 and 1650 and was manifest in the rise of the nation-state.

Jürgen Habermas (1987) tells us a related term, "modernization," was introduced into our technical vocabulary as late as the 1950s. It was a theoretical approach that carried forward Max Weber's problem of universal history. However, it did enlarge on Weber's project via the tools of social-scientific functionalism. For Habermas, the concept of modernization refers to

a bundle of processes that are cumulative and mutually reinforcing: to the formation of capital and the mobilization of resources; to the development of the forces of production and the increase in the productivity of labor; to the establishment of centralized political power and the formation of national identities; to the proliferation of rights of political participation, of urban forms of life, and of formal schooling; to the secularization of values and norms; and so on. (p. 2)

School administration as a profession, seems particularly committed to modernization as Habermas has outlined it here.

It is important to note that it is not a foregone conclusion that either modernity or modernization are finished projects. Habermas in *The Philosophical Discourse of Modernity* (1987) argues that the modern project lies incomplete and the focus upon "postmodernity" is a misappropriation of the critical posture required for any rational project to continue. Christopher Norris (1990) rejects postmodernist theory *qua* theory, pointing to the vacancy created by the nihilism inherent in it. Modernity is neither complete nor is it out.

On the other hand, Richard Bernstein (1992) speaks of a "new constellation" of radical postmodern critiques on the horizon that have certain shared assumptions, commitments, and insights regarding the deficiencies of the modern era. He calls for "postmodern interventions" marked by critical distance and independent thought. This critique will witness individual and differing voices and will itself defy and resist any reduction to a single common core (1992, pp. 7–8).

The selected chapters in this text seem to reject, at least tacitly, the assumption advanced by Habermas that modernity is unfinished, while accepting Bernstein's proposal that postmodern interventions are indeed necessary for the reform of administration. Many of the authors of the chapters to follow will take on the question of whether or not modernity is terminal in their arguments.

A number of scholars prefer to work with the conceptual guidance of a new "poststructuralism," both a kind of subspecies of postmodernity as well as an independent phenomenon in research circles. Poststructuralism emerged in response to "structuralism," a family of theoretical views that share much with "modernism," but was derived from the work of French linguistic philosopher Ferdinand de Saussure and his followers. Saussure was relatively unknown until the 1950s and 1960s when his lectures, published posthumously as the *Course in General Linguistics* (1916; 1966), were revived. His writings established the notion that language was a structured system of signs. Rather than study the logic of these signs, Saussure proposed that the signs formed a structure and could be studied scientifically. Language had an abstract structure (*langue*) as well as concrete speech manifestations (*parole*); but unlike his predecessors, Saussure believed that the rules of language underwrote speech games. Language as a structured system of signs expresses ideas for convenience, more than for truth. Signs like "man" were arbitrary "signifiers," for the things they stood for (the "signifieds"). The three letter word *man* could be *mensch* in another sign system (German). Most importantly, it is the relationships among the different elements of a sign system or language that constitute the signs. Saussure's version of structuralism was built upon the study of signs; a science he called "semiology."

Claude Levi-Strauss moved the structuralist project into anthropology to embrace culture. Essentially, he took Saussure's structuralism to reveal the fact that language was the most distinctive feature of the human species. While other philosophers (notably Ernst Cassirer) had arrived at the insight that symbol creation marked humans as special, Levi-Strauss focused on primitive societies and sought to uncover how the cultures expressed their sign systems. Once these features were located, the anthropologist would have depictions as to how the rules operated in the culture. Myth proved a certain fascination for Levi-Strauss. In his book *Le cru et le cuit, mythologiques* (1964), he was able to demonstrate the fact that there were certain unconscious mental structures that expressed themselves through myth. Moreover, he recognized within these structures key binary oppositions, such as raw and cooked, hot and cold, which resurfaced in myth after myth and from culture to culture. Myths expressed a priori structures that predispose humans to speak and act in certain ways. These embedded "codes" in language and culture predetermined human thought and action. Structural anthropology found structures made humankind, not the other way around.

Intellectuals gravitated to structuralism and applied its methods to the disciplined study of a variety of phenomena. Roland Barthes (1972; 1976) examined the sign systems that occurred in literary texts and argued that reality was a form of narrative. Jacques Lacan (1977) applied structuralism to psychoanalysis. Michel Foucault, an historian of ideas, developed a branch of structuralism in the late 1960s and early 1970s that centered on the changes in institutional discourse and how this impacted on the lives of human beings over time. His book *The Order of Things* (1973) revolutionized the study of culture history. However, Foucault also disliked the term "structuralist" and refused to be linked to the movement. His antipathy to grand theory and metanarrative found him embracing the "poststructuralist" agenda as he rose in scholarly prominence. And,

Foucault, with his concern for power and the manner in which it worked in complex social phenomena, led many out of the structuralist school to the higher ground of poststructuralism.

At the heart of structuralism was the unanswered question of human freedom. The implicit structures were deterministic and human beings were seen as merely slaves to the force emanating from these patterns. Myths and folktales became rich indicators of sublimely rational beliefs that were perpetuated over time. Primitive man became a kind of "homo naturales," unknowingly practicing rituals and speaking profundities. Assumed (in the sense of taken for granted) were large-scale patterns that revealed themselves only through synchronic and dyachronic cross-cultural investigations. The research agenda pointed to replicated studies of narratives and practices that traced binary relations cross-culturally and over time. Lost was the free-spirited individual.

The primary problems of structuralism were (1) its conception of the human subject as unimportant viz the territory of signs, (2) the collapse of identity into meaning, (3) the notion that history is a stand-alone process that can be queried, and (4) the elevation of reason over all.

The bearings of modernism and structuralism on educational administration and leadership theory were pervasive. Educational researchers sought to engage in efforts to determine through technically precise, "scientific" means administrator tasks and impacts on school, teacher, and student dependent variables. To trace variables across the playing field of human behavior was to assume the privileged eye of the rational observer and to sanitize the participants and settings.

In the real world of schooling "school executives" came to act as if they were controlling, managing, and implementing effective, efficient means for producing educational outcomes in the form of higher standardized test scores, greater teacher accountability, and so forth. The "enlightenment ideal," dualistic to the core, of the rational controller versus the culture of the school comes to be played out in the research literature on school principals and superintendents, supervisors and evaluators.

POSTMODERNITY AND POSTSTRUCTURALISM

Postmodernism

Postmodernism came on the scene first as an artistic and literary movement, but later it moved to the arena of a general cultural and political critique of modernism/structuralism. Poststructuralism, on the other hand, has operated both as a subspecies of postmodernity as well as carving out, in the hands of some theorists, a quite narrow reconstruction of scientific discourse. To compound the confusion, "postmodernity" and "poststructuralism" are frequently used interchangeably. Finally, since theoretical orientations rarely remain static, poststructuralist theorizing is tending toward greater specificity, with differences in the two domains becoming discernable and significant.

In the chapters to follow, the reader will see poststructural and postmodern used to describe educational leadership and educational administrative revision and transformation. This practice mirrors the essentially open texture of critique as it reacts to modernism/structuralism, and the freshness of the postmodern and poststructural theorizing.

As we have seen, the precise dating of the collapse of modernity has generated controversy. It is not possible to say that "naturalistic inquiry," "critical pragmatism," or any other particular strategies have laid structuralism to rest. When we witness the break-up of Soviet Russia into separate sovereign states with their own culture, language, and national will, there seems to be some evidence for modernism's end. On the other hand, science and its handmaiden technology seem to linger as the penultimate means for determining truth; this despite the crystal-waving savants of the New Age. There is a paradox at work here. While some of modernity's rapture has waned, we still find solace in the values of the modern age. Toulmin (1990) tells us that "modern" has taken on the meaning of the newest or latest in cultural fashions. In this sense, the modern is always at the forefront and will never recede into the past. Postmodernity, therefore, must be a break with this succession of moderns. But this is a tall order, for as Toulmin tells us, to be postmodern we must be critical, novel, and creative, without being Kantian or Cartesian, trendy, trivial, or accidental.

Jean-François Lyotard focused Western interest on postmodernity with his text *The Postmodern Condition: A Report on Knowledge* (1984). An interest among scholars in bringing philosophy to bear on culture, critically examining modernity and its assumptions, and deciphering the legitimacy of modernist tradition led to the formation of new "postmodern" discourses/practices. Theorists have attempted to move beyond Descartes and Kant and their legacy. To this end, a new interest in the works of Friedreich Nietzsche, John Dewey, Alfred Whitehead, Martin Heidegger, and Ludwig Wittgenstein has surfaced. These thinkers, more than others, represent the virtues of nonfoundational and pluralistic thought.

Certainly, the term postmodern is not free from ambiguity and contradiction. One must be on one's toes to protect against jingoism. There appear to be at least three strong candidates for meaning here: (1) postmodern in the sense of a populist attack upon elitism found in modernism; (2) postmodern as a critical deconstruction of and resistance to modernity; and finally (3) postmodern in the sense of neo-conservative antimodernism (H. Foster, 1983, ix–xxi). Viewed from the standpoint of postmodernism and education, the second meaning seems most fruitful. This meaning of postmodernism stresses resistance and

arises as a counter-practice not *only* to the official culture of modernism but also to the "false normativity" of a reactionary postmodernism. In opposition (but only in opposition) a resistant postmodernism is concerned with a critical deconstructionism of tradition, not an instrumental pastiche of pop- or pseudo-historical forms, with a critique of origins, not a return to them. In short, it seeks to question rather than exploit cultural codes, to explore rather than conceal social and political affiliations. (H. Foster, 1983, p. xxi)

Foster's postmodernism of resistance and critique offers much for the reconstitution of educational leadership as we move toward the *fin de siècle*.

Poststructuralism

Poststructuralism is a movement that emerged in the late 1960s, had an essentially antistructuralist mentality, and was an emerging literary critique of French theoreticians and their work in the fields of anthropology, literature, and philosophy. Whereas structuralism was antihumanist, believing that human beings were unable to solve their own structure-induced problems, poststructuralists adopted a decidedly humanist view.

Viewed from a political science perspective, poststructuralists reacted to political conservativism, centrality of state, and de-emphasis on human rights associated with the post–World War II era. Poststructuralism, to differentiate it from simple "antipositivism," sought to provide a means of characterizing human experiences without reducing these claims to a logic of "independent-dependent variables" (the so-called "scientific method"). In the sciences, structuralism was critiqued by Thomas Kuhn in his book *The Structures of Scientific Revolutions* (1962). Kuhn depicted the mechanism by which changes in scientific belief occurred as largely a matter of a paradigm shift, rather than the emergence of some more significant "truth." Although not a radical relativist, Kuhn's arguments were popularly read as explanation and justification for divergent belief systems arising out of sociocultural pressures for conformity. Thus, unlike Saussure and Levi-Strauss who believed the rules or sign system was an embedded mental structure, Kuhn suggested that humans made and broke the rules as they went along.

Jacques Derrida (1982) adopted a unique strategy of attempting to "deconstruct" the structures that the structuralists seemingly discovered through their semiological sciences. Rather than speak of signs being set in place by speakers, Derrida argued that signs were arbitrary and their meanings endlessly deferred. It was a myth to believe that a signifier and a signified would ever be characterized once and for all. In addition, he found structuralists embracing dualisms of the most dangerous kind: conscious and unconscious, inside and outside, and so on. Since meanings were not fixed, Derrida set about in playful ways to show the tricks performed by speakers. He demonstrated how we privilege some terms and suppress others in our speech and writing. Moreover, he advanced the sublime notion that the subject, as a privileged observer, was a nonentity. Neither writer intention nor observer observation was sacred in Derrida's scheme. We are in the business of marginalizing and excluding as we seek to characterize and describe. "Which is legitimate?" becomes the burning issue.

Poststructuralist Hans-Georg Gadamer (1985) moved the critique further when he proposed that the notion that humans could arrive at "truth" through the means of such a young discipline as "science," was absurd. Hermeneutics was far older a study and would yield not truth, but *understanding,* he argued. However, while

Gadamer's version of poststructuralism is fruitful for the teacher in the classroom, it is not evident that his techniques will help in dealing with the political and moral/ethical dimensions of school leadership. More is required.

APPLICATIONS OF POSTMODERNISM/POSTSTRUCTURALISM TO CONTEMPORARY CRISES IN EDUCATIONAL ADMINISTRATION

When we shift our lens to the American cultural scene, few intellectuals have moved to embrace postmodernism/poststructuralism. Two exceptions are Richard Rorty (1991) and Richard Bernstein (1983; 1992). They have popularized in the United States the new genre of philosophical discourse/practice, operating under the terms "postmodernism" and "poststructuralism." Rorty calls for the end of epistemology and proposes a search for "edifying discourse." Bernstein moves "beyond objectivism and relativism" to a nonfoundational, pragmatic, and humanist view of cultural and social praxis.

Much earlier, the educational philosophy of John Dewey (1934) embraced the tenets of postmodernity/poststructuralism when he sought to challenge the modernist assumption that there was a foundational discourse/practice. For Dewey, dualisms were something to be attacked and shown up for what they were: artificial poles in the rationalist kit bag. And, Dewey's emphasis on experience as the unifying theme around which all else be bound took him into the postmodern/poststructural camp albeit decades before these labels became popular.

Today, in curriculum theory, Cleo Cherryholmes pays homage to Dewey in his work *Power and Criticism* (1988). He fuses critical theory, hermeneutics, and pragmatism into a poststructural critique and solution of the problems encountered in curriculum, teaching, and research.

In the field of educational administration, the first postmodern/poststructural essays were penned by Thomas B. Greenfield (1973; 1975). He led the poststructural attack on positivist assumptions underwriting administration "science." William P. Foster (a co-author of one of the chapters in this book) centered the critique by calling for a critical theory approach in his *Paradigms and Promises: New Approaches to Educational Administration* (1986). Australian Richard Bates (1990) provides a poststructural account of leadership and educational administrative reform. My own text, *Educational Leadership: A Critical Pragmatic Perspective* (Maxcy, 1991) offers a postmodern/poststructural dissection of "leadership" in schools.

The postmodern "critical administration" movement—if it is possible to speak of this loosely affiliated set of new administration theorists as forming a movement—challenges the traditional emphases in educational administration research. Rather than take for granted the simple derivation of administrative science from positivist social science, the postmodern administration theorists draw on new philosophy, literary theory, qualitative research methods, and other nontraditional intellectual backings. Educational administration, viewed from this *metastructural* perspective, is informed by a wider variety of disciplines than the earlier structuralist narrative and will be more aesthetic than strictly scientific. However, the concern for judgment and choice is not overlooked, and we see poststructuralist writers, like those in this text, focusing on new, more edifying discourses/practices.

In the pages that follow we shall examine a sample of the writing of some of the poststructural scholars working in the field of educational administration as they address the problems of educational governance. The themes explored range from educational inquiry to the actual restructuring of schools. These chapters will raise questions regarding the moral and ethical dimensions of school leadership, as well as the nature of empowerment in school redesign. The chapters address all levels of administration from elementary school to university. The pieces assembled here are remarkable for their shared commitment to the importance of thinking more critically and with greater concern for the educationally driven future we shall all inhabit. What is apparent from the pieces is the discovered need and importance of a set of new administrative perspectives/interventions. Educational administration research and publication has been traditional, conservative, and naive: Postmodernist critique reveals this fact while pointing to normative moves that may correct and improve administrative theory and practice. The essays develop an understanding of contemporary changes in schools as well as point the way to a new postmodern "critical administration."

THE ARRANGEMENT OF THE TEXT

The chapters in this text are clustered in three parts: postmodern knowing, postmodern processes, and postmodern organization. Collectively, these chapters move the reader from the critique of modernist/structuralist epistemology, processes, and organization to radically new, emancipated reflection and understanding of leadership and the educational administrative crises.

Postmodern Knowing

James Joseph Scheurich's chapter is grand in scale and profound in its implications. Professor Scheurich proposes we adopt a "postmodern or social relativism." While the author acknowledges "scientific realism" to be the best effort to date to move beyond positivism, he finds his own social relativism more adequate for the purposes of inquiring into educational matters. In carefully constructed arguments, criticisms of social relativism are set out for our consideration and then refuted. "Postfoundational" or pragmatic alternatives to social relativism are also interrogated and revealed to be inadequate to the task of furthering educational inquiry. Strongly influenced by Michel Foucault's writings, Scheurich argues that epistemology or "truth games" are located in diverse and shifting historical discourses/practices: Truth game enactments are, finally, political or ethical enactments.

Jackie M. Blount's chapter offers a feminist analysis of educational leadership. Identifying the difficulties in "essentialist feminist" arguments, she launches a postmodern feminist vision that recognizes the theoretical tools available, as well as the political necessity of social critique and political action to remove oppression. Traditional research perspectives on educational leadership are revealed to be biased relative to gender. Business and professional groups slant leadership characterization, the academic community exercises its power over the picture depicted of educational leadership, and university school administrator training programs have perpetuated skewed and elliptical versions of leading. Ms. Blount displays the problems of a gendered and hierarchical leading and asks of us that we listen to the heretofore "unheard voices" of leadership.

Jon S. Davies and William Foster examine university educational administration preparation programs in chapter 4. They argue (1) such university programs in educational administration present a received "text" that is essentialist (modernist) in nature; (2) this text is tied to certain conceptions of power, resources, legitimacy, and status; and (3) new educational administrator preparation curricula ought to be informed by a critically pragmatic postmodernism.

The authors delineate the essentialist foundations of educational administrator preparation in the United States and then each assumption in this modernist pattern is tested against postmodern criteria. Davies and Foster unmask the assumptions that: research will generate theories; time-tested concepts explain administrator behavior; competing frameworks or perspectives play no role; and the essentialist model reifies concepts, such as leadership. The adequacy of the popular programs in administrator training are challenged through an interrogation of each of these assumptions.

Davies and Foster find educational administrators have impact primarily through their personal influence and not owing to any essentialist foundational knowledge of the field. The role of power in the text of educational administration is highlighted and a critical pragmatic posture advocated.

Postmodern Processes

After tracing the first two waves of educational reform in the last decade, with wave one stressing accountability and wave two introducing teacher empowerment, Joseph R. McKinney and James W. Garrison ask, "What may wave three offer that is truly alternative in educational administration?" in chapter 5.

McKinney and Garrison suggest that postmodernists/poststructuralists take a serious look at the traditional technocratic discourse/practice in education. Schools in chaos have not reacted well to rational choice models. The authors suggest adaption of the "garbage-can" model of decision making to replace the rational choice approach. Here decisions are set in context and are not deemed longitudinal and logically derived. Choices are taken to be made by resolution, dissolution, flight, and oversight.

After choice is radically postmodernized, power is reconceptualized drawing on Foucault's work and his use of the "panopticon" prison of Jeremy Bentham's design. Since the self is historically, socially, and linguistically derived, the panopticon is an excellent illustration of how the modern self came to be defined. McKinney and Garrison demonstrate that the individuals in the modern school are subject to the same technology of power in which surveillance, observation, and comparison are used to guide and control prisoners.

"Technocratic education" is traced historically in chapter 5 to its roots in E. L. Thorndike's philosophy and is offered as a particular illustration of this effort to exercise power over individuals via testing and Frederick Taylor's "scientific management" as it found expression through Franklin Bobbitt's work.

The authors are led to conclude that the third wave of reform as it embraces postmodern thinking and addresses administration in the schools ought to explore alternative modes of decision making and power wielding.

Charles J. Fazzaro, James E. Walter, and K. Kelly McKerrow critique the ideology of "techno-science" as this has impacted schools and school administration in chapter 6. Arguing that the two domains of "knowing" and "recommending" are based on values, they propose that public education policies have raised technical knowledge (process knowing of science aimed at true/false) above that of normative knowledge (just/unjust). The version of technical knowledge dominating educational thinking has taken on the epithet "structuralism."

In the techno-language of structuralism, the individual person is submerged under the organization; the status quo is preserved; a technical language game is elevated above talk of morals and ethics; performativity becomes the means of legitimizing; and educational leadership is turned into "scientific management." Social institutions come to control through language the very people who compose them. The authors turn to postmodernism/poststructuralism as it attacks and rejects this totalizing structuralist view with its supposed objectivity and quantifiablility.

The postmodern solution to the question, "What shall replace the technological language of structuralism?" is, according to Fazzaro, Walter, and McKerrow, a moral/ethical discourse/practice that seeks to impact both public schooling and the private conscience of administrators. The skeleton of this new language is laid out and the authors argue for a core curriculum based on *meanings* rather than technical knowledge. This core is to include personal knowledge (synnoetics); history, religion, and philosophy (synoptics); and knowledge of good/bad, right/wrong (ethics).

James D. Swartz takes on the postmodern task of fusing qualitative research and critique to develop "qualitative criticism" as educational decision-making in chapter 7. Swartz draws on the ideas of George Herbert Mead and Richard Rorty as he counters such naive modernist conceptions as "objectivity" and "individualism," to posit a new vision of the individual as artist in educational organizational life. Swartz's qualitative criticism entails five axioms: reality seen as multiple, constructed, and holistic; knower and known as interactive, inseparable; working hypotheses time and context bound; mutual simultaneous shaping (no causes no effects); and, inquiry as to what is value bound. Engaging in qualitative criticism will enrich both the community and the knowledge base and lead to a new critical administrative praxis, we are told.

Postmodern Organization

In chapter 8, Bill J. Johnston tells us that new goals for educational organizations require change in organizational structure: This is the central problematic he reasons. Postmodernity is defined and its fruitfulness set forth. He concludes on the postmodern recommendation that schools be seen as texts in which teacher/administrative narratives are written.

Louis F. Miron and Richard J. Elliott find in poststructural theory a warrant for a new "moral leadership" for education in chapter 9. The authors caution us regarding current school reform efforts, reject the flawed features of structuralist and modernist conceptions of school administration, critique and rebuild the concept of power in organization, and call for a new poststructural leadership in education. At the heart of their project is a rejection of modernist/structuralist efforts to make administrators into "instructional leaders," and to shift to "school based management/shared decision making," or both. The authors favor a poststructuralist reconsideration of the role of persons. Moral power is set to yield a true, "transformative school leadership."

Barbara Curry moves our discourse on postmodernism and leadership to the field of higher education and the problematic of institutional change (chapter 10). She calls for a reconceptualization of the academy as a "learning organization," consultative in nature and cycling toward adaptation and innovation. Paying attention to the narratives of constituents in the academy will result in a new malleability, reforming higher education along emerging lines of social concern.

A final caution is in order: The following chapters lie mid-way between the traditional framework that has guided administrative thought and practice for nearly 100 years, and a new paradigm that simultaneously challenges the old and suggests novel approaches to educational orchestration. Postmodernist in spirit, the views expressed here are neither ideological nor dogmatic. Suggestive, open-textured, and fresh vision provided here encourage the reader to appreciate both the unfamiliar and the less-traveled in this landscape of an emerging critical administration.

PART I
Postmodern Knowing

2
Social Relativism: A Postmodernist Epistemology for Educational Administration

James Joseph Scheurich

> How far the perspective character of existence extends or indeed whether existence has any other character than this; whether existence without interpretation, without "sense," does not become "nonsense," whether, on the other hand, all existence is not essentially an interpreting existence—that cannot be decided even by the most industrious and most scrupulously conscientious analysis and self-examination of the intellect; for in the course of this analysis the human intellect cannot avoid seeing itself in its own perspective forms, and only in these. We cannot look around our own corner.
> —Nietzsche, quoted in Spivak, 1976

EPISTEMOLOGY: AN INTRODUCTION

Epistemology is the study of how we know or what the rules for knowing are.[1] From my perspective how I see (my epistemology) must precede what I see (my ontology), because how I see shapes, frames, determines, and even creates what I see.[2] This description, however, could not be said to be accurate for all epistemological positions. Positivism, for instance, has attempted to derive rigorous "scientific" rules for creating a one-to-one correspondence between what "reality" is and how it is represented in research so that the representation is untainted by researcher bias or the ambiguity of language, among other possible threats to claims of validity. From the positivist perspective, then, how knowing is accomplished does not shape, frame, determine, or create what is known; the positivist epistemology claims to mirror reality.[3] This position, according to Foucault (1977) assumes "an eye whose entire substance is nothing but the transparency of its vision" (p. 45).

For positivists the rules for knowing (the positivist epistemology) guarantee or warrant the fact that the research representations of reality truly re-present reality. If the researcher follows the positivist rules, the results are certified to represent reality accurately. Very few epistemologists think that the positivists succeeded in developing such rules: "all of the main forms of positivism are now regarded as false, their key tenets clearly refuted" (Evers & Lakomski, 1991, p. viii).[4] As Minh-ha (1989) asserts, "There is no such thing as a 'coming face to face once and for all with objects'; the real remains foreclosed from the analytic experience" (p. 76). Popper, however, as a friend and critic of the Vienna Circle put it most succinctly, "Everybody knows nowadays that logical positivism is dead" (quoted in Culbertson, 1988, p. 18).

Polkinghorne (1983), though his epistemological target is more encompassing, contends that "the logical-empirical philosophy of science . . . has failed to hold up under continued self-examination" (p. x). In fact, it could reasonably be argued that, as implied by Polkinghorne with his use of the word "self-examination," much of the contemporary ferment in epistemology derives directly from the questioning of the positivist rules by the positivists themselves and their successors. Rorty (1979), for example, has argued that the analytic philosophers of England and the United States, who in many ways could be said to be in the positivist tradition, have played a major role in undermining their own tradition. Wittgenstein would later be the most well-known example of this tradition that was turning against itself.

REALISM

Though positivism is now seen as a failed attempt to create rigorous scientific rules for mirroring reality,[5] most social science research, including that in education, continues to take place within the general parameters derived from positivism, though largely without the almost fanatical logical purity sought by positivists. Social science researchers who want to retain the scientific method could be said to have returned, at least in terms of epistemology, to the general scientific frame that in many ways preceded the positivist heresy (e.g., John Stuart Mill). Currently, realism has generally been divided into two groups—naive realists and scientific realists.

The most commonly practiced of these two epistemologies is labeled naive realism (Mishler, 1991), a somewhat unfair though also fairly accurate label. The overwhelming preponderance of research in education administration and in education in general, as in many other social and psychological science disciplines, is of this type. This perspective assumes that conventional social science research methods unproblematically insure accurate or valid representations of reality. It thus proceeds unreflexively as if the perspective of the researcher has no effect on what is seen. Accordingly, most of the scholarly work in education pays little, if any, attention to its epistemological assumptions.[6]

As an unselfconscious stepchild of positivism, naive realism assumes that the "seen" or "researched" world is reasonably transparent to conventional consciousness or, at least, to a consciousness trained in conventional social science research methods. For this transparency to exist the mind of the conventional researcher must be in a virtual one-to-one correspondence of understanding to "the world." That is, what the researcher thinks she or he sees accurately reflects that which the researcher is looking at in the world. In addition, the researcher assumes that the language used to represent the world in the linguistic presentation of the research is not so ambiguous that meaning becomes problematic.[7]

The second group of realists, whom I have labeled scientific realists, is itself divided into smaller subgroups under labels such as neorealism, scientific realism, coherentist realism, or critical realism, each of which is somewhat different from but mainly similar to the others. The entire group is much more sophisticated or reflective in terms of the numerous epistemological problems that have been raised against positivism. Indeed, this second group has tried to adjust the epistemology of science in terms of the criticisms that have been made of positivism so that the orthodox scientific method, albeit through a realist reconstruction, remains defensible as the preferred method of research.

The differences between the two groups of realists are fairly obvious. If, for instance, in studying a classroom a researcher assumes that the facts she or he "sees" are unproblematically "there" in the world without reference to any particular theoretical perspective, this researcher is a naive realist.

Scientific realists, however, recognize that, even in the natural sciences, facts are always theory-laden because "something" can only become a fact due to the theory that makes it recognizable as a fact. Naive realism, which is certainly incorrect, must be distinguished from the scientific brand. Naive realists, when viewing a lemon, for example, hold that the observed object is really what it appears (yellow), without benefit of any theoretical mediation. The scientific realist, on the other hand, believes that the lemon appears yellow because of the way light waves refract off its surface, the particular structure and nature of the human eye, and so on. Perceptions thus invoke the causal entities and the structures that produce the phenomenon of what we term "yellow lemon." Thus, the analysis of the process does not halt with the events occurring on the surface of the object, but goes deeper, into the underlying schemes and proclivities (House, 1991, p. 4).

When it comes to describing events in a research setting, more often than not naive realists assume that what you see is what you get. When they look at a classroom they are unaware that what they see, what they pick out as facts, are theory or perspective dependent. Different theories yield different facts: whereas one researcher may see yellow in a classroom, another researcher, looking at the same classroom as the first, may see red. Scientific realism recognizes the theory dependency of facts. Our world comes to be known through particular descriptions or theories. Theory in this scientific view never mirrors reality as a naive realist might typically claim (House, 1991, p. 4).

Another criticism that scientific realists have of naive realism is the latter's view of causation. The naive realists, House (1991) tells us, assume a view of causation that is derived from the philosophers David Hume, John Stuart Mill, and Bertrand Russell. Within this view the classic example is that of one billiard ball striking another. House (1991) depicts this phenomenon as a "flat ontology" in which there is a flow of events and experiences such that our observations produce regular patterns. The goal of science is to locate these regularities in the flat configurations. The problem with the naive realist conception of causality, according to the scientific realists, is that their primitive understanding of causation sees social reality in an analogously simple way. In contrast, a realist's view of cause takes events as the product of the interaction of a large number of underlying causal entities operating at many levels (House, 1991, pp. 5–7).

As an example of the difference between naive and scientific realist conceptions of cause, House (1991) cites the evaluation of planned change. In the naive realist view, an evaluation of the same reform applied in several sites would expect the same result at each site. In other words, the naive realists have a traditional experimentalist orientation toward evaluation. But scientific realists, assuming that like causal features do not necessarily produce like results, would take a different approach as they viewed different sites or contexts (House, 1991, p. 7). Scientific realist program evaluators would accept the assumption that the program being evaluated would differ from site to site owing to the fact that the multiple factors yielding the program would differ. Different teachers and students, for example, would impact upon the program differently in the different settings. The program may not be conceived of as a set entity, or the x in a design, but as varying from site to site as it came to be implemented. And beyond this, the same program could yield differing results owing to the complex interactions of all the various patterned events that impact the results derived (House, 1991, p. 7).

Scientific realists would have very different expectations with regard to program evaluation. The conception of causation shared by scientific realists prompt an approach to evaluation that anticipates and seeks to chart the variability and irregularities in patterns of events. Programs can thus be characterized by their influences, causes, and interactions; and these traced to outcomes. For the scientific realist, inferences may be drawn from experiments (with the aid of substantive information) but never produce the critical tests of the program, as the naive realist would believe (House, 1991, p. 8).

Thus, while naive realists see evaluation as similar to a traditional experiment that tests the effects of a specific reform at different sites, scientific realists see a multisite evaluation as tracking and explaining differences that are not comparable in an experimental sense.

Scientific realists have several other criticisms of naive realists that I will not address here. For those who want to pursue a more thorough understanding of scientific realism, the House (1991) article and its references are a good beginning. Another good example, though much different in the approach taken and in the references cited, is Evers and Lakomski's *Knowing Educational Administra-*

tion (1991). Chapters 1, 2, and 10 of this work are more specifically focused on epistemological issues, while the other seven chapters apply scientific realism to the theory debates in educational administration.

Simply put, from the scientific realist perspective the world and our judgments about it are substantially more complex and problematic than the naive realist view usually assumes. Indeed, in my opinion, epistemological judgments of the nature of reality are more problematic than even the scientific realists assume. As Greenfield (1978) has said, "The relationship between explanation and reality is *at best* [emphasis added] uncertain" (p. 19). The next section will address my point of view on this issue.

SOCIAL RELATIVISM

While I agree that the scientific realists have made the best attempt to date to reconstruct the scientific method in the face of the broad array of criticisms that have been made of positivism by both the positivists themselves (Phillips, 1983) and various postpositivists, including Popper, Toulmin, Kuhn, and Feyerabend, I find their perspective to be inadequate. Instead of any version of realism for the social sciences, I would support what I call social or postmodernist relativism, even though relativism is, as Barnes and Bloor (1991) have said, "everywhere abominated" (p. 21). (See also, Donmoyer, 1985; Bernstein, 1988; Harding, 1991; Lather, 1991b; and Phillips, 1983 among numerous others who oppose relativism.)

What I mean by this term "social or postmodernist relativism"[8] is the unabashed recognition that all epistemology, ontology, and the ways of thinking that yield such categories as epistemology and ontology are socially conditioned and historically relative or contextual.[9] More simply, "ways of knowing are inherently culture-bound and perspectival" (Lather, 1988, p. 570). This is the same point that Habermas makes in *Knowledge and Human Interests* (1971) when he says:

> the interpreter cannot abstractly free himself from his hermeneutic point of departure. He cannot simply jump over the open horizon of his own life activity and just suspend the context of tradition in which his own subjectivity has been formed in order to submerge himself in a subhistorical stream of life that allows the pleasurable identification of everyone with everyone else. (p. 181)

Foucault (1977) makes a similar point in his essay "Nietzsche, Genealogy, History." In this work he criticizes historians who write history as if they write from outside of history; instead Foucault praises Nietzsche's embrace of his own perspectival positionality. Similarly, in this study I criticize social scientists who do science as if they work from outside of their own historical positionality; instead I praise the embrace of the relativity of the social scientists' positionality.[10]

By the word "social," I intend to signal that this postmodernist version of relativism is not "anything goes," because there are always social and historical constraints on what is allowed, though what is allowed is always open to challenge and change. I also intend to signal that this postmodernist relativism is social and not individual. Although there are individual perspectives based on the idiosyncratic differences among individuals, the "stuff" with which individuals construct and interpret "reality" and are constructed and interpreted by "reality" is social and not individual.

This social relativism flies in the face of any positivist or realist efforts to develop foundational or ahistorical truths or truth claims: "paradigms and language games—to borrow from Kuhn and Wittgenstein—have been relativized" (Apple, 1991, p. vii). This position also undermines seemingly postfoundational efforts to establish some kind of criteria, standards, procedures, decision rules, or rationality that rises above the relativity of history. Both truth and any kind of postfoundational metacriteria for establishing truth are, in my view, socially relative to a particular time and place. Even though in that particular time and place there may be a variety of truths competing with one another and even though there will be many possible truths or truth methods that are not allowed in that particular time and place, both the competing truths and the excluded truths are socially and historically located.

For instance, currently positivism, realism, critical theory, feminism, interpretivism, constructivism, and poststructuralism, among others, are all competing within the Western social sciences to name truth (or, as with some deconstructionists, to leave truth nameless). There are other truth games, such as fundamentalist Christianity, Tibetan Buddhism, or even earlier versions of science, which are not allowed within the social sciences. This does not mean that these or other alternatives are not viable possibilities for the social sciences, but only that they are outside the current, socially defined boundaries of what is considered valid approaches to the generation of knowledge. It also does not mean that the alternatives that I have named or other unrecognized possibilities will not in the future become allowable.

Social or postmodernist relativism, thus, accepts that there are social and historical constraints on what can be claimed as truth, or whatever other word we use to designate knowledge, in any particular social and historical location. It does not accept, however, that such social and historical constraints cannot be questioned or altered. While the acceptance of such social and historical constraints may at first appear conservative, it is in fact the opposite. It specifically locates where the struggle for truth or knowledge occurs. Truth is a social, historical, and, therefore, political struggle. Truth is not power-free; it is powerladen. "Discourse and politics, knowledge and power are . . . part of an indissoluble couplet" (Apple, 1991, p. vii). "Power and knowledge directly imply one another" (Foucault, 1979, p. 27). In the sense that this social relativist epistemology uncovers the truth–power relationship, it is radical rather than conservative: "to politicize [knowledge production] means not to bring politics in where there were none, but to make overt how power permeates the construction and legitimation of knowledges" (Lather, 1991b, p. xvii).

The struggle for truth is a struggle for power because different truth games establish different relations between people or, as Foucault (1977) would say, between different "constellation[s] of bodies" (p. 39).[11] For example, Habermas in *Knowledge and Human Interests* (1971; 1972) claims that the application of the positivist truth game to social issues inappropriately removes social decisions from the democratic community to the small, select community of truth game experts. It could also be argued, as Foster (1986) has done, that one of the reasons positivism and its sociological ally, functionalism, have been so dominant in the social sciences is that the advocates of positivism and functionalism have claimed to be value-free and apolitical. Positivists and functionalists could then avoid addressing the inequitable arrangements of power within which they worked.

Truth games, however, always imply, in my view, how people are arranged in relation to each other—different truth games, different relations. Another way of saying the same thing is that all truth games are political.[12] All truth games imply political arrangements, though what those political arrangements are for a particular truth game is itself open to argument. Habermas (1971; 1972), for example, argued for a more democratic truth game than the scientific one he saw dominating the West. Others (Antonio, 1989, or Bernstein, 1988, for example) have contended that Habermas' truth game has an inherently elitist basis because of Habermas' transcendental claim that the fundamental nature of communication, a central facet of his theory of truth, is ahistorical and, thus, foundational. This would be elitist because Habermas could then argue that his truth was the real truth in relation to other possible truths that were not founded on the same communicative basis as his.

Poststructuralism, another example of a truth game, with its claim that the establishment of a truth game necessarily means the repression of other truth games, yields an ongoing critique of the dominance of any truth game, whether the game is scientific, Marxist, or any other one (Merquior, 1985).[13] Foucault (1977) contended that "humanity installs each of its violences in a system of rules and thus proceeds from domination to domination" (p. 151). This poststructuralist truth game implies a social arrangement in which there is a constant undermining of unitary dominance in any form. Habermas, however, in his criticisms of Foucault claimed that poststructuralism was inherently conservative because it undermined key democratic values developed through the Enlightenment (Bernstein, 1992). According to Habermas' critique, Foucauldian poststructuralism would, in effect, support social relations in which the most powerful were unchecked in their actions by any commitment to such Enlightenment values as democracy and individual liberty.

THREE CRITICISMS OF SOCIAL RELATIVISM

The latter contention—that relativism undermines protections against "might makes right"—is in fact one of the criticisms of the type of relativism I support.[14]

The argument goes as follows: If there is no foundational truth, no right way to determine what is the good, the true, and the beautiful, whichever group is strongest will simply establish its choices for these categories, and, most certainly, establish self-serving choices at that. More simply, might makes right. Harding (1991), the widely respected feminist epistemologist, makes a similar point when she says, "There have to be standards for distinguishing between how I want the world to be and how, in empirical fact, it is. Otherwise, might makes right in knowledge-seeking" (p. 160). This argument, however, depends on the positivist assumption that a nonpower related truth game is possible.[15] It is doubtful, at least in the social sciences, that such a power-free truth game has ever existed.

This argument against relativism also depends on a totalizing view of power. Choices about truth games are always made within specific social and historical contexts. Such contexts are never simple, and they are rarely totally dominated by a single "might." For example, there is little question that the most powerful group in a particular community has more ability to establish its truth game than other, less powerful groups; for example, people of color or working people do not dominate such truth games. So on average the most powerful group is going to "win" more often than any other group whenever and wherever the more powerful group chooses to fight for its interests. (The more powerful groups in a community often ignore many decisions, such as many decisions about schools, because they see no vital interest of theirs at stake.) But this is only part of the picture: "power in a society [or in any community, school, etc.] is never a fixed and closed regime" (Gordon, 1991, p. 5). There are, as Fraser (1989), a poststructuralist-oriented feminist, says, "multiple axes of power" (p. 10). The more powerful groups are often divided among themselves. In such cases they sometimes make alliances with other less powerful groups.[16] Less powerful groups are sometimes sufficiently united to defeat the more powerful. The less powerful also tend to resist domination in multiple and creative ways both as individuals and as groups (Apple, 1982; Giroux, 1983; Weiler, 1988).

In addition, there are often social constraints on the powerful that are historically rooted in values that both the powerful and the less powerful accept to a greater or lesser degree. For instance, in the West the emerging capitalists, along with other social groups, used the promise of democratic values and practices like universal suffrage to "defeat" the royalist truth game, but now, at least to some extent, the capitalists have to abide by those democratic values and practices. This is not to say that the powerful do not often abrogate, ignore, or corrupt such historical arrangements; this is also not to say, though, that they always abrogate, ignore, or corrupt such arrangements. In other words, the powerful are also constrained, to some extent, by their truth games.

The same picture could be drawn of schools. On average the formal power hierarchy usually dominates. In specific contexts, however, there are often multiple centers of power in constant struggle, conflict, compromise, and negotiation.

Sometimes within a particular school district a principal is more powerful than is the superintendent. Sometimes a teacher is more powerful than a principal. Sometimes teachers are more powerful in some areas, while principals are more powerful in other areas. Sometimes a student or group of students is more powerful within a particular classroom than the teacher. Often these relations of power shift over the course of a school year.

While there may be a dominant truth game in a particular school, there are virtually always alternative truth games with different degrees of power in different situations. There are, in addition, consensual values and interpretations that constrain what is allowable within a school or a classroom. For instance, in many states corporal punishment is not allowed even if the formally most powerful person in the classroom, (i.e., the teacher) wants to use such punishment.

Similar things could be said about the dominance of the social sciences by the conventional science approach to epistemology.[17] While it is true that conventional science has dominated methods departments in education and while the advocates of this approach have often acted arrogantly like the powerful often do, many in education (like Lincoln and Guba [1985]) have fought against this dominance. Sometimes the new alternatives are supported by conventional scientists who think like Feyerabend that science should remain very open to new ideas and methods. The advocates of alternative orientations have thus been able to gain ground in educational research partially because there are constraints within which the conventional social scientists had to exist. For many reasons, then, those who have resisted the dominance by conventional social scientists have attained some power and, in some situations, could now be said to have established a new dominance.[18]

Consequently, while "might" or the more powerful groups certainly make right or truth more often than anyone else does (and this inequity must repeatedly be emphasized), the most powerful in any situation only rarely, and perhaps never, possess totalized control for a very long period of time. To argue, then, that relativism in the social sciences leads to a totalized control by the most powerful is to ignore the past historical connections between power and truth (which positivists only assumed they had overcome) and to ignore that power is rarely or only fleetingly totalized. Instead of permitting a dominance of power over knowledge, social or postmodernist relativism leads to an unmasking of the historical relations between these two and of the illusion that any dominance is comprehensive or total.

A second, and related, criticism of relativism is that it undermines emancipatory struggles and epistemologies: The "undercutting of foundational Enlightenment tenets causes many intellectuals with emancipatory concerns to question the politics of postmodernism" (Lather, 1991b, p. 37).[19] Those who make this critique, such as some feminists (see Nielsen, 1990 or Lather, 1991b, pp. 26–31, for example), argue that relativism undermines factual or empirical determinations that certain social groups, such as women or people of color, are oppressed or have less power or are exploited.[20] These critics are reluctant to set aside some kind of foundationalism or empirical criterion from which they can argue that it is really *true* that certain groups are socially oppressed.

Another argument that some feminist critics have made is that the current fascination with relativism is a male response to the growing power of feminism. Since feminists have effectively questioned masculinist versions of foundationalism, so this argument goes, males have strategically switched to a relativist philosophy that makes all positions equal and thus undermines foundationalism as successfully revised by feminists. According to Harding (1991), the feminist epistemologist, "Historically, relativism appears as a problematic intellectual possibility only for dominating groups at the point where the hegemony of their views is being challenged" (p. 153).

While I too would sometimes wish that there were ahistorical foundations for justice and equality, I do not agree that the social relativism I support is a threat to feminism or other emancipatory positions. Indeed, I would argue the opposite. The Enlightenment values of justice and equality were never ahistorical or foundational. These Enlightenment values have evolved out of multiple historical struggles reaching back hundreds of years. The idea or the belief that women are equal to men is not an ahistorical truth but a social creation constructed within historical human activity.

Women, and the men who supported their struggles, have fought to create the "truth" of gender equality in the face of immense opposition, an opposition that, not incidentally, often couched its resistance to equality in foundational truth claims, such as the "natural" role of women. The equality of women as a truth was not created by Enlightenment values; instead both the equality of women and other Enlightenment values are historical social constructions. This does not mean that feminists did not in their struggles draw on already recognized Enlightenment values. They certainly did. Feminists obviously used Enlightenment values with which to develop rationales that would convince other women and men of the justice of their cause. Many or even most of the early feminists may have believed that these values were foundational or ahistorical. Nonetheless, such values or truths and the partisan use of such values always arise out of and evolve within historical conditions and struggles.

A third criticism of relativism is that it has meaning only as one side of a binary opposition between a correspondence theory of truth and an "everything is relative" truth (Bernstein, 1988; Harding, 1991; Lather, 1991b). One way of pursuing this critique is to contend that once a correspondence theory of truth is disposed of the other side of the binary, relativism is no longer meaningful. This is similar to the argument Barone (1990) used to say that since objectivism was dead, subjectivism had lost any useful meanmg.

Another way of pursuing this critique is to make both sides of the binary problematic as some poststructuralists and feminists have done (Haraway, 1988; Harding, 1991; Lather, 1991b). While I agree with the effort by feminists and poststructuralists to think outside of the traditional sexist or logocentric binaries,

I do not agree with how this has been done by Haraway, Harding, and Lather. The effort to move beyond the foundationalism/relativism binary violates a basic tenet of postmodern thought, according to Derrida (1981). This tenet is that it is not possible to completely free oneself from the discourse out of which the issues arose in the first place. Decisive breaks are not possible: "I do not believe in decisive ruptures. . . . Breaks are always, and fatally, reinscribed in an old cloth that must continually, interminably be undone" (Derrida, 1981, p. 24). In fact, Derrida would claim that our concepts are "marked through and through by referential . . . assumptions, and there is no way of simply breaking their hold by a kind of deconstructionist fiat" (Norris, 1987, p. 54). That is, the social-cultural academic matrix, which includes the foundationalist/relativist binary and within which Bernstein, Lather, and Harding think and write, cannot be escaped by simply declaring one's escape. One Derridian alternative is

to criticize . . . from *within* [his emphasis] an inherited language, a discourse that will always have been worked over in advance by traditional concepts and categories. What is required is a kind of internal distancing, an effort of defamiliarization which prevents concepts from settling down into routine habits of thought. (Norris, 1987, p. 16)

Another postmodernist response is to think and write at the margins of the old binary and thereby signal an awareness of one's own limits (Hutcheon, 1989). An additional postmodernist alternative, and the one I have tried to pursue, is to transform the binary from within by recognizing and using its classical meaning, moving with and against that meaning, and altering it by pushing it in new directions.

Several of those who want to move beyond the foundationalism/relativism binary, and I count Bernstein (1988), Harding (1991), and Lather (1991b) in this group, want to retain some degree of foundationalism, especially in terms of the idea that there is a "real" that can be known in some sense.[21] But all three are difficult to pin down because they all have commitments that straddle both sides of the binary. While I have no quarrel with their relativist commitments, I do disagree with their foundationalist ones. For Bernstein (1988) this retained foundationalism is contained in such statements as, "We must avoid the fallacy of thinking there are no fixed, determinate rules for distinguishing better from worse interpretations" (p. 91).

For Harding (1991), who for me is more complex and persuasive than Bernstein (1988), this retained foundationalism is "a strong objectivity." While this strong objectivity recognizes that all views are historical," a strong notion of objectivity requires a commitment to acknowledge the historical character of every belief or set of beliefs" (Harding, 1991, p. 156), it still includes a commitment to a scientific idea of objectivity that is inescapably ahistorical. For example, she claims that it is possible to have "a critical evaluation . . . [that would determine] which social situations tend to generate the most objective knowledge claims" (Harding, 1991, p. 142). Her expansion of objectivity from the traditional sphere of the context of justification to the sphere of discovery leaves the idea of objectivity intact. Even her argument that the "bias" of feminism leads to a stronger objectivity leaves the idea of objectivity intact. In fact, she takes a position that is similar to Bernstein's when she indicates that strong objectivity can discriminate between, "Which ones [truth claims] generate less and which more partial and distorted accounts of nature and social life" (p. 161).

Lather (1991b) has a range of criticisms of relativism. It has no meaning outside of the binary. It undermines the objective reality of the oppression of women. It is a masculinist maneuver to undermine feminism. It ignores context and positionality. Of the three scholars discussed in this section—Bernstein, Harding, and Lather—she is the most thoroughly committed to a postmodernist social relativism and, thus, is more willing to undermine foundationalist ideas of all sorts. She is, however, somewhat divided in this commitment as is appropriate to her deconstructionist inclinations. For example, she says her goal, and the goal of deconstruction as a method, is to transcend, "a binary logic by simultaneously being both and neither of the binary terms" (Lather, 1991b, p. 13). It is not surprising then that in "being both" she is committed, like Harding (1991), to retaining an objectivism that confirms inequitable power arrangements in terms of class, race, and gender.

Contrary to Bernstein (1988), Harding (1991), and Lather (1991b), I resist the idea of placing anything outside of the relativity of specific social and historical conditions. I would suggest that what Bernstein, Harding, Lather, and others are against is a modernist definition of relativism, one that is "anything goes" and individualistic and one that is idealistic and separated from its moorings in particular historical contexts. Their idea of relativism is itself ahistorical. "Anything goes" is a phantom; historically "anything goes" is never possible. What is possible, truth games or otherwise, is always embedded in historical conditions. The argument against individualistic relativism proceeds similarly. Humans are social, historical beings. While an individual may become an idiosyncratic (individual) combination of the bits and pieces of her or his social and historical positionality, she or he cannot reach outside time and place for these bits and pieces. In fact, what most of us become individually is well within the accepted patterns of our time and place. Social relativism, rather than resisting our positionality, recognizes and valorizes the social and historical contingency of human existence and our truth games.

I would argue that a poststructuralist view of relativism, as I am trying to develop here, dissolves many of the prior problems with relativism. This, I think, is the point of view that Alcoff (1987) arrives at in her meditation on the problems of positivism and relativism for a feminist social science:

what happens to the problem of relativism if we drop out from the above picture of the transcendent, independent reality lying beyond our discourse or web? It seems to me this is what Foucault and Gadamer at least want to do. Our beliefs [truth claims] are still relative to a discourse, but they cannot be characterized as therefore "less true" because they are not being compared to a transcendent reality. . . . it is not just the criterion of truth that is relative, but truth itself is relative. . . . it would appear to make relativism less formidable by undercutting the usual ground its critics take. (p. 98)

It would, thus, seem to me that it is possible to maintain the ongoing critique of foundationalist truth games and to posit nothing—no criterion, no rationality, no objectivity of any kind, no anything—as outside particular historical contingencies and positionality without falling into the problems that Bernstein (1988), Harding (1991), and Lather (1991b), among others fear. I have, for instance, no problem with "strong objectivity" as a criterion according to Harding's (1991) definition, but I strongly resist the idea that this criterion is not historically mediated. I can see that this criterion is useful and meaningful for the social struggle to establish equitable social arrangements, but I cannot see that arguing that this criterion is itself unmediated by socially located truth games is helpful to that struggle.

And, finally, I am not as sanguine as Harding is about a standpoint approach. In fact, I am not sanguine about any one position, mine included. I am as suspicious as Fraser (1989) of the claim that a standpoint approach, like that of Harding and others, solves our epistemological dilemmas. I would agree with the poststructuralists that all perspectives imply political arrangements and invariably exclude some groups, some voices. Some sort of social relativist or postmodernist epistemology is necessary but certainly not a romanticized "everyone is equal" one or an "all positions are equal" one. A contentious, self-critical pluralism, an Ellsworth (1989) style pluralism of shifting coalitions and conflicts, might be best.

TWO POSTFOUNDATIONAL OR PRAGMATIC ALTERNATIVES TO SOCIAL RELATIVISM

As was briefly mentioned in the prior section, there have been numerous efforts to develop postfoundational or pragmatic alternatives to relativism. A wide range of scholars have attempted to derive postfoundational alternatives that would provide us with a middle range choice between the Scylla of foundationalism and the Charybdis of relativism.[22] Bernstein's *Beyond Objectivism and Relativism* (1988) is obviously a classic example of this approach, but here I want to consider two other scholars whose work is more specifically located within the field of education. In both cases, however, I will contend that their postfoundationalism or pragmatism fails.

Donmoyer (1985) in an article that was partially entitled "The Rescue from Relativism" used Toulmin's claim

that there are ways to rationally assess the relative worth of conflicting claims . . . [and] that differing purposes [of the particular research] will inevitably result in different criteria for appraising the relative adequacy of conflicting conceptual schemes or languages. (p. 18)

Donmoyer does recognize that "different theoretical languages [different perspectives] will lead researchers to employ quite different dependent variables, and these variables will profoundly influence research findings" (1985, p. 19). He, nonetheless, wants to privilege some sort of rationality procedures that rises above politics, tradition, and error (i.e., metaparadigmatic standards that rule over all truth games):

Whenever they [educational researchers] make decisions about funding research or allocating journal space, questions of purpose must be answered. Answers, however, normally emerge more from the exercise of political power or from an appeal to tradition or from an inappropriate application of methodological canons than from *rational deliberation* [emphasis added]. There is a need, therefore, for methodologists to develop [such rational] procedures. . . . The development of such procedures will not be easy. The work remaining, however, is *largely procedural rather than epistemological* [emphasis added]. (Donmoyer, 1985, p. 19)

The oppositional deployment is clear: "political power," "tradition," and "inappropriate application of methodological canon" on the negative side and "rational deliberation" on the positive. He follows this rhetorical strategy with a further valorization of "rational deliberation" by citing the need for "methodologists to develop procedures" that would facilitate the implementation of such rationality. Finally, he makes sure we understand his commitment by stating that the epistemological issues are settled and only procedural work remains. In short, rationality, rational deliberation, and rational procedures provide the warrant for decisions about knowledge claims.[23]

Mishler's (1990) application of disciplinary exemplars, which are adapted from Kuhn (1970), is a second example of an effort to develop postfoundational standards. In this case, however, it is not standards or procedures of rationality that are privileged but the research exemplars that come to dominate "a community of scientists as they [the scientists) come to share nonproblematic and useful ways of thinking about and solving problems" (Mishler, 1990, p. 421). That is, Mishler sees respected exemplars of past research within specific disciplinary contexts as postfoundational guides to social science research. Obviously he is more oriented to a relativistic point of view than Donmoyer (1985) by the fact that such exemplars are socially and historically embedded. For example, Mishler (1990) agrees with my contention that epistemological issues are located in "the social world—a world constructed in and through our discourse and actions, through praxis" (p. 420). He also agrees that "Since social worlds are endlessly being remade as norms and practices change, it is clear that judgments . . . may change with time, even when addressed to the 'same' findings" (Mishler, 1990, p. 420).

From my social relativist perspective each of these examples commit different errors, but the source of the errors, in my view, is due to their desire or need to avoid relativism. While Donmoyer (1985) agrees that there are "different theoretical languages" (p. 19), he appears to think that there are rationality procedures that rise above such languages.[24] Is there, however, only one kind of rationality that is applicable to all situations and all theoretical languages? Are there rationality procedures to which all theoretical language advocates would agree? Could we not have different rationalities and different sets of rationality procedures, a condition Bachelard (who both mentored and strongly influenced Foucault [Eribon, 1991]) suggests already exists even in the natural sciences (Gutting, 1989), or could we not have different "logic fragments" as Barth (1991, p. 125) suggests?

Merquior (1985) says that Cassirer in *The Philosophy of the Enlightenment* concludes that

the Enlightenment significantly changed the concept of reason. While, for Descartes, Spinoza or Leibniz, reason was "the territory of eternal truths," the next century no longer saw reason as a treasure of principles and fixed truths, but simply as a faculty, the original power of the mind, to be grasped only in exercise of its analytical functions. (p. 69)

Foucault (1977) suggests that what we label as reason historically "arose from the passion of scholars, their reciprocal hatred, their fanatical and unending discussions, and their spirit of competition—the personal conflicts that slowly forged the weapons of reason" (p. 142). Deleuze (1992) asserts that "reason is forever bifurcating; there are as many bifurcations as there are foundations, as many collapses as there are constructions" (p. 163). Derrida says the rule of reason is logocentric (Flax, 1990). Habermas (1971) argues that "Representations and descriptions are never independent of standards. And the choice of these standards . . . cannot be either logically deduced or empirically demonstrated" (p. 312). In addition, feminists and race-oriented theorists (see, for example, Stanfield, 1985, or Minh-ha, 1989) among others have contended that privileging the rationality of conventional social science is unfairly or unduly providing legitimacy to only one kind of possible rationality. These critics would advance other kinds of rationality.

If there are multiple rationalities and multiple sets of rationality procedures, as I would contend there are, Donmoyer (1985) has simply moved relativity from one domain of concern to another without settling anything, without establishing the apparently desired Archimedean point. My critique, though, does not mean that rationality and rationality procedures do not exist. They do. My point is that there are many rationalities and many sets of rationality procedures (some of which overlap, some of which conflict, some of which are incommensurable), all of which operate within particular social, historical, and disciplinary contexts.

Mishler (1991), though he is closer to my position than Donmoyer (1985), makes a different set of mistakes. First, he unproblematically appropriates

Kuhn's natural science-oriented "shared exemplars" approach to the social sciences. While I agree that the old, assumed epistemological differences between the social and natural sciences are less meaningful or defensible than they once were, an exemplar that is guiding research in the social sciences is different from an exemplar that is guiding research in the natural sciences. According to Kuhn (1970), a particular discipline within the natural sciences is guided by the same paradigm, except in the rare revolutionary periods. Thus, those using an exemplar in a natural science discipline generally agree epistemologically; the exemplar simply guides their research within that agreement.

The social sciences, as Kuhn himself has pointed out, are much different. Rarely does any particular discipline in the social sciences have the kind of epistemological consensus that Kuhn saw in the natural sciences. In addition, the history of the social sciences looks more like succeeding ideologies (Bernstein, 1988; Polkinghorne, 1983), rather than Kuhn's "normal [progressively accumulating] science" followed by occasional eruptions of "revolutionary science." Consequently, in the social sciences presiding exemplars serve more to establish the dominance of one epistemological voice over others. The research that such exemplars guide serves to exclude alternative research voices as much as it supposedly serves to simply guide research.

Shakeshaft's (1987) feminist research in educational administration well illustrates this point. She contends that the dominant exemplars in educational administration privilege male administrators and the viewpoint of those men over women administrators and the viewpoint of those women. The result, according to Shakeshaft (1987), has been that male perspectives and experiences are privileged while female perspectives and experiences are marginalized or silenced. Mishler's privileging of a discipline's "shared exemplars," thus, tends to privilege the discipline's status quo over other possible contending voices.

This same point was also made by Scheurich and Lather (1991). They found that in a specific journal conversation about epistemological perspectives in supervision, only two of several possible epistemological perspectives were being included in the exchange within the journal. Even if the two included perspectives, and the exemplars representative of those two, are considered the "normal science" of supervision, they were not the only perspectives possible. Other perspectives exist in supervision; they were simply not represented within this journal's conversation. Consequently, an acceptance of the dominant two perspectives in supervision, as was done by those conducting the conversation, reinforced the dominance of the status quo and the exclusion of other voices.

A second problem for Mishler (1990) is that he argues, following Kuhn, that "shared exemplars" are an accurate description of the way that scientists do science. I would suggest, following Bachelard, Canguilhem, and Foucault, that scientists are much more nonstandardized than this in how they do science (Gutting, 1989). I would contend that some follow exemplars, some follow orders, some pursue various other approaches, and most do all three of these. (For descriptions of scientific works that are different than "exemplar-oriented" approaches, see Latour and Woolgar's *Laboratory Life: The Construction of Scientific Facts,* 1986.) In addition, Mishler (1990) ignores how idiosyncratic the individual scientist is in her or his perception and use of a particular exemplar. In other words, Mishler in a certain sense totalizes the use of exemplars both by assuming that exemplars are the best description of how scientists proceed and that the use of exemplars proceeds in the same fashion for all scientists. This privileging of a totalized version of shared exemplars serves, once again, to marginalize or silence other, equally defensible research approaches. In response to Donmoyer's and Mishler's postfoundational approaches I counsel extreme suspicion toward any effort to privilege or totalize any postfoundational approach, whether that approach be some kind of metacriteria or metaguide to how research ought to be done. Instead I would call for the literal multiplication of *bricolage*[25] methods that are reflectively aware of their social and historical contextuality and of their politics.[26]

A SOCIAL RELATIVIST CRITIQUE OF SCIENTIFIC REALISM

Earlier, after reviewing scientific realism, I indicated that although I thought that it was superior to either positivism or naive realism, I still considered it to be inadequate.[27] I make this judgment primarily on the basis of two conclusions. First, although scientific realists think that "knowledge is a social and historical product," they still believe that a body of knowledge can be developed that accurately describes the "complex and stratified" "real world" (House, 1991, p. 3). This combination of assumptions hides two connected problems. One is that "social and historical" implies a single, unified social and historical context; otherwise many knowledges would be elicited from many social and historical contexts, which is what I as a social relativist or *bricoleur* would say. The other problem is that the scientific realists, subsequently, assume that one knowledge/one context produces essentially one best description. While there may be conflict between various contending descriptions of the "real world," one will be eventually judged the best, according to the scientific realists. If the scientific realists do not support this "one best description" conclusion, then they must accept the existence of a range of equally possible but different descriptions, which is what I would accept.

A second way that scientific realism is inadequate is similar to Doñmoyer's (1985) postfoundationalism. They assume that they can develop rational criteria that rise above historically positioned and mediated social and cultural constructions. This is clearly apparent in the work of Evers and Lakomski (1991), who consider themselves scientific or coherentist realists. They privilege a set of coherency standards, but they would not agree that their standards are metaparadigmatic because they think that only realism is acceptable and that a multiple-paradigms position is unacceptable. They call their coherentist standards "extra-empirical." In their view theory choice needs to be guided by a consideration of the extra-empirical virtues possessed by theories. These virtues of system include simplicity, consistency, coherence, comprehensiveness, conservativeness, and fecundity, though they are often referred to collectively as coherence considerations or as elements in a coherentist account of epistemic justification. (p. 4)

These "extra-empirical virtues" are meant to guide choices between theories. From my perspective Evers and Lakomski (1991) have several problems with these "virtues." First, they have the linguistic problem of how to define each of their criteria, a problem logical positivists and analytical philosophers have found to be difficult indeed. What I think they will find as they attend to these definitional issues is that relativism will simply reappear in decisions about appropriate definitions. Second, the decision of which criterion is more important in any particular situation is equally difficult. What if, in comparing two theories, one is high (whatever that means) on simplicity, consistency and coherence and the other is high on comprehensiveness, conservativeness, and fecundity? Which is better? What is the appropriate balance amidst all of these terms?

Third, and most devastating, these extra-empirical virtues themselves have no empirical foundation even though they are supposed to rule over empirical judgments. Even Quine, on whom Evers and Lakomski (1991) assert much of their theory is dependent, indicates that "these extra-empirical criteria are based neither on empirical nor rational foundations" (Hesse, 1980). If no empirical or rational reasons exist for these coherency criteria, they are historically relative to derivation in particular social or disciplinary contexts (i.e., socially relative). As Hesse (1980) argues, the "adoption of such criteria, which can be seen to be different for different groups and at different periods, should be explicable by social rather than logical factors" (p. 33). Moreover, she contends that, even in the natural sciences,

Conflicting [natural] scientific paradigms or fundamental theories differ not just in what they assert as postulates, but also in the conceptual meaning of the postulates and in their criteria of what counts as a good theory; criteria of simplicity and good approximation: of what is to be an "explanation" or a "cause" or a "good inference", and even what is the practical goal of scientific theorizing. All such differences are inexplicable by the logic of science, since they are precisely disputes about the content of that logic. The historian must make them intelligible by extra-scientific causation. (Hesse, 1980, p. 33)

All three of these issues — definition of the coherence terms, the weight given to each term in relation to the others, and the lack of foundations for the coherency criteria — will simply lead back to relativity. As Hesse (1980), following Barnes (1974), says,

all attempts to find demarcating criteria, that is, necessary and sufficient conditions for a belief system to be a science, have failed. These failures include all verifiability and falsifiability criteria, and all specific appeals to experimentation and/or particular kinds of inductive or theoretical inference. At best, he [Barnes, 1974] argues, the concept "science" must be regarded as a loose association of family resemblance characteristics involving, among other things, aversion to all forms of anthropomorphism and teleology, and consequent tendencies to secularism, impersonality, abstraction and quantification. Moreover, we must not impose our own scientific criteria on the past; the subject matter of the historian of science can only be demarcated by recognizing [ex post facto] what it is in the past that exhibits causal continuity with present science. (p. 47)

As with Donmoyer (1985), Evers and Lakomski (1991) have attempted to solve the "problem" of relativism but have only succeeded in moving it elsewhere. More importantly, however, I do not accept that reality, whatever that is, can be encapsulated under the sign of any single, dominant epistemology, scientific or coherentist realism in this case. As Foucault (1991) says, "I am a pluralist" (p. 53). Further, as fits my emphasis on the politics of all epistemology, I find such single-epistemology dominance highly dangerous. Again, I would support the proliferation of many ways of seeing and the dominance of none. Foucault (1977, p. 168) puts this much more poetically when he says, "we should welcome the cunning assembly that simulates and clamors at the door" of knowledge.[28]

A POSTMODERNIST POLITICS OF EPISTEMOLOGY

If, as in my view, epistemology or truth games are "grounded" not in foundational truth claims nor even in such apparently postfoundational claims as rationality procedures (Donmoyer, 1985) or disciplinary exemplars (Mishler, 1990) but are located in shifting and diverse historical human practices, politics and power become central epistemological or doxological issues. As Eisner (1988) says, "There is no such thing as a value-neutral approach to the world" (p. 19). Epistemology as doxology is then no longer limited either to the explication of particular truth games or to the competition between truth games. Epistemology is thus expanded to include the history, sociology, and politics of truth games.[29]

For example, scientific realism, as discussed previously, is a currently advocated truth game. In the earlier discussion I covered in a traditional way some of what this position was about and how it compared to other positions, such as positivism and naive realism. From the social relativist position I have been exploring, a consideration of scientific realism would be expanded to include an additional set of questions. If scientific realism were the ruling paradigm, who would benefit? Does it require expert knowledge and thus privilege experts over others? Is its view of the technological products of science unproblematically positive? Does it view science and technology in an idealistic way or does it view science in terms of its "real" practices? What is its social history? Under what social and historical conditions did it arise? As a way of thinking, does it privilege some social groups over others? From what social groups in terms of class, race, and gender would it tend to draw its advocates? What does it mean if its advocates are chiefly members of a single social group? Does it then, historically and socially, serve particular class, race, and gender interests?

Fraser (1989), a feminist who rejects both a correspondence-oriented positivist approach and a standpoint approach (pp. 181-182) like that of Harding (1991), raises similar kinds of questions in reference to choices about better or worse "interpretations of people's needs" (Fraser, 1989, p. 181). She says that

> First, there are procedural considerations concerning the social processes by which various competing need interpretations are generated. For example, how exclusive or inclusive are various rival discourses? How hierarchical or egalitarian are the relations among the interlocutors? In general, procedural considerations dictate that, all other things being equal, the best need interpretations are those reached by means of communicative processes that most closely approximate ideals of democracy, equality, and fairness.
>
> In addition, considerations of consequences are relevant in justifying need interpretations. This means comparing alternative distributive outcomes of rival interpretations. For example, would widespread acceptance of some given interpretation of a social need disadvantage some groups of people vis-à-vis others? Does the interpretation conform to, rather than challenge, societal patterns of dominance and subordination? . . . In general, consequentialist considerations dictate that, all other things being equal, the best need interpretations are those that do not disadvantage some groups vis-à-vis others. (p. 182)

In this more specific application, Fraser (1989) illustrates the kinds of political analysis that needs to be applied to epistemological questions in general and to specific applications of particular epistemologies. When she asserts that there are no privileged foundational, postfoundational, or, even, standpoint reasons for judging one interpretation better than another (Fraser, 1989, pp. 181-182), and she turns instead to political judgments, she is evidencing the kind of approach I have tried to develop and explain in this work.

Similar kinds of questions would also be applied to the definition of such key research terms as "empirical," "data," or "reality." Such terms draw their meaning from the epistemology in which they exist. For example, Farran's (1990) feminist constructivist definition of data or Lather's (1991b) postmodernist feminist definition of "data" are different than Kerlinger's (1986) meaning of the same word within his positivist orientation. Farran (1990) says that " 'data collection' is 'data construction' " (p. 91). Lather (1991a) says that "Data might be better conceived as the material for telling a story where the challenge becomes to generate a polyvalent data base that is used to *vivify* [her emphasis] interpretation as opposed to 'support' or 'prove' " (p. 10). It is not difficult to imagine that Kerlinger would have formidable problems with Farran's and Lather's definitions.

Similarly, what is "really" happening in a classroom and what "facts" are used to support a particular perspective may be different for a naive realist, for a critical theorist, and for a poststructuralist. As Kuhn (1970) says of two groups of scientists working out of two different paradigms, "Practicing in different worlds, the two groups of scientists see different things when they look from the same point in the same direction" (p. 148). A naive realist might say that what is really happening is the teacher is attempting to teach a particular lesson to the students. A critical theorist might say that what is really happening is that the teacher is attempting to get the students to believe in the dominant ideology even though doing so is not in their own interests and even though some students are resisting. A poststructuralist might say that what is really happening is all of the above and more: The teacher is teaching subject content and dominance among many other things, and the students are learning, accepting, and resisting dominance, socializing, fighting, sleeping, and so forth. Which of these is "true," however, depends on whose truth story is being told.[30]

The issue, in this instance, is not that different perspectives "see" different "facts." Most contemporary epistemologists agree that they do (though they would certainly not agree that all of the currently competing epistemologies are equally valid). The issue is the political dimension of the definition of specific terms like *empirical facts,* or *reality.* From a social relativist viewpoint the issue is not whether or not the term "empirical" refers to some observable reality. "Observable" and "reality" are also relative terms. As Minh-ha (1989) notes, "The real . . . [is] nothing else than a [social] *code of representation* [her emphases]" (p. 94). The contestable meanings of these terms—empirical, data, reality, facts—float historically within particular epistemologies or within certain disciplinary communities dominated by particular epistemologies.

While the advocates of these epistemologies or the members of these communities may claim that "empirical" is a referent to "observable reality," I would say that their claim is simply relative to their epistemology or their community, both of which exist within specific historical and sociological contexts: "the categories or concepts by and through which we structure experience [or reality or research] are themselves historically and culturally variable" (Flax, 1990, p. 35). None of these terms—empirical, data, reality, facts—rise above their location in space and time and thus point somehow to a reality; they are all contextually relative. This contextual relativity leads then to the issue of what are the politics of a particular use of such terms as "empirical" or "facts."

An example will serve to illustrate this point. Suppose we take the question of whether or not a generalized bias against people of color and women exists in the U.S. public school system. This would conventionally be considered an empirical question. Bias would be defined. Data or facts would be gathered. An empirical determination would be made. This process, though, is problematic or relativistic in at least two ways. First, there would be disagreements over the definitions of bias, and there would be no external standards by which to solve the disagreements. In addition, each definition would have certain politics. For instance, a radical feminist might suggest that the educational system is not only biased in terms of test composition or teacher wait time but also in terms of the basic idea of what knowledge is. A conventional social scientist of liberal inclinations might want to define bias only in measurable or behavioral terms. Each of these researchers embed their politics in their definitions.

Second, what are considered data or facts is open to epistemological debate.

Naive realists would see facts in one way; scientific realists would see facts in another way. A critical theorist might see facts in still a different way, and so on. Therefore, in social science research the nature of reality, according to certain definitions and facts, is debatable. Furthermore, since the nature of reality is debatable and since different portraits of reality include different political arrangements of people, debates over the nature of reality are, in effect, political debates. Determinations of whether the U.S. public school system is generally biased against people of color and women only become "empirical" questions once several prior issues are decided, issues that are fundamentally political or ethical.

Perhaps my position can be illustrated better by comparing truth game enactments to policy enactments. Donmoyer (1985) says that Toulmin specifically exempts policy studies from being a social scientific discipline, but I would argue that the social sciences are in much the same situation as policy studies. We seem to have no problem recognizing that different policy enactments yield different arrangements of people (i.e., have a politics). We also seem to have no problem accepting that policy enactments are political or, even ethical, enactments. Finally, we also seem to have no problem recognizing that it is acceptable for people to differ on policy enactments. But we want truth games to be special sorts of games that rise above such relativistic political struggles. I would, in contrast, claim that epistemological enactments are very similar to policy enactments. Truth games in the social sciences are not about some sort of privileged truth; they are socially constrained perspectives that have significant political implications. In short, truth game enactments are political or ethical enactments (Hesse, 1978).[31]

The result is that researchers in terms of their epistemological enactments are in the same position as a school administrator or teacher who has to make policy choices. An administrator or teacher can choose to base her or his decisions on effectiveness, cost, equity, career needs, or on some combination of several possibilities. Each decision will have a certain politics (i.e., it will benefit some people or groups over others). For example, cutting funds for a gifted program will tend to hurt upper-middle-class white families, while cutting funds for an at-risk program will tend to hurt lower-class families of color. Each policy decision of the administrator or teacher will express, explicitly or implicitly, the politics of that person and her or his social, historical positionality.

It is, thus, not the purposes of research that drives these choices about which epistemology to use, as suggested by Donmoyer (1985). Critical theorists like Foster (1986) or Bates (1980; 1982) who contend that positivism is politically questionable cannot ethically or politically choose a positivist perspective from which to conduct their research no matter what the purpose of the research is. The same is true for feminists or Afrocentrists who have similarly criticized conventional social science research approaches. Those who assume that they can choose any epistemology to fit the needs of the research situation restrict the array of epistemologies to only those that are considered to be value-free, believe that only value-free epistemologies are acceptable in the social sciences, or ignore the politics of the research they conduct. Obviously, in my view and others, such as critical theorists, feminists, or race/culture theorists, the third possibility—ignore their politics—is the most likely.

From a social relativist position, each epistemological enactment, like the policy enactments of the administrator or teacher, is a political enactment. No specific epistemology or particular research situation can remove the researcher from this predicament. The result is that the enactment of an epistemology can no longer be founded on picking the best epistemology in terms of which one brings the researcher closer to some sort of foundational truth or in terms of which one coheres most closely to some postfoundational standard or criterion. It is now based on which epistemology best expresses the politics of the researcher.[32] Truth game enactments or epistemological enactments are ultimately political or ethical enactments.

NOTES

1. In this case I am using a very broad and loose definition of the word "epistemology," a use that is common throughout education and the social sciences in general. For those who might label themselves as epistemologists or as philosophers, there are often more technical or exacting definitions of epistemology. For example, Bernstein (1978) indicates that epistemology as an endeavor is more connected to scientific methodology than to the methods of other paradigms. Polkinghorne (1983, pp. 9–10) makes a similar point. He says that Plato in *Theatetus* distinguished between *doxa* ("what we believe to be true") and *episteme* ("what we know to be true"). Thus, "epistemology (the *logos* or study of *episteme*) has become the search for methods and foundations which enable us to be assured of the truth of our beliefs." I would claim, however, that the use of the word "epistemology" is not restricted in this way. But if we were to restrict ourselves to the classical definition, I would label what I do and what everyone else in the social sciences does as doxological rather than epistemological.

Also, in this discussion of epistemology I will focus exclusively on the social sciences for which there is little evidence of a succeeding accumulation of better and better approximations of the truth of the kind that Popper and Lakatos, for instance, argue can be found in the natural sciences. There are, however, numerous scholars who argue against the idea of steadily improving knowledge even in the natural sciences. This latter group would include Feyerabend, Rorty, and Bernstein, among others. There are also, more recently, scholars of the natural sciences who argue that the natural sciences are more like the social sciences than has previously been recognized (see Rouse, 1987, for an excellent example of one such an approach).

2. In my opinion the separation of epistemology and ontology is artificial. In practice and in theory my epistemology cannot be separated from my ontology. What I see and how I see are intimately interwoven.

3. If we look across many of the texts addressing these issues, we find that the definitions of such terms as epistemology, positivism, realism, and the like are different in different texts. For instance, Polkinghorne (1983) uses the phrase "pragmatic science" to mean something similar to House's (1991) "scientific realism." Though there are differ-

ences in their descriptions, there is also considerable overlap. There is, thus, really no way to stipulate definitions that would apply across all or most texts, nor is there even really a need to do so. Instead my approach is sometimes to define explicitly a term I am using, but more often I let the context implicitly indicate the meaning, which always remains somewhat slippery and ambiguous.

4. See, also, Phillips (1983) who contends there are at least four versions of positivism, some of which are considered to be dead and some of which are considered to be "still alive in one form or another" (p. 6). Donmoyer (1985) argues that Phillips in this same article is defending a "reconstructed version of positivism" (p. 14), a kind of pragmatic or common sense version of positivism. Lincoln and Guba (1985), however, vilify positivism, as do many others. In fact, positivism is the most common straw-philosophy of those interested in defending alternative viewpoints. Lather (1991b), on the other hand, is a good example of a scholar who positions herself as thoroughly and deeply critical of positivism but does not give much space to attacking it. She is much more interested in developing a postmodernist emancipatory perspective than maligning positivism. Lather (in press) does assert that "Positivism is not dead, as anyone knows who tries to get published in most journals, obtain grants from most funding agencies or have research projects accepted by theses and dissertation committees. What is dead, however, is its theoretic dominance and its 'one best way' claims over empirical work in the human sciences" (pp. 6–7).

5. I would contend that positivists were not a complete failure because through their self-critique they showed that the positivist dream was not possible. In addition, it is often forgotten in the current vilification of positivism that the positivists saw their rigorous rules as an enhancement of democracy. As Fuller (1988) says, "Returning to the positivists, it is well known that their chief ideologue, Otto Neurath (1962), saw the Unified Science movement as, in part, a way of driving out the politically conservative and elitist tendencies of hermeneutical thinking in the 'human sciences' . . . and driving in the more radical and egalitarian, specifically Marxist, politics associated with a naturalistic approach to the 'social sciences.' Less well known is how Neurath's preoccupation with the status of 'protocol statements,' those fundamental building blocks of evidential warrant in the natural sciences, contributed to the overall project. . . . Neurath's concern with protocol statements, along with other positivist attempts at formulating a principle of verification, may perhaps be seen as raising to self-consciousness the values of *equality* [his emphasis] (of the individual knowers) and *progress* (of the collective body of knowers) which were first asserted in the Scientific Revolution" (pp. 6–7).

6. One example of work that does not attend to its epistemological biases is the new work on micropolitics (e.g., Blaise, 1991). While I think this work is very important in expanding our understanding of the complexity of classrooms and schools, I find Blaise to be unreflexive in an epistemological sense. The proponents of the micropolitics of school settings seem to understand the complexities of such settings but not the complexities of their own epistemology. How they see what they see and thus what they see itself is much more problematic than they seem to understand.

7. Naive realism would accurately describe the epistemological basis of most work in educational administration, just as it does in almost all areas of education. Positivism itself became influential in educational administration in the 1950s with "the theory movement" under the leadership of Getzels, Griffiths, and Halpin, but only a few of its practitioners were serious theorists in a positivist sense. By the 1960s, however, Halpin himself had begun to question the legitimacy and limitations of positivism (and functionalism, the

sociological version of positivism) for educational administration (Culbertson, 1988; Griffiths, 1988). In retrospect, naive realism would be a better descriptor for the research practices of most adherents of this movement. Whatever label is applied, however, this perspective continues to be influential among the great majority of professors of educational administration as shown by a study of the syllabi and textbooks used in the United States by participants in the University Council for Educational Administration (UCEA) (Nicolaides & Gaynor, 1989), which incidentally was founded to further the theory movement (Culbertson, 1988).

8. As with the other perspectives that I address in this study, I will not try to present an exhaustive description or explanation of socially constrained relativism. I think that a comprehensive coverage is not only impossible in practice but theoretically impossible. Instead I will discuss certain aspects of this perspective or certain issues raised by it that I think are particularly important. This will obviously and necessarily leave a range of issues unaddressed and questions unanswered, some of which may or may not be encountered in future conversations or written work.

9. Nielsen (1990) maintains that "the critical tradition," of which I would, in general, consider myself an advocate, supports a similar position as mine: "the critical tradition rejects the idea that there can be 'objective' knowledge. Proponents of the tradition argue that there is no such thing as an objectively neutral or disinterested perspective, that everyone or every group (including themselves) is located socially and historically, and this context inevitably influences the knowledge they produce. Knowledge, in short, is socially constructed" (p. 9).

10. One important theme that will not be developed in this work is an explication of positionality. This is obviously a complicated concept, especially in terms of social relativism. In lieu of a more extended discussion, I would say that positionality encompasses history, class, race, and gender, among other possible factors. One's historical position, one's class (which may or may not include changes in one's class over the course of a lifetime), one's race, one's gender, one's region, one's religion, and so on, all of these interact and influence, limit and constrain productions of knowledge. Without a doubt these interactions are extremely complex. Nonetheless, they cannot be overlooked, especially where one social group, like white middle-class males, tends to dominate knowledge production. The social positionality of such dominant groups and the maintenance of that positionality has an immense impact on knowledge production. Many, however, would dispute that positionality and relativity, even as I have defined them, are related. Indeed, positionality is a position that is often used to escape the bane of relativism. As can be surmised by the end of this chapter, I disagree that the nonrelativist version of positionality attains this escape.

11. Foucault (1979) takes the relation between power and knowledge several steps further when he asserts that

> Perhaps, too, we should abandon a whole tradition that allows us to imagine that knowledge can exist only where the power relations are suspended and that knowledge can develop outside its injunctions, its demands and its interests. Perhaps we should abandon the belief that power makes mad and that, by the same token, the renunciation of power is one of the conditions of knowledge. We should admit rather that power produces knowledge (and not simply by encouraging it because it serves power or by applying it because it is useful); that power and knowledge directly imply one another; that there is not power relation without the correlative constitution of a field of knowledge, nor any knowledge that does not presuppose and constitute at the same time power relations. (p. 27)

12. I define the word "political" somewhat differently from what is most common. Most frequently the word "political" is used in such statements as "The principal's choice as to which teacher is to chair the committee was very political." My definition encompasses this latter use for the most part, but it is also much broader than this. I use the word to indicate alignments, arrangements, or relationships of power, resources, and people.

13. One line of thought in poststructuralism, following Nietzsche (Taylor, 1986), suggests that the pursuit of knowledge is a facade for a will to power on the part of Western civilization. Lubiano (1991, p. 181) calls it the "Euro-American territorial and cultural will to power." Foucault (1977, p. 163) says that Nietzsche thought that "The historical analysis of this rancorous will to knowledge reveals that all knowledge rests upon injustice . . . and that the instinct for knowledge is malicious." Young, in an excellent work entitled *White Mythologies* (1990), contends that the Western knowledge project is an academic version of Western imperialism.

14. As I have said previously, I will not attempt to be comprehensive. In this instance I will not try to answer all of the criticisms of relativism. Even if this task were possible, there would be little room in this work for anything else. Instead I will attempt to address three criticisms that are particularly important to me and are relevant to developing my perspective. I will not address, in particular, the argument that is widely thought to destroy relativism (i.e., that it is self-refuting). According to one way this argument goes, if everything is relative, then relativity itself is relative and thus refuted. Hesse (1980) has successfully, in my opinion and in the opinion of Barnes and Bloor (1991), answered this criticism of relativism. Nonetheless, I do not think that someone who is strongly against relativism will accept her argument. In a certain sense, the unwillingness to listen to Hesse's arguments reasserts relativism.

Poststructuralism addresses the apparently self-refuting character of relativism in a different way. Poststructuralists such as Minh-ha (1989) and Spivak (1988) have developed a way of writing that both asserts and undermines the assertion. Lather (1991b) in education has also focused on this manner of rhetorical presentation of a text. In this way these authors always foreground the contingency of all statements. Although this poststructuralist style was not specifically developed to answer the critics of the supposed self-refuting character of relativism, it flows out of a similar understanding that all positions are problematic.

15. See feminist (Alcoff, 1987; Harding, 1986; 1991; Lather, 1991b; Minh-ha, 1989; Nielsen, 1990; Shakeshaft, 1987), race-oriented (Gordon et al., 1990; Stanfield, 1985), and critical theorist (Bates, 1980; 1982; Foster, 1986; Habermas, 1971) critiques of positivism as a power-free truth game.

16. Stone (1989) has written a book about Atlanta, Georgia, that details the long-term alliance between the African-American community (middle-class and lower-class) of Atlanta and its largely white business community. Because African-American leaders were able to develop a large, consistent block of voters and because the white business community saw its success dependent on the support of that block of African-American voters, a reasonably successful coalition was developed between what is traditionally seen as a less powerful group, the African-Americans, and a more powerful group, the business community.

17. See, for example, Merquior's (1985) comment about epistemological dominance as seen by Foucault in *The Archaeology of Knowledge* (1972): "the dominance of an episteme does not mean that every single mind thought along the same line in a given age and culture" (p. 61).

18. Another good example is the Greenfield-Griffiths-Willower debates. Greenfield raised what he called a phenomenological challenge to the positivism of the theory movement in educational administration. Proponents of the theory movement, like Griffiths and Willower, responded with aggressive repudiations of Greenfield. Although this debate continues to simmer (Culbertson, 1988; Greenfield, 1991), in many ways the challenger, Greenfield, has "won" the debate, at least theoretically. This was verified by Griffiths (1988, p. 30) himself when he admitted that "the demise of the theory movement came at the 1974 meeting" where Greenfield first presented his phenomenological critique. This powerful effect of Greenfield's critique was also verified by Culbertson (1988) when he concluded that Greenfield "fired a shot at the theory movement that was heard around the world. Striking hard at the key suppositions of the theory movement, he precipitated controversy which is not yet ended" (p. 20). That most professors of educational administration continue to operate from within the positivistic frame of the theory movement (Nicolaides and Gaynor, 1989) means, though, that while the theory movement may be dead theoretically, it is still thriving in departments of educational administration and, presumably, among school administrators.

19. This criticism is particularly important to me because I am a strong advocate for the numerous emancipatory perspectives, such as feminism, critical theory, Afrocentrism, and so on. In fact, my perspective is located amidst the work of scholars who position themselves within one of the critical perspectives. Part of my purpose in this work, however, is to disagree with such scholars that relativism is not the threat it is seen to be and that relativism is a "better representation" of their work than foundational or the various postfoundational perspectives. (For examples of two critical theorists who, as Lather, 1991b, says, are both "attracted" and "ambivalent" toward a relativist position, see Giroux, 1988b and McLaren, 1988.)

20. For example, Lather (1991a), who considers herself to be working at the "intersection of postmodernism and the politics of emancipation" (p. 1), says that "While 'the real' is mediated through language, it has not disappeared" (p. 31), especially the "realities of poverty, racism, sexism, imperialism" (p. 30). I would argue otherwise: these "realities" are not real in the sense that Lather hopes they are; they are historically located social constructions that have arisen out of past and present political struggles. Bakhtin (1986) says that the meanings of all words "always exists among other meanings as a link in the chain of meaning, which in its totality is the only thing that can be real" (p. ix). I will have more to say, however, about this as this particular section progresses.

21. One of the arguments that I would pursue in opposition to Bernstein's (1988), Harding's (1991), and Lather's (1991b) ideas of the "real" is that the very idea that there is a something called reality that is "out there" to be known by humans is itself a cultural construction. To go around thinking that there is something out there is a Western cultural construct. Other cultures—some Native American cultures and some African cultures, for instance—do not appear to think this way. To think in the Western way is to assume that there is some kind of separation between the thinker and the "out there" reality. In addition, the insertion of something called "knowing" that is located inbetween the thinker and this thing called reality is equally dependent on the same dualism of humans and reality. Some non-Western cultures and some marginalized cultures within the West think, instead, that humans and reality are one interdependent whole. They would thus not posit some process like "knowing" that existed between human existence and the larger world, nor would they posit the humans/world dualism.

22. Rorty (1989) argues, and I agree, that these postfoundational efforts arise out of the

same impulse or needs that lead to foundational standards. He advises that we simply give up this way of thinking.

23. Donmoyer (1991) has an article in *Educational Administration Ouarterly* that, in my opinion, suggests a very different position from the one he maintained in "Rescue from Relativism." In this more recent "postpositivist" article he suggests that the evaluation of a school program be conducted as a parent-teacher committee process. He even suggests, contrary to his prior position on rationality (Donmoyer, 1985), that there are "limits . . . [to] rational discourse" and that these limits "challenge some of the fundamental assumptions that undergird a deliberative approach" (p. 285). Such an approach seems very social relativist to me. It apparently posits that there is no correct evaluation of the program that rises above the socially located committee process. Thus, in this case, "knowledge" is a social production with no ahistorical foundation or postfoundational metacriteria. Moreover, he even discusses the fact that the parent-teacher committee process is basically political. In this case the ideology of the teachers was able to dominate complaints about the program by the parents with the result that the evaluation was judged to be inequitable by Donmoyer. The main limitation of the article from my point of view, however, is that Donmoyer is not self-reflective of his own positionality and politics within the study.

The issue could be raised that this case raises the very problems that are cited in reference to relativism (i.e., relativism leads to might makes right). I would simply say, as I have said previously, that power and knowledge are always operative in all knowledge production situations, no matter what epistemology was used. Knowledge production is always a political process: "The postpositivist critique suggests that ideological issues can never be avoided, they can only be unconscious" (Donmoyer, 1991, p. 293). That the more powerful or the more articulate usually win is nothing new, as the less powerful and less articulate well know. But social relativism foregrounds that there is always a politics. In addition, as I have also contended, the powerful rarely, and perhaps never, have total dominance for any meaningful period of time. It is my opinion that if Donmoyer (1991) had been looking for indications that the dominance of the teachers on the committee was not total, he would have been able to find such evidence.

24. Poststructuralists would suggest that the only way one sort of rationality can be privileged over other possible alternative rationalities would be through a (hidden) violent suppression of these other alternatives. They would argue that any kind of epistemological privilege involves a kind of violence (Flax, 1990; Foucault, 1977; Minh-ha, 1989; Norris, 1987; Scheurich & Lather, 1991; Young, 1990).

25. *Bricolage* is a French word that means "the ad hoc assemblage of miscellaneous materials and signifying structures" (Levi-Strauss, quoted in Norris, 1987, p. 134). Spivak (1976) says "the *bricoleur* makes do with things that were meant perhaps for other ends" (p. xix). Levi-Strauss used this word to describe how pre-Western cultures "made sense of the world in a way quite remote from our own, more logical and regimented habits of thought" (Norris, 1987, p. 134).

The *bricoleur* is a kind of Heath Robinson figure, happy to exploit the most diverse assortment of mythemes—or random combinatory elements—in order to create a working hypothesis about this or that feature of social life. The opposite approach is that of the typecast "engineer," one who starts out with a well-defined concept of a machine (or explanatory theory) he wants to construct, and who follows this blueprint through to its logical conclusion.

26. I think my socially constrained relativism also overcomes postpositivist positions, as typified by Donmoyer (1987), that argue that relativism eliminates any possibility of

making decisions or judgments about theories or paradigms. My reply is simply that decisions or judgments are made, but they are made within the political struggles of a particular social, historical, and, often, disciplinary context. From a relativist position the decisions or judgments made are not "better" according to any postfoundational reasoning that is itself ahistorical or apolitical. Such judgments are only "better" in terms of a particular perspective within a specific context.

27. In light of this statement and the prior discussions of social relativism, it might be argued that I have no basis for judging any position as inadequate. If this argument, however, is thought to be inconsistent with my explanations of social relativism, then I have failed to communicate clearly. A social relativist does not contend that judgments cannot be made between various perspectives or various theories within a single perspective. Instead a social relativist claims that such judgments, including those made in this work, are themselves within social, historical contexts and are, thus, relative. In addition, I have tried repeatedly to make the point that all perspectives, theories, and judgments have politics, though what those politics are for (a particular perspective, theory, or judgment) is always debatable.

28. For a critique of realism in philosophy, see Rorty (1982, pp. xxi–xxxvii). Rorty's pragmatism has been criticized as being relativistic. Thus, the realist based "anti-pragmatist backlash" (p. xxi) that he is responding to would be similar to criticisms that might be made of relativism.

29. There are numerous scholars who claim that epistemological discussions should include historical, sociological, and, especially, political issues. See, for example, Bernstein (1982; 1988), Burrell and Morgan (1979), Clegg (1989), Foster (1986), Greenfield (1991), Habermas (1971), Harding (1986; 1991), Lather (1986a, 1986b; 1991a; 1991b), Richardson (1988), and Stanfield (1985). These examples, of course, reflect my political and epistemological interests; there are many other examples reflecting other political and epistemological interests.

30. Donmoyer (1990) makes this same point but from a more practical angle:

Few people would disagree with the proposition that schools should promote learning, but the term *learning* [his emphasis] will mean different things to a kindergarten teacher influenced by Piaget, a process-product researcher, an art teacher who wants to promote productive idiosyncracy, and a parent who wants the schools to go back to basics. Each of these meanings reflects a different conception of what learning is, and what teaching ought to be. Each can be said to reflect a different paradigm of reality. (p. 179)

31. Fraser (1989), whose work I greatly admire, insists that "you can't get a politics straight out of epistemology, even when the epistemology is a radical antiepistemology like historicism, pragmatism, or deconstruction. On the contrary, I argue repeatedly that politics requires a genre of critical theorizing that blends normative argument and empirical sociocultural analysis in a 'diagnosis of the times' " (p. 6). To some extent I simply disagree with her if she defines politics as a general political orientation. In fact, I would say that you do not "get a politics . . . out of epistemology"; instead I would say that an epistemology is a politics, again if by politics is meant a general orientation that arranges bodies and things. Moreover, I would also suggest that this issue is best examined in terms of specific applications or practices of particular epistemologies. In such cases, it seems to me, the equation of epistemology and politics is even more evident. I would emphasize, however, as I have before that what the politics of a particular epistemology is in general or in a specific application is always debatable.

32. See Lather (1986b) and Gitlin et al. (1988) for discussions that move beyond this one to the necessary political relationship between the researcher's epistemology and her or his research methods.

3

One Postmodern Feminist Perspective on Educational Leadership: And Ain't I a Leader?

Jackie M. Blount

INTRODUCTION

I am not an educational administrator. However, after a career teaching in a public high school where I led several student and teacher organizations, I have spent the last few years working to understand the multiple ways in which women have provided leadership in education. The scope of my inquiry ranges from formally designated leadership positions, such as the superintendency, to more informal, though no less important, actions such as engaging students, other educators, and members of the community in discussions about the meanings they attach to their lives and work in schools. Rather than finding that "women's true profession" holds great opportunities for women to speak, act, and lead, I have instead been repeatedly reminded that our public schools are an enormously complex and shifting culture in which women are oppressed with "endless variety and monotonous similarity" (Rubin, 1975, p. 160). Through the years women's multifaceted efforts at leadership have consistently been ignored, resisted, and squashed in a variety of ways by oppressive social structures.

It is tempting to explain this oppression with structuralist metanarratives of sexual/gender identity that cut across cultural, social/economic class, and racial lines. Proponents of such theories claim that men and women possess essential characteristics either born out of biological differences or differing native mental, emotional, or psychic qualities. Two movements among women illustrate the range of essentialist thinking. In the 1970s, liberal feminists voiced a belief that in order for women to break free of sexual discrimination, they should minimize their *natural* female qualities and instead adopt characteristically masculine values and behaviors. Women were encouraged to "dress for success" and learn to play the games of the "good old boys." While this advice probably enabled a few women to advance in some spheres, they doubtless did so at the expense of their respecting themselves as women.

Cultural feminists countered the liberal feminist agenda with a variety of theories describing women's positive native qualities, such as caring, compassion, and other relational values (Gilligan, 1982; Noddings, 1984; and Belenky et al., 1986). These writers offered women much needed support by highlighting and appreciating what they perceived as the essential goodness of feminine qualities; and that these values should be highly regarded in our society, especially in comparison with described masculine values, such as competitiveness, isolation, and a belief in a transcendental sense of justice. Though these feminist positions have certainly improved the way many women identify and value themselves, the problem remains that these qualities can and often do become reified and limiting. When this happens, women lose latitude in developing nontraditional gender identities and characteristics. Linda Alcoff (1988) explains:

To the extent that [cultural feminism] reinforces essentialist explanations of these attributes, it is in danger of solidifying an important bulwark for sexist oppression: the belief in an innate "womanhood" to which we must all adhere lest we be deemed either inferior or not "true" women. (p. 266)

Beyond this reification of gender qualities inherent in any essentialist argument, another compelling problem remains. When people face oppressive conditions, they often develop strengths and attributes that many in our culture admire. Women may have developed qualities like caring and compassion as survival responses to societywide sexual oppression (Ferguson, 1984, pp. 92–99). Critics of essentialist feminisms caution, then, that we should work to eliminate oppressive conditions, even those that may foster the development of positive traits. Failure to criticize the basic mechanisms of sexism can invite them back into any possible solutions we might entertain (Alcoff, 1988, p. 267).

Postmodern approaches to feminist theories can provide conceptual tools for breaking free of these limitations in essentialist feminist arguments. Although disparate thinkers have articulated a variety of theories under the banner of postmodernism, Nancy Fraser and Linda Nicholson (1990, p. 21) describe their understanding of the postmodern agenda:

With the demise of foundationalism comes the demise of the view that casts philosophy in the role of *founding* discourse vis-à-vis social criticism. That "modern" conception must give way to a new "postmodern" one in which criticism floats free of any universalist theoretical ground. No longer anchored philosophically, the very shape or character of social criticism changes; it becomes more pragmatic, *ad hoc,* contextual, and local.

A postmodernist, then, might contend that feminist theories attributing certain characteristics to all women fail to recognize the great diversity of women's lives.

For example, some women manifest supposedly masculine qualities. Also, a generalized theory of gender identity does not account for differences associated with race, class, sexual orientation, ethnicity, and numerous other qualities that position individual women in particular and ever-changing social spaces. A postmodern approach ameliorates this shortcoming by accommodating the diversity of women's experiences, the meanings they attach to their lives, the complexities of their social contexts.

One tactic for theorizing about such complexity, deconstruction, aims to dismantle taken-for-granted assumptions about the unitary nature of our sociocultural organizations, assumptions such as those held by essentialist feminists. Deconstruction, when successful, exposes the historical contingency of structural theories and practices previously thought to be ahistorical and somehow transcendent. With such tools as deconstruction at their disposal, postmodernists create sophisticated criticisms of essentialism; however, Fraser and Nicholson (1990) argue that these critiques alone lack the power to provoke social change (p. 20).

Postmodernists, then, offer theoretical tools for challenging essentialist feminist tendencies toward limiting, grand narratives; but on the other hand, feminists offer strong theories for social critique and political action geared toward dismantling oppressive systems. In isolation either approach suffers limitations; however, a complementary relationship is possible. A postmodern feminist practice incorporates the most useful features of each separate approach: tailoring "its methods and categories to the specific task at hand, using multiple categories when appropriate, and forswearing the metaphysical comfort of a single feminist method or feminist epistemology" (Fraser & Nicholson, 1990, p. 35). To maintain integrity, a postmodern feminist also discloses her unique social contexts and history, "and therefore remains critical of [her] own complicity in writing gender and writing others" (Luke & Gore, 1992, p. 7).

Finally, believing that a postmodern feminism is a means by which my knowing informs my action and vice versa, I write this piece "to challenge the legitimacy of the dominant order and break its hold over social life" (Lather, 1991b, p. xv), including the lives of men as well as women. In this work I attempt to bring a postmodern-feminist analysis to bear on the notion of educational leadership and administration in the hope that I might take a few chips out of what seems like a vast and formidable social structure.

EDUCATIONAL LEADERSHIP AND ADMINISTRATION

We are told that our schools face a crisis in leadership. Over the past decade numerous education reform studies, such as *A Nation at Risk* and *Action for Excellence,* have provided documentation and credibility for the notion that our schools desperately need excellent, visionary leaders because our schools are performing poorly. To repair schools, the reports intone, our central concern should be to choose more capable leaders and provide them with careful, thoughtful training. If the authors of these reports are correct in this assertion, then a critical examination of the notion of leadership is in order. In what follows I describe our prevailing cultural conceptions of educational leadership, providing some of the historical and social contexts of their origins. In so doing, I aim to locate structuralist notions of leadership in their temporal and culturally specific frames.

Cultural Conceptions of Educational Leadership

Spencer Maxcy (1991, pp. 2–5), in *Educational Leadership: A Critical Pragmatic Perspective,* opens his critical examination of educational leadership by outlining three prevalent views of leadership that have emerged in research: leadership as a collection of character traits, leadership as behavior, and leadership as a function of social and environmental contexts. These views developed as a means of facilitating discussion on the control of public education, each view is useful for the particular social context and historical moment of its origin.

The first view, that leadership consists of distinct character traits, predominated in education early in the twentieth century as college and university professors, prominent administrators of large school systems, and business leaders filled publications with lists of leadership characteristics. Raymond Frazier (1926, p. 205), for example, outlined what he viewed as the qualities necessary for the ideal principal: "the personification of courage, rugged honesty, sincerity, . . . not too serious, . . . able to play as well as work, . . . he should heartily enter into the wholesome plans and ambitions of his workers . . . just as does the ideal business man."

Those who compiled lists like Frazier's intended to normalize the pool of persons from which to select school administrators. These lists, however, rarely contained explicit mention of particularly desirable demographic characteristics, such as race, gender, economic class, and so on. The authors only purported to list leadership qualities. Men were clearly envisioned for positions of school authority, though, since many of the highlighted character traits were, at the time, generally attributable to men rather than to women. For example, Frazier, himself president of a large bank in Seattle, believed that principals should model themselves after successful business *men,* men rather than women not only because of his use of the masculine pronoun, but also because few women ran businesses or corporations then. He did not overtly express that women should not be principals; however, in the wake of the Suffrage campaigns, influential community members like Frazier commonly stopped speaking openly on issues of employment by sex lest the organized and newly powerful women's groups protest (Blount, 1993). Instead, explicit language was replaced with either coded language, such as trait characterizations, or with silence. Silence on sex discrimination became standard practice in public education during this time as organizations like the National Education Association (NEA) stopped compiling statistics on sex ratios of school administrators, such as superintendents (Hansot & Tyack, 1981).

Around the middle of the century the second view of leadership emerged, that leadership consists of value driven actions of persons in leadership positions. Behavioral psychology, sociology, and other empirical social sciences deemed useful by the American military in World War II figured into this view. In the wake of the war, Herbert Simon's influential work, *Administrative Behavior* (1947), nudged the field of educational administration in the direction of the behavioral sciences. Simon asserts in this work, for example, "that *rational* decision making is a linear series of steps for choosing among established alternatives: (1) listing all the alternative strategies; (2) determining all the consequences that follow upon each of these strategies; and (3) comparatively evaluating these sets of consequences" (Garrison et al., 1991, pp. 84–85). This formalist, functionalist approach assumes that there is a best means for handling any situation a manager is likely to encounter. By following procedures such as those Simon outlines, that means can be objectively determined. Waves created by this and other fast-emerging developments in the social sciences eventually provoked the Kellogg Foundation to provide significant funding for the establishment of several school administration research and training programs (Culbertson, 1988, pp. 14–15). Researchers at these institutions mainly concentrated on such leadership behaviors as decision making, task directing, goal accomplishment, goal setting, and activity directing. Generally, researchers tended "to postulate causal models of leadership, vectoring force, and control over groups" (Maxcy, 1991, p. 14).

Many feminists have argued that these studies of leadership behavior have presented problems for women in general because the scientific, positivistic underpinnings of such works are inherently gender biased. Feminist philosopher of science Evelyn Fox Keller (1985, pp. 3–4) explains that science is not a discipline defined only "by the exigencies of logical proof and experimental verification," but rather is a socially constructed body of knowledge and set of practices. Since the people largely responsible for the creation of modern science have been white, middle-class males, any attempt to claim the value-neutrality of science in effect conceals its masculine gender bias (Garrison et al., 1991, p. 115).

In addition to confronting implicitly gender biased social science research, women who aspired to educational leadership in the middle of the twentieth century faced another problem. As the body of empirical research findings on educational leadership grew, the training of school administrators in the resulting methods became a requirement for their employment and their professional development. Educators found they could no longer rise through administrative ranks solely on the basis of their experience. In compliance with new professional standards developed in part by Kellogg Foundation pilot programs, educators seeking promotions also needed academic credentials.

Women faced limits on their access to these credentialing programs in several ways. First, some of the schools that hosted Kellogg programs, such as Teachers College, were primarily male institutions. (See Campbell et al., 1987, p. 14 for some of the Kellogg sites. Also, see Solomon, 1985, pp. 53–58 for dates women were admitted to men's colleges and universities.) Second, institutions of higher education that kept enrollments up during World War II by recruiting women, changed their policies after the war and pushed women out to make room for returning veterans (Solomon, 1985, p. 190). Third, male veterans not only displaced women in colleges and universities, but they also pushed school enrollments to record highs in large part because they received G.I. Bill education benefits. Future school administrators were among the recipients of this governmental largess—an AASA Survey of Superintendents revealed that in 1971, nearly three quarters of all school superintendents had obtained their masters degrees with G.I. Bill assistance (AASA, 1971, p. 48). These three factors and a host of others contributed to an overall pattern of the inaccessibility to women of educational administration credentialing programs, programs that developed as means of implementing research based on the view that leadership consists of value-driven behaviors.

Finally, the third view that researchers have held is that leadership is a function of social and environmental contexts. Maxcy explains that the goal of this approach is "the identification of particular characteristics of the setting which seem to impact on leader behavior." Researchers attempt "to isolate specific situation variables determining leadership" (Maxcy, 1991, p. 34). The usual method employed in these studies is a search for controlling variables that affect leadership; however, a significant weakness with this approach is that researchers have difficulty defining leadership. Also, the questions remain: In the event that researchers manage to define leadership and clearly identify its contributing environmental factors, who then will control these factors and for what purposes?

The Purveyors of the Educational Leadership Crisis

When the three main views of leadership are examined for the historical contexts of their emergence, the agents of their construction, as well as their popular implementation, several patterns emerge. First, questions about educational leadership have been posed by groups of persons in authority positions who have had sufficient socially derived power to effect change in the qualities, behaviors, and contexts of school administrators. Second, these persons in authority have been able to control the discussion of educational leadership by defining the accepted discourse parameters, such as whose leadership deserves scrutiny, which aspects of leadership are of interest, and how leadership will be investigated. Third, the persons who have controlled discourse about educational leadership generally have not included women and other oppressed groups either in discussions of leadership or in consideration for formal administrative positions. As a feminist, it has often seemed to me as though this discourse has treated *women* and *leaders* as two mutually exclusive categories.

Who, then, are the people controlling the discourse about educational leadership? Joel Spring (Spring, 1993, p. 3) begins an answer to this question by listing the powerful political actors affecting public education including politicians, the courts, private foundations, teachers' unions, the corporate sector, educational-interest groups, and knowledge creators, gatekeepers, and distributors. Politicians, for example, at the national, state, and local level both engage in discussion about *leadership* and commission research to study it. A host of national blue ribbon panels and expert commissions appointed by politicians have issued reports and recommendations for improving the training, practice, and conditions of school leaders. Often the views conveyed in these reports influence national policy as well as government and private philanthropic funding for education. Many governors, legislators, state superintendents of education, and state school board members call for research on school leadership to guide the development of state law and policy. Local politicians and school board members likewise commission their own research, call in leadership consultants, or read extant literature to best determine how school leadership should be controlled.

Regardless of the level at which they serve, politicians enjoy similar positional advantages, but they also feel comparable pressures. Elected officials benefit from the somewhat public forum from which they speak on issues of educational leadership. They also have funds with which they may solicit "expert" opinions, then later implement and control programs designed to better affect leadership. To a certain extent, though, politicians accept risks with their positional power. They are accountable for their cumulative actions at each election. They may receive or be denied funds from various educational-interest groups depending on their individual positions on education issues. They also face the scrutiny of the media.

The business and corporate worlds also participate vigorously in discussions about educational leadership. Joel Spring (1993) summarizes the motives driving their interest:

The corporate sector is interested in increasing profits, and one way of enhancing profits is to maintain low wages and tax rates. On the basis of these assumptions, businesses might want public school systems to: (1) educate potential employees at the lowest cost to the corporate taxpayer; (2) reduce the cost of labor by educating a steady stream of employees for particular segments of the labor market; (3) concentrate on skills needed by business; (4) present knowledge as instrumental for work as opposed to knowledge as a means to develop a critical awareness of politics and the economy; (5) socialize the student to be a compliant worker who will not rock the corporate boat; (6) avoid teaching about unionism and collective action as a possible means of improving working conditions and wages, because these would increase labor costs and reduce profits; and (7) teach the student a pro-business ideology that would not question increasing concentrations of wealth. (p. 16)

With these considerations in mind, the business sector clearly has vested interests in working closely with and attempting to control the direction of public education leadership.

Besides politicians and members of the business community, some educational researchers also invest substantial time and effort in the discourse on educational leadership. These researchers tend to work in institutions of higher education, private research organizations, or in government-sponsored research institutes.

Individuals or organizations interested in changing leaders and/or their conditions usually fund this work. Some researchers, while professing objectivity, maintain an awareness that they must provide the kind of information for which they are being commissioned. The resulting research often reflects the inherent biases of fund providers as well as of the researchers who need to continue to please their clients/employers. These researchers may not ask important questions; they might fail to consider the perspectives of certain seemingly unimportant constituencies in schools; and they may not explore particular alternatives that would adversely affect the conditions of those supporting the research.

Academic researchers in universities and colleges tend to enjoy greater latitude than private and some government-sponsored researchers in the sense that their paychecks are not written directly by those for whom their work is intended. Academics, however, face different pressures. First, some college and university professors are concerned with educational leadership issues because their work consists of preparing the people who will become school administrators. It is in the best interests of these professors to convince law and policy makers that academic preparation programs have important services to offer. Otherwise, these professors would find themselves out of work.

One way that researchers in educational leadership have demonstrated their competence in assuming the task of preparing school administrators is by generating a large corpus of research literature, of legitimating knowledge. The educational leadership professor, then, becomes both a creator and a broker of knowledge—knowledge that separates the credentialed from the uncredentialed. Researchers and professors find they must generate this knowledge for the continued existence of educational leadership preparation programs, and thus their livelihoods.

The experiences of one of the earliest educational leadership researchers/professors, Ellwood Cubberley, provides clear illustration of this problem. David Tyack (1974, pp. 135–36) explains that Cubberley was hired by Stanford in 1898 and was expected to build the school's education program with leadership components. Stanford's president instructed him to make the program "intellectually respectable in three years or see it abolished. . . . Thus Cubberley had to discover what it was he should be teaching, had to convince his colleagues that it was worth academic credit, and had to recruit students who thought the training was worth their tuition." Cubberley then went about the task of writing the textbooks that he would need for his newly created programs. Although Cubberley's situation was extreme in the sense that he was told up front that he faced program termination, academics today still endure the pressure to produce and convey legitimating knowledge. Who determines that this knowledge is legitimate? A very important component of academic work is the production of research that is discussed mainly within academic circles. In an insightful analysis, Deborah Eaker and Jane Van Galen (1992) reveal a system where institutions of higher education reward professors for writing and presenting research intended mainly for other academics. Universities and colleges hire and promote professors in part on their record of publications in academic journals and presentations at academic conferences. This practice creates a closed system where researchers maintain a vested interest in producing particular types of works for their peers. In an arrangement like this, there is little incentive for creating either research or administrator preparation programs that aim to change significantly the practice of teaching/leading.

Not only does the academic community tend to exclude nonacademics, but in the field of educational administration, academic women also face barriers to the discourse of their own profession. Charol Shakeshaft and Marjorie Hanson (1986) illustrate this phenomenon by analyzing the editorial practices of the influential *Educational Administration Ouarterly* for evidence of androcentric bias. Not only do they find numerous instances, but they also cite the relative absence of women among article authors (8% for the decade of the 1970s). Shakeshaft (1989, p. 43) highlights another barrier women have faced: until the 1970s, the educational honor fraternity, Phi Delta Kappa, formally excluded women.

Ortiz and Marshall (1988, p. 130) argue that not only is the work of female educational leadership professors difficult, but also that entrance into the profession in the first place is fraught with hazards. They found, for example, that the 1983-1984 *Educational Administration Directory* lists only 200 women among a total of 2,553 professors of educational administration. They further describe that "detailed information on some 196 of the 200 positions reveal that (a) 63 were temporary and 133 were permanent; (b) of the 133 permanent positions, 49 were at the assistant professor level, 50 at the associate professor level, and 34 at the full professor level." Proportionately fewer women, then, formally engage in the academic discourse on educational leadership. This situation exists even though women's enrollment in educational administration doctoral programs has increased significantly since the 1972 passage of Title IX of the Education Amendments: from 11% in 1972 to 39% in 1981-1982 (Fishel and Pottker, 1975, pp. 300-310).

In addition to politicians, business persons, and educational researchers/professors, there are certainly other individuals and groups of people, such as educational administrators themselves, who are deeply interested in the subject of educational leadership. These people have in common their relative power to change the selection process for and practice of school administration. Despite these commonalties, each group also has its distinct interests in defining and controlling educational leadership.

Unheard Voices

Many people have been conspicuously absent from public discussion of educational leadership. Teachers and school employees subservient to administrators, for example, have rarely been included on expert commissions, consulted on policy-making decisions, invited to submit articles or opinion pieces, or been permitted substantive power when issues of educational leadership are at stake.

Students, the persons whom schools allegedly serve, are consulted less frequently. Even parents and other community members find that though they have some political power as adults with voting privileges, their voices are usually far from the fray on this issue. It is not that these people have few or unimportant opinions in a discussion of leadership. Many undoubtedly have deep and passionate ideas about who educational administrators are, how they should behave, and perhaps most important, how they should interact with the people whom they are designated to lead. These people have in common not only a lack of public voice, a voice denied them by the exclusionary practices of those who control the discourse, but also the fact that educational administrators are not directly accountable to them.

In a limited sense, parents, adult community members, and local teachers can hold school administrators accountable. They can vote for school board members who in turn usually have the power to appoint administrative personnel. However, this electoral accountability has grown weaker for some groups of persons since, through the years, school board elections have become highly centralized and increasingly costly undertakings for those seeking office. As a result, usually only the affluent and influential members of a community have the resources to mount successful campaigns. Writing in 1927 (p. 4), George Counts observed that school boards are "controlled by the employing classes, that labor is without representation on boards of education and that, as a consequence, the interests of the laboring classes are not adequately recognized in the shaping of educational policies." In addition to excluding the working classes, it has also been rare for school boards to have many female members (Counts, 1927, p. 42; Ortiz & Marshall, 1988, p. 129). Not surprisingly, school boards have come to resemble elite corporate boards rather than representative democratic assemblies for the local citizenry. Any accountability that may exist for underrepresented groups is weak and a couple of layers of hierarchy removed.

This weak accountability of school administrators to the voting public has not always existed. Earlier in the century, for example, a number of superintendents staged and won political elections without appointment by school boards. Because of school suffrage, women often voted in these and other school-related elections even before individual states granted them complete suffrage. (Thomas Woody [1929, pp. 441–44) explains that leaders of the women's suffrage movement used the success of school suffrage in western states as a wedge for demanding expanded suffrage.) A number of women, then, with the support of the suffrage movement managed to win elections for county, intermediate, and some rural superintendencies, often in far greater percentages than men (Blount, 1993). Eventually, though, a nationwide trend toward superintendent appointments replaced the elective process and not coincidentally, men assumed this position in increasing numbers. Then as now, since school boards were not usually demographically representative of their constituency, it is not surprising that the persons they appointed were not either. School boards' members have tended to choose people most like themselves: white males amenable to the needs of the affluent and influential members of the community.

Essentially, then, educational leaders and those who discuss leadership issues are persons who operate within a hierarchical structure where the lines of accountability run mainly in one direction—from those with great positional power to those with little. Voices in conversations about leadership also run in one direction—from those with interests in manipulating/controlling the subject of leadership to those who must listen and comply. As a result, a number of persons intimately involved with public schooling have been excluded from discussions on the shape and direction of education in this country.

Problems with the Notion of Leadership

When framed in their historical and social contexts, the initiators of and participants in discussions of educational leadership can be seen operating from privileged positions in a rigidly hierarchical system. These actors have sought to define the rules by which the structures of public education operate. Further, they have worked to normalize not only the practice, but also the selection of educational administrators in their own images. By setting the discourse parameters, these powerful persons have also determined the practices deemed undesirable, the voices to be silenced, and the persons to be oppressed.

Although educational *leadership* has been a central expressed concern of the discourse-privileged over the last century, the term has largely escaped critical scrutiny in several problematic areas. First, those in control of this discourse have traditionally viewed leadership as a theoretical construct for which an ideal exists, an ideal free of the whims of social definition. Supposedly, then, the purpose of research has been to discover these ideals and devise ways to assure their manifestation. When this discourse is grounded in its social and historical contexts, though, leadership ideals can instead be seen as manifestations of modernist assumptions about a hierarchical structure that tends to preserve the positions of the discourse-privileged. When leadership is idealized, the term's definers escape responsibility for the results of its application. Their complicity is thus concealed.

Second, those who subscribe to traditional views of leadership assume that a leader can be defined as a person who displays leadership traits, behaves like a leader, or operates within a particular context defined as that of a leader. This assumption, however, covers over another important conceptual alienation: When we construct such models, we neatly remove the notion of leadership from the person who leads. This schism makes it relatively easy for the privileged to exert control since finding ways to manipulate a theoretical practice such as leadership presents much less difficulty than directly attempting to control leaders. A leader, or anyone else who faces overt control efforts, might mount resistant challenges especially if they are not instigators or complicitors in the attempt.

Third, there is a tendency within this privileged discourse to assume that educational administrators are leaders even though marked distinctions between the two exist. Administrators are appointed by the persons to whom they must later account. Essentially, administrators tend to serve as functionaries whose roles are carefully defined, their hierarchical positions fixed. As such, administrators find themselves expendable; they can be replaced by others who also meet the same structure-bound requirements. To keep their positions, administrators discover that first and foremost, they must preserve the hierarchical structure, even to the exclusion of attending to the complexities of their social and temporal contexts.

Leadership, on the other hand, is a term that implies a context based relationship among people. Where a leader exists, there must be a follower, and where a follower exists, there must be a leader. The leader/follower relationship implies the existence of at least two persons in a particular kind of relationship. "Follow" and "lead" are intentional act verbs: Those who follow or lead do so willingly. When persons choose to follow or lead, they consider the contexts of their situation as well as their relationships with others, their mutual bonds. A leader, then, is unique to a situation, arising from its particular challenges rather than operating as an interchangeable part of a relatively acontextual administrative structure. A leader has bonds with followers and cannot exist in functional isolation from others as do administrators.

Fourth, when discourse-privileged persons in hierarchies define leadership, they assume that one leader (administrator) exists for each discrete group of people. These persons, in turn, must report to individuals higher in the hierarchy. Leadership, by these definitions, seems to connote a system of one-way accountability where those in subservient roles must be accountable for their actions to administrators in higher positions, one administrator per group of people. This limitation on the number of administrators would seem to necessitate either that only one person per group desire to play the role of the administrator, or that if more than one desires this position, a system of competition or other selection mechanism be in place for appointment. Leadership in this hierarchical system, then, is centered at the top of the power structure.

In contrast with this system, leadership is decentered to within the group of persons constituting the leader/follower relationships when persons willingly choose to lead or follow particular others. One who leads, then, does so by maintaining caring, trusting, constant relationships with those who follow. Those who follow reciprocate in ongoing relationships of mutual responsibility. Each influences the other. As leaders and followers maintain these relationships, however, the notion of leadership begins to break down. A leader cannot lead another who does not choose to follow. Accountability in a mutually consenting relationship runs in two directions, rather than in one direction as in a hierarchy. Traditional views of leadership in the context of this type of leader/follower relationship, then, cease to make sense because followership seems to imply a sort of leadership.

CONCLUSION

When the actors and settings of the educational leadership discourse are revealed through historical deconstruction, the seemingly objective assertion that we face a crisis in educational leadership begins to sound contextually contingent. Those holding to structuralist assumptions about social organization must believe the crisis in leadership is real since leadership has traditionally served a key role in maintaining and reifying hierarchies; and these hierarchical structures now face criticism from diverse individuals and groups, each with their own interests and needs, each with their own conceptions of leadership, and each endeavoring to join the discourse on education.

This brief piece is a humble attempt to strengthen the challenges to gendered hierarchies in our educational systems. To dismantle these and other existing modernist structures, much more work needs to be done to understand the historical contexts of educational leadership as it has developed over the last 150 years. This work must be done explicitly from the vantage points of women and other silenced groups so that their socially constructed realities may consciously be put at the center of inquiry.

Who am I, though, to discuss educational leadership when I, like most of the other persons who have traditionally been privileged in this discourse, am outside the immediate contexts of public schools? I am not presently an educational administrator, teacher, or student. However, I am a woman who has taught in public schools, believed passionately in the meanings I attached to my work, adored my students and colleagues, labored to improve educational practices in my school and local system, and ultimately felt frustrated by the utter silence with which the restrictive and rule-bound layers of administration greeted constructive innovations. I have spent much time pondering why other voices and mine, particularly those of women, were deemed unimportant. My solution to this situation has been to move from one position in a hierarchical system to another with greater voice. Paradoxically, however, in order for my structure-chipping voice to be heard, I have found that the structure assuring my newly privileged speech is the same structure continuing to deny that of others.

A ruthless self-reflexivity helps me to maintain some integrity while attempting emancipatory work from within this oppressive system. This self-conscious analysis is essential for anyone undertaking such ideological work as feminism since otherwise, the line between ideology and dogmatism is thin and elusive (Lather, 1991b). It is also important for one who critiques structuralism to watch for her own theory-reifying, oppressive tendencies. While this close examination may reveal paradoxes and the uneasy, often painful coexistence of multiple truths, it is a necessary precondition for theory directed toward the demise of operant oppressions in our culture. It is to this end I wish my actions to lead.

4

A Postmodernist Analysis of Educational Administration

Jon S. Davies and William Foster

Educational administration is a discipline taught at major universities in both Western and Eastern countries. It is a discipline an understanding of which is recognized as a prerequisite to secure licensure for practicing in administrative positions, such as the principalship and superintendency (in the United States). As a discipline, albeit a professional one, educational administration rests on a foundational base of knowledge and makes a claim to a certain coherence of structure within its academic framework. Like other professional disciplines—nursing, law, social work—educational administration theorists present a foundational core of concepts considered necessary to the practice of the profession. These foundations include courses in areas such as supervision, school law, organizational and administrative theory, and so on.

This chapter argues that, first, educational administration presents to its audience a received "text," a text that includes uncontested definitions of the field and certain beliefs in particular procedures. Second, such received texts are in themselves only one way of interpreting the social world of administration, and this one way is itself intimately tied up to conceptions of power, resources, legitimacy, and status. This argument is developed through an analysis of postmodernism and its implications. Finally, the chapter argues that educational administration programs, deprived of their foundational basis and informed by a postmodernist theory, have to become critically pragmatic in order to better serve their constituency.

THE ESSENTIALIST BASE OF EDUCATIONAL ADMINISTRATION

By essentialist, we mean a set of assumptions about the nature of knowledge. In particular, an essentialist perspective suggests that there is an essential set of basic beliefs and a foundation of knowledge that undergirds the field. Here theorists and practitioners alike assume that there are essential doctrines that support a knowledge base, that further research is necessary to enhance such a base, and that the eventual outcome of both research and theory development will be the discovery of universal laws.

Each of these assumptions exists in educational administration and its various disciplinary spin-offs. Certain of the foundationalist assumptions for the field are compelling; among the more frequently mentioned are these:

1. Research will generate theory, which in turn will produce law-like generalizations. Hoy and Miskel (1982) define applying knowledge to "administrative and organizational problems" (p. 27) and then go on to observe that "the road to generalized knowledge can lie only in tough-minded scientific research" (p. 28). Knezevich (1984), while admitting the "artistic" side of administration, suggests that "the goal of the scientific approach to administration is the more precise determination and realization of institutional outcomes through reliance on theory, models, sophisticated tools in administrative planning, decision making, and leadership behavior" (p. 9). The emphasis in the teaching of educational administration is on how theory and research can guide practice, and on how increasing scientific research will yield reliable, foundational knowledge for the practice of administration.

2. There are well-established concepts that can explain administrative and organizational behavior. Hanson (1979) comments that the objective of his text on educational administration is "providing decision makers with concepts and theoretical frameworks that aid them in determining what to look for in diagnosing and analyzing what they will see" (p. 17). Campbell and associates (1985), in the fifth edition of their text on administration, conclude that "behavioral scientists have developed some useful concepts about organizations and much empirical work has been done to test these concepts" (p. 17). Textual material used in administration generally accepts what it labels "administrative science" or "management science" and assumes that their concepts are foundational for the preparation of administrators. These concepts include motivation of employees, effective communication strategies, authority relationships, organizational climate, and models of leadership behavior.

3. Competing perspectives and alternative frameworks are not acknowledged, or if acknowledged, done so only in passing. An examination of popular texts in administration will show little concern by such texts with continental scholarship, neo-Marxist accounts of schooling, revisionist histories, critical theory, feminist critique, constructivism, and other nonparadigmatic deviations from orthodox, functionalist approaches to understanding human action. The outcome, of course, is to present assumptions 1 and 2 as necessary, satisfactory, and sufficient.

4. The reification of concepts is considered a normal and necessary outcome of an administrative science. The traditional approach to educational administration is to see such concepts as "organization," "leadership," "administration," and so on as things that can be researched, prodded, changed, and otherwise manipulated. They stand not as artificial creations of human minds but as concrete entities, and are presented as such to the audience of educational administration texts. This, indeed, must be the case if the model under which educational administration research operates is to justify itself, for if there were no concrete, "real" organizations much of the research program would falter for lack of a subject.

These four assumptions are the major ones that underlie the discipline of educational administration as it is conceived in colleges and universities. There are other approaches to administration, but they remain on the fringe of that tight circle of believers in a positivistic science of educational administration. It may not be excessive to say that this circle is a wide one indeed; a network of actors ties together a unified approach to the field. In addition to the college professor, state credentialing agencies design "competencies" that university programs must meet; by and large, these competencies reflect the foundationalist assumptions already discussed. They often have to do with teaching about the nature of organizations, the tasks of administration, the legal and financial systems, and so on.

The popular literature in educational administration demonstrates a foundationalist bias as well. The rash of "school effectiveness" articles certainly shows this, with their certain correlates of effectiveness and their basic principles for achieving an effective school environment. National reports call for change and many times change in basic institutional arrangements; however, they generally accept the basic structure of American schooling, and in so doing accept the foundationalist basis for it. A report by the Carnegie Forum (1986), for example, suggests that "school systems based on bureaucratic authority must be replaced by schools in which authority is grounded in the professional competence of the teacher, and where teachers work together as colleagues, constantly striving to improve their performance" (p. 55). Thus, the essentialist concepts of authority, competence, and performance remain as measures of a profession, whether located in bureaucracy or collegiality.

Our argument has been that educational administration programs, themselves caught up in a web of interdependence between universities, state departments, popular journals, and practitioners, have demonstrated certain essentialist tendencies; this means that such programs have assumed that either a certain, essentialist base for such programs has been achieved, or that such a base is imminent in the not-far-distant future.

If this argument is correct, as we believe it to be, then it reflects a basically modernist position on the administration of schooling and even on its reform. (We are here using the terms "modern" and "structural" interchangeably.) Cherryholmes (1988), for example, points out that "structuralist and positivist modes of thought dominate texts and discourses-practices of contemporary education" (p. 13). A modernist position assumes the existence of a foundationalist base and a deep and underlying rational structure to programs and projects in education, including those that involve administration. The four assumptions developed earlier reflect an essentialist approach to administration and a modernist perspective on it. A modernist perspective suggests that there is indeed an underlying order to things, whether in language, culture, or educational administration. A modernist lens would have us look at the underlying order to which an essentialist project aspires, although it would not necessarily engage in the type of positivistic presumptions about regularities, knowable laws, and systemic generalities that much of administrative science uses. Nevertheless, both the essentialist and the modernist positions believe that it is possible to discover the basic operating rules of a social system, to understand the obvious or hidden assumptions of such systems, and to uncover the glue that holds such systems together. It is this with which postmodernism disagrees. In particular, it would disagree with the essentialist nature of educational administration.

The Modern and the Postmodern

Thus far, we have argued that educational administration is organized as a discipline that makes a claim to a coherent structure and foundational base and that this claim merely reflects the pervasive modernist view of the educational field in general. A modernist view is governed by certain principles that are accepted as "givens" and that become problematic when subjected to a postmodernist analysis. In order to conduct a postmodernist analysis, then, we need first to delineate what these modernist principles are and then to critically examine the implications of them for educational administration.

Structuralism or modernism assumes that a given phenomenon or discipline has an underlying rational structure. Miller stated that this rational structure is characterized by "agreed-upon rules of procedure, given facts, and measurable results" (in Culler, 1982, p. 23). These rules and facts serve to "force order on things" (Cherryholmes, 1988, p. 166) and to fix meaning through an "appeal to a transcendent idea that rises above the text or discourse [or structure]. . . . These ideas come to form the origin of truth" (p. 32). Culler (1982) maintained that "the structuralist enterprise extends the methodological models developed by linguistics to all aspects of culture and studies signification as the product of underlying systems of rules and norms, like the grammar of a language" (p. 17). Structuralism, thus, "is a systematic way of thinking about whole processes and institutions whereby each part of a system defines and is defined by other parts" (p. 13). Reed (1992) argues that in postmodern organizational theory:

Belief in an independently existing and objective "organizational reality," knowable through scientific reasoning and discourse, is replaced by a conception of theories as self-justifying representational forms or "intelligible narratives" which allow groups or communities of researchers and scholars to make shared sense of their collective engagement with a predefined phenomenon. (p. 11)

The terms discourse and text are used in particular ways in a modernist perspective. In a modernist context discourse and text are categories that contribute to the formulation of the underlying structure. A discourse, for example, is that which "refers to what is said and written and passes for more or less orderly thought and exchange of ideas" (Cherryholmes, 1988, p. 3). This orderly thought is "constituted by . . . sets of rules that organize and give . . . coherence" (p. 4). These oral and written expressions of thought, governed by sets of rules, form "organized bodies of knowledge and practice" (Major-Poetzl, 1983, p. 5).

From a modern perspective, text assumes a more amplified definition than the more narrow one usually associated with the term. "Texts are discursive and contribute to discourses. . . . They are speech acts, and we act when we project texts and discourses onto the world around us" (Cherryholmes, 1988, p. 7). Text and discourse, then, when projected onto the world, serve as the basis for the reification of structure. In this way, discourse and text come to be accepted as foundational and unquestioned.

A postmodernist analysis is, in part, an analysis of how discourses and texts are formed. This analysis includes a rejection of the notion that there can be objective truth or that foundational, transcendent first principles can form the basis for a discipline. According to Culler (1982) "modernists are convinced that systematic knowledge is possible; postmodernists claim to know only the impossibility of this knowledge" (p. 22). Rather than serving as the harbinger of a new and improved truth, though, poststructuralism is instead a methodology for criticism (Cherryholmes, 1988, p. 40). This methodology includes the questioning of essentialist first principles, "modernist 'givens' are not foundations but provisional starting points which the analysis must question" (Culler, 1982, p. 25), and the uncovering of an ultimately nonrational structure, "the thread of logic leads . . . into regions which are alogical, absurd" (Miller, 1982, in Culler [1982], p. 23). Postmodernist criticism, then, "attacks modernist assumptions and the arguments built upon them" (Cherryholmes, 1988, p. 13).

The basis for a postmodernist critique developed in part from the works of Foucault on interpretive analytics and Derrida on deconstruction theory. According to Foucault, for example, "It is inescapable that discourses are materially produced by specific social, political, and economic arrangements" (Cherryholmes, 1988, p. 33). These social, political, and economic arrangements reflect the unequal distribution of power in a society. Discourses, then, "are generated and governed by rules and power" (p. 35) that determined what is said, what remains unsaid, and who is qualified to speak. The "truth" of a discourse is historically situated and, thus, the notion of a transcendent idea governing truth is illusory.

Derrida challenged the modernist claim that meaning can be fixed by an appeal to a transcendent idea. His argument is based on the notion that "meanings are dispersed throughout language and texts and are deferred in time" (Cherryholmes, 1988, p. 36). The paradox in this is that the meaning of any given word is always ultimately unattainable because its definition depends on other words, whose definitions depend on other words, and so on. Since the meanings of the other words also depend on words, one is trapped in a never-ending search for transcendent meaning, which is always just out of reach. Thus, meaning cannot be fixed by an appeal to some transcendent truth; instead, "settling upon a foundation is situational and pragmatic" (p. 38). Texts and discourses, then, which depend on language for their meaning and which contribute to the formulation of structure, are situational and pragmatic as well. This results in "texts [and discourses that] are often not what they claim to be. Their rhetoric is often not supported by their logic" (pp. 38–39).

Since Foucault argues that discourses are materially produced rather than foundational, and Derrida argues that meanings in language and text are dispersed and deferred rather than transcendent, then the rational basis for a modernist logic is undermined. In its place is a postmodernist skepticism that questions how discourses and texts come into being, reinforce the unequal distribution of power, and legitimize some voices while silencing others.

A postmodern analysis leads to the identification of themes that problematize educational administration. Two concepts that emerge from a poststructural analysis and serve to problematize educational administration are legitimacy and power. Examining the four assumptions in educational administration through a postmodernist lens framed by legitimacy and power, then, calls into question the foundational basis for their existence as unquestioned or unexamined. Legitimacy serves to create a certain status and rightful position within the structure of society. As already stated, by adhering to foundational assumptions, educational administration begins to assume a status in society not unlike medicine or law, in which foundational principles serve to inform the practices of these professions. Power serves to create a social class with special privilege, and one that appears to hold specialized information. In educational administration this class is primarily university professors, who by the specialized information that they hold create a certain mystique about educational administration as a discipline. This kind of mystique, of course, reinforces asymmetrical power relationships in that some people are "in the know" and others are not.

By this we are not suggesting that administrators do not have an effect; rather, it is that their effect is due primarily to their personal influence and not as a result of generalized knowledge about the field. Yet, the pretension to generalized knowledge is used to create power differentials. The foundational base allows for the creation of classes of bureaucrats (e.g., federal/state government, district offices) who act as if they had certain control over the field, as if shoring up their need for personal status.

Given legitimacy and power as they have been defined here, it is evident that they are not entirely independent concepts: Power is derived in part from legitimacy and legitimacy is derived in part from power. Power, for example, is derived in part from the legitimacy provided by social status and position. Conversely, legitimacy is derived in part from the power of holding specialized information. Both are in operation simultaneously in the creation and reification of the discipline of educational administration. By framing an analysis of the essentialist assumptions of educational administration through the postmodernist lens of power and legitimacy, we find that their discourses and texts are materially produced, reflecting the unequal distribution of power in society, and legitimized by an illogical appeal to transcendent meaning. Framing the first essentialist assumption from a postmodernist perspective, namely, that research will generate theory, which in turn will produce law-like generalizations, reveals that the concepts of research, theory, and generalizations contained in the field, and which serve as discourses, are situational and pragmatic rather than foundational. In other words, the text and discourses generated under this assumption are not what they claim to be. They arose not as part of the ongoing discovery of foundational truth, but rather as a result of serving certain power interests in a privileged social class. Rather than leading to a unified general theory, as is implied by the rhetoric contained in the assumption, the discourse exists because it serves to reinforce the legitimacy and power of the status quo. Hoy and Miskel's statement that "the road to generalized knowledge can lie only in tough-minded scientific research" (1982, p. 28) is a good example. The metaphor created by the phrase "the road to generalized knowledge" alludes to the Biblical proverb "The road to hell is paved with good intentions," with the understanding that as sure as there was a hell for an eighth-century Christian, then there must be generalized knowledge for a twentieth-century administrator. The adjective *tough-minded* used to describe scientific research reinforces the Biblical significance, suggesting a Puritan work ethic. The overall effect of the statement, then, is to set up rigorous scientific research as the only legitimate means to achieve generalized knowledge, thus branding all other frameworks or forms of research as somehow illegitimate. Only those who ascribe to scientific research, then, have access to power: Their voices are the ones that are heard.

A postmodernist analysis of the second assumption, that there are well-established concepts that can explain administrative and organizational behavior, suggests several problems as well. Rather than resting on foundational truth, the discourse and text generated by the assumption instead reinforce symmetrical power relationships through a hierarchical organizational structure and bureaucratic administrative procedures that have come to be reified. Campbell and associates' statement that "behavioral scientists have developed some useful concepts about organizations and much empirical work has been done to test these concepts" (1985, p. 17) is a good example. The legitimacy of this statement depends on an appeal to privileged class-behavioral scientists, who, through specialized work and information, have arrived at foundational knowledge about organizations. Because these scientists are a legitimized class who have followed correct empirical procedures, their truth statements tend to assume a reified position.

A postmodernist analysis of the third assumption clearly demonstrates the struggle for legitimacy and power: Competing perspectives and alternative frameworks are not acknowledged, or if acknowledged, done so only in passing. The rhetoric contained in the discourses and texts of educational administration clearly reinforces status quo views of schooling and the school's function in society. Calls for reform do not challenge the existing structure or the underlying socioeconomic conditions in society from which the educational structure emerges. By excluding alternative perspectives and frameworks that challenge the dominant socioeconomic view (for example, feminist critique or critical theory), educational administration discourse legitimizes the power of a predominant Anglo, male, privileged class.

Finally, a postmodernist analysis of the fourth assumption—the reification of concepts is considered a normal and necessary outcome of an administrative science—serves to reinforce existing power arrangements as well, because if such administrative constructs are viewed as concrete, then changing them becomes a much more difficult task. This also serves to legitimize some voices, while silencing others. By ignoring that concepts, such as organization, leadership, and administration, are constructs of the human mind rather than foundational, mainstream researchers, legitimated by membership in a privileged class, dismiss competing views. To do otherwise would present a threat to their own legitimacy and power.

To examine these assumptions separately is, in fact, somewhat misleading. A closer look at the assumptions demonstrates their interconnectedness. It is no surprise that a pursuit of law-like generalizations, for example, also serves to exclude competing frameworks, especially those frameworks that are not based on essentialist principles and that, in fact, challenge the existing structure of education and the social context from which it emerged. The fact that they do so renders them illegitimate, thus silencing their voices. This process of silencing becomes institutionalized when a process of reification is adopted, since that process in turn rejects other ways of conceptualizing organizations.

CONCLUSION

A postmodernist analysis suggests that there is more to educational administration than just technical procedures and scientific research strategies. It reveals the tendency of people to create networks of power, entry into which requires suspending belief in the diversity and mystery of human voices, and sustaining beliefs in unquestioned foundational principles. The outcome, in effect, is to create a closed system that legitimizes the unequal distribution of power, status, prestige, and resources.

PART II
Postmodern Processes

5

Postmodernism and Educational Leadership: The New and Improved Panopticon

*Joseph R. McKinney and
James W. Garrison*

It has been well documented that public education in the Western democracies is managed according to the dictates of Taylorist scientific management, expert systems analysis, and technocratic rationality (Callahan, 1962; House, 1978; Wise, 1979; Lyotard, 1984).During the 1980s the debate on education was dominated by educational reform initiatives linking the needs of corporate America to the American public schools. The overriding emphasis during the 1980s and continuing into the present has been on creating schools that provide the skills necessary for increasing domestic productivity. Three interrelated and continuous waves or periods of educational reform initiatives can be identified. The first wave of education reform, relying on reports like *A Nation at Risk* (1983) and *Action for Excellence* (1983) stressed accountability in a setting that reaffirmed the familiar structuralist strategies of technocratic rationality (e.g., standardization, hierarchy, testing, centralization, and formalized procedures) aimed at administrative management for maximum efficiency and productivity. The second wave of reforms centering on the Carnegie Task Force (1986) and Holmes Group (1986) reports sought to restructure education through programs emphasizing teacher empowerment, decentralized site-based management, and professionalism. One important result of the second wave has been a tendency to subordinate administration to a faculty-initiated leadership activity to facilitate teacher empowerment. The emerging third wave reforms have begun to address matters of administrative leadership. The Danforth Foundation and the University Council for Educational Administration (UCEA) have called for the reform of administrator training that would be more rigorous and full-time and less committed to narrow technocratic models of administration (Johnston, 1991). Unfortunately, both the Danforth Foundation and the UCEA response to the reform movement has been to rely on the administrative internship as a way to connect with the field. This is problematic because in so doing they rely on what already is and tend to perpetuate the status quo. The internship becomes the culprit. Further, the waves of national reform have created a high tide for educational research aimed at school improvement. The result has been the production of "effective schools" research aimed at identifying the characteristics of the "effective school." Again, this research relies on existing practice and is sure to reproduce more of the status quo.

What is missing are any clear images of what administrative alternatives emerging from the third wave might look like. In this chapter we would like to propose one such alternative to narrow technocratic management strategies, the "garbage-can" model of decision making and the more general notion of accountability through organizational choice in organizations characterized by ambiguous situations or what is often called "organized anarchies." Further, since major social reforms like that found in education at the moment are usually symptomatic of larger cultural concerns, we will try to put the garbage-can model into the larger context of the poststructuralist and postmodern critique of modern Enlightenment culture. It will become apparent that the garbage-can model of decision making and accounting in organized anarchies resonates with a number of important postmodern themes.

SCHOOLS AND ACCOUNTING IN ORGANIZED ANARCHIES

Garbage-Can Models of Organization Management

Most theories of organizational decision making are theories of willful and rational choice. Within such traditional models of economic rationality the following assumptions regarding the rational agents (or organizations) are usually made:

1. Agents (or organizations) have knowledge of all alternatives for action and the alternatives are unambiguously defined by the situation (March & Olsen, 1986).
2. Agents always know the consequences of all alternatives at least to some degree of probability (March & Olsen, 1986).
3. Agents can always make a decision when confronted with a range of alternatives (von Newmann & Morgenstern, 1947).
4. Agents can provide a consistent transitive preference ordering of alternatives (von Newmann & Morgenstern, 1947).
5. Agents always select the highest-ranking alternative (von Newmann & Morgenstern, 1947).
6. Agents will always apply the same rule of rationality (i.e., will always make the same decision) when confronted with the set of alternatives (von Newmann & Morgenstern, 1947).

This highly instrumentalist or functionalist view of rational decision making was questioned as early as the 1950s by a number of prominent theorists including the future Nobel laureate Herbert Simon (Simon, 1955; March & Simon, 1958). Some of the most serious criticisms include the following: (1) decision makers in real situations have limited information and ability to process it; (2) most decision makers do not have well-defined preferences; (3) goals are usually multiple and conflicting; (4) alternatives are usually not well specified and, therefore, their specifications are part of the decision and action process; and (5) usually consequences are unclear and must also be included in the decision and action process.

Cyert and March (1963) developed a model of bounded rationality for decision making in ambiguous organizations and circumstances. It looks upon ambiguous organizations as a loosely coupled collection of participants (departments, administrative units, and so on) with different demands, changing goals and interests, and limited capacity to confront all the problems perceived by all participants. March and Olsen (1976) and Weick (1976) applied the term "loosely coupled" to educational organizations. They suggest that substantial evidence reveals that public schools lack close internal coordination, especially of the content and method of instruction. Schools are viewed as organizations with ambiguous goals, unclear technologies, fluid participation, uncoordinated activities, and a structure that has little effect on outcomes. Instruction tends to be removed from the control of the organization structure, in both its bureaucratic and its collegial aspects. Teachers work individually and relatively unobserved in their classrooms. Teachers exercise wide discretionary authority over their pupils. According to Weick (1976) even such school personnel as principals and counselors, often assumed to work hand-in-hand, retain separateness characterized by infrequent, unimportant, and weak interactions. This results in structural looseness at the school. Similarly, Weick argues that loose coupling defines the relationship among school units in the system. Other elements found in loosely coupled educational systems include voters–school board, process–outcome, administrators–teachers, parents–teachers, and administrators–classrooms.

Studies of actual decision-making processes present strong evidence that decision making in organizations is not generally the result of deliberate choices driven by a rational organizational system. Rather, decision making in organizations, including public schools, is characterized by ambiguity in decision making, loose coupling within organizations, and apparent confusion and disorder. Organizations such as public schools can aptly be described as "organizational anarchies" where decision processes do not function according to rational choice models. School administrators will recognize the exquisite fit with their work. A principal's activity is typically characterized by brevity, fragmentation, and variety (Martin & Willower, 1981). It is unusual for a principal to spend more than ten minutes on a single task. Principals make as many as 150 different decisions in the course of a typical day (Martin & Willower, 1981). This image supports the view of educational administration as an "organized anarchy."

To overcome the apparent disorder in organizations, loose couplings within organizations, and the ambiguities of decision making, models of accounting in organized anarchies were developed (see, among others, Allison, 1971; Cohen et al., 1972; Cohen & March, 1974). The most prominent among these is the garbage-can model. According to March and Olsen (1976, pp. 26–27), the decision process can be viewed as a "somewhat fortuitous confluence" of four fairly independent streams within the organization.

1. *Problems* of many types arising in the personal and organization lives of people in and outside a particular organizational context.
2. *Solutions* that are somebody's product, an answer looking for a question. Frequently the question is not identifiable until the solution is known.
3. *Participants* who come and go at various times in the choice process. Variations in participation usually stem from sources extraneous to the specific decision context.
4. *Choice opportunities,* occasions when an organization is expected to produce a behavior that can be called a decision (hiring and firing, signing contracts, choosing a curriculum, etc.).

Some important aspects of garbage-can models include a partial uncoupling of problems, solutions, participants, and choices into what March and Olsen (1986) call a "temporal order" of simultaneity instead of a logical consequential order. Decisions are made when solutions, choice opportunities, participants, and problems come into fortuitous confluence in the garbage can. Decisions are made by resolution, dissolution, flight, and oversight and can be very culturally and context-dependent. Education is a commonly cited example of the kind of organized anarchy that will benefit by modeling or adapting to a garbage-can model of administrative decision making (Cohen et al., 1972; Cooper et al., 1981; March & Olsen, 1986).

March and Olsen (1986, pp. 12–13) recognize that garbage-can models of rational decision making run counter to "the ideologies of the Enlightenment and associated definitions of the nature of the species." The Enlightenment ideal of rational decision making relies on the Cartesian ideal of an historically and socially autonomous center of individual willful choice. Emphasizing the organizational context and culture, as garbage-can models do, runs counter to the modern Enlightenment ideal of autonomous decision-making action. This different emphasis suggests an entirely different function for accounting, especially in organized anarchies. Instead of being merely descriptive of the efficacy of decisions, accounting may actually, in large part, *constitute* the organization (or culture) and *legitimate* its decisions and actions (Cooper et al., 1981; March & Olsen, 1986; Cunningham, 1990). It does so in several ways.

First, and foremost, systems of accounting can often provide a common language for everyone in the organizational community whether they are superintendents, principals, parents, teachers, or school board members. A common language is capable of generating a sense of social order with a developed history and future, all resting upon a single value system. Organizations come to possess a self-image and consciousness (Daft & Wiginton, 1979; Cooper et al., 1981). A common accounting language can provide a common "world-picture" of shared beliefs and values. March and Olsen (1986, p. 21) observe that decision processes "are sacred rituals, and decision making is linked to important symbolic concerns of society." Cooper et al. (1981, p. 183) go so far as to write: "Ritual, magic and myths are some of the means by which organizational cultures are sustained. . . . By possessing specialist skills and language as well as arcane knowledge, the accountant and accounting systems may be regarded as mystical, cosmological and charismatic."

A second function of systems of accounting is that of legitimation. Organizations need to legitimate themselves to others and to themselves as well. March and Olsen (1986, p. 22) observe,

Organizations [cultures] establish that they are good decision makers by making decisions in a way that symbolizes the qualities that are valued. They consult relevant people, consider alternatives, gather information, and act decisively but prudently. Decision making is, in part, a performance designed to reassure decision makers and others that things are being done appropriately. . . . Where, as is often the case, decision quality is difficult to measure directly, the competition for reputation is likely to lead to an emphasis on displacing process attributes.

Internally, March and Olsen (1986, p. 22) note: "The idea of intelligent choice is a central idea of modern ideology, and organizations are institutions dedicated to that vision of life. . . . The decision process is a ritual by which we recognize saints, socialize the young, reassure the old, recite scripture and come to understand our existence." Sounds like a school board meeting to us.

In light of the cultural-linguistic and especially the legitimating roles played by accounting systems, particularly in organized anarchies, Cooper et al. (1981, p. 175) recommend, "Relaxation of traditional prohibitions in choice behavior against imitation and rationalization." Rationalization is often required because, as they indicate, "the sequence whereby actions precede goals may well be a more accurate portrayal of organizational functioning than the more traditional goal-action paradigm." The traditional goal-action paradigm is, needless to say, that of technocratic-instrumentalist rationality.

Imitation and coercion provide a way of understanding how accounting systems can constitute the process of administrative decision making in organizational cultures. Cooper et al. (1981, p. 182) write,

the process of arriving at a common world-view . . . may be one of domination or negation as individuals and groups struggle to form a basis for understanding and controlling the organization. . . . Accounting systems encourage imitation and coercion by defining the problematic (by choosing which variables are measured and reported) and they help to fashion solutions (by choosing which variables are treated as controllable). . . . the structure of an accounting system helps to create the appropriate and acceptable ways of acting, organizing, and talking about issues in organizations.

Said differently, "internal accounting systems by *what* they measure and to whom they report can effectively delimit the kind of issues addressed and the ways in which they are addressed" (Cooper et al., 1981, p. 182).

Cooper et al. (1981) conclude: "Power is not just overt behavior forcing or coercing others to comply with a particular individual or way of doing things. It also has a latent or unobservable aspect, such as the ability to control agendas and issues" (see also Lukes, 1974; Wrong, 1979; Clegg, 1979).

Garbage-can models decenter and distribute power in loosely coupled systems and at least raise possibilities of redistributing power in ambiguous organizations like schools. We should not forget the following paradox of freedom; that is, freedom without control and constraint (including self-control) is not freedom but capriciousness. Cooper et al. (1981, p. 185) note that "there seem to be few accounting systems that encourage playfulness, creativity or experimentation." The garbage-can model, as you might expect, is the exception.

THE POSTMODERN PERSPECTIVE

Foucault and the Panopticon

The modern age, the age of Enlightenment, places the greatest emphasis on the ideal that it is possible to secure progress through reason. Progress toward what and the meaning of the abstract noun "reason" remain at the center of conversation in modern liberal democracies. Closely related to this ideal is that of the autonomous individual detached from the influence of tradition, history, and cultural context who relies solely on the natural light of reason to illuminate all aesthetic, moral, and cognitive judgments as well as willful action. Descartes' *cogito ergo sum* was arrived at only after rejecting tradition as a source of knowledge and even confronting himself with an evil genius with an infinite capacity to deceive him. Self-identity could only be secured by individual, autonomous, and entirely interior rules of reason. The self was seen as the center of rational choice and action. Newton and Locke applied a similar line of reasoning to frame Enlightenment ideals of the constitution of science (empirical rationality) and the relations of self and society, the constitution of the civic state out of the brute state of nature. Whatever the nature of pure reason, it was assumed that practical reason was governed by instrumentalism, functionalism, and means-ends reasoning. The rules of rational decision making enumerated by von Newmann and Morgenstern assume a Cartesian center of choice operating in an unambiguous, rationally *structured* world.

Postmodernism and poststructuralism deny many of the most important principles of modernity. We will only look at a few of the most important while focusing our attention on the thought of Michel Foucault. It will become clear that the garbage-can model of decision making and accounting in organized anarchies are replete with significant postmodern themes.

Michel Foucault has connected political power to the psychological and moral development of the self in a manner that leads to a new "post-modern" challenge to the Enlightenment ideals of autonomy, rationality, and progress. Foucault places great emphasis on the historical, social, and linguistic construction of the rational self. He finds no essential humanity, no essential self, no cosmic rationality, and certainly no Hegelian cosmic purposes operating in society or history. He "decentered" the self by displacing subjectivity into webs of shared linguistics and social practices and their histories. By his own admission he was influenced by Nietzsche, especially the latter's *On the Genealogy of Morals*, and the idea of the will to power, especially the will to power as knowledge. In his own genealogies, Foucault sought to call into question the supposed rationality of modernity by rendering it discontinuous with the past and displaying how past practices were perfectly "rational" in their sociohistorical context and no more or less effective than present social practices in their contemporary settings. In many of his genealogies, Foucault focused on a critique of the modern instrumentalist "technology of power" and coercion in social control, and more generally, in the relation between rational knowledge (e.g., science) and power. He seems oftentimes to have read Bacon's bromide "knowledge is power" backwards, thereby exposing the dark side of Enlightenment. His goal was self-awareness through an understanding of the social and linguistic practices, including the "technology of power," that determine our completely contingent identity as well as the identity of rational discourse and the idea of progress itself. Finally, Foucault's work tends to reflect on the literature of transgression. We have been struck by how accurately Foucault's description of the "technology of power" fits public schooling in the Western democracies and especially in North America. We will look closely at only one chapter of his *Discipline and Punish* (1977) titled "Panopticism."

The Panopticon is a piece of prison architecture proposed by the utilitarian philosopher Jeremy Bentham. The construction was composed of a ring-shaped building with a second structure, a tower, at its center. This tower has wide windows that open onto the inner side of the ring. The outer ring structure is divided into cells along the entire width of the building. These cells have two windows, on the inside corresponding to the windows of the tower; on the outside permitting light to enter the cell. Guards may be positioned in the central tower, while inmates [or schoolchildren] are to be confined to each cell. It is thus possible to see constantly and to recognize instantly (p. 200).

In the Panopticon each person is secured in a cell. He can be observed by the guards, but he cannot see them. Foucault characterizes this prisoner as an object of information, but someone who is never a part of any communication. The cell is opposite the central tower and imposes on him an "axial visibility." However, the manner in which the separated cells are arranged yields a "lateral invisibility." It is this invisibility that guarantees order for Foucault (Foucault, 1977, p. 200).

Now, conjure up the image of the teacher confined to the classroom, lunch, or bus duty with no occasion for lateral communication with other classroom teachers.

The Panopticon contains two important ideas. First, the Panopticon induces in the prisoner a state of consciousness and permanent visibility that operationalizes power. Bentham had specified that power should be visible, in the sense that the inmate would always have before him the central tower from which he is watched. Power was to be unverifiable, in the sense that the inmate could never know at what moment he was under surveillance (Foucault, 1977, p. 201). Furthermore, the Panopticon makes power automatic and disindividualized. Any inmate could function as the machine, no matter what motivates him. The anonymity and temporal nature of the observation means the inmate is always at risk of being surprised. He thus becomes anxious, aware that he is always being observed (Foucault, 1977, p. 202). Unlike earlier times when society merely controlled the body by crude force, the modern world controls the mind. Once we internalize constant surveillance so that we monitor ourselves, we affirm the final horror of self-enslavement.

The Panopticon yields another important idea. As Foucault (1977) points out, the Panopticon also served as a laboratory, and the ideal venue for research, for pedagogical experiments in which individuals could be experimented with and analyzed (p. 204).

Beyond its application to prison reform, the Panopticon also served as a device for grasping the power relations in everyday life in general and in schools in particular (p. 205). Without confinement, surveillance could be seen in a system of permanent registration and careful documentation. Within an organized setting with a disciplinary regime (like a school), individuation is "descending." Where power becomes more anonymous and more functional, the objects of such power tend to become more individualized. This shift is prompted by surveillance, observation, and comparative measures that are norm referenced (p. 193). And it is this bureaucratic record-keeping and technical devices of control that make up the image of the modern administrator—the technocrat.

Tests and examinations, joined to a formation of knowledge, were a certain form of the exercise of power for Foucault (1977, p. 187). This linkage was accomplished in three ways. First, the examination changed the economy of visibility (p. 187). Unlike earlier centuries, in modernity disciplinary power makes the ruler invisible and the ruled visible. In an earlier age the political ceremony, the triumph, gave rise to display, to excess, to spectacle, and explicitly to displays of power. The monarch was visible. Later, the "infinite examination" age, found subjects compulsorily objectified by the examination. Individuals are ordered and ranked by their scores. Examples are the yearly testing of students in public schools, the SAT, minimum competency tests (MCT), GRE, and others.

Second, the examination introduced individuality into the field of documentation (Foucault, 1977, p. 189). The examination constitutes the individual as a describable, analyzable object within a comparative system of measurements that permit the characterization that there are gaps or distributions among individuals in a given population (p. 190). The examination placing individuals in a field of surveillance also places them in a network of writing. A mass of documents exists to capture and fix these individuals. Testing procedures are accompanied by a registration and documentation system. This "power of writing" becomes a primary portion of the mechanism of discipline (p. 189).

Personality inventories, work interest inventories, aptitude tests, job tests, and psychological tests are all part of the disciplinary power of writing that help put us in our social place. So, too, is the teacher's permanent record.

Third, Foucault (1977) tells us, the examination turns each person into a "case" within which his individuality may be described, measured, compared with others, and judged. The case also provides a means whereby the individual is to be trained, corrected, classified, normalized, excluded, and so forth (p. 191).

At the same moment when the human sciences became possible, a new technology of power and a new political anatomy of the body were implemented, Foucault points out (p. 193). A historical reversal of the methods of individualization, from primarily ritualistic to scientifico-disciplinary took place. In this way, there was a substitution of the calculable man for the memorable man (p. 193).

It is interesting in this Foucaultian context to look at some of the statements of Thorndike, the founder of modern educational psychology. In her book *The Sane Positivist* (1968), a biography of Thorndike, Geraldine Joncich begins a chapter with a passage from Thorndike's *Educational Psychology;* it reads, "We conquer the facts of nature when we have made them our servants" (p. 282). Thorndike's commitment to measurement was almost metaphysical. Elsewhere he would write, "Whatever exists, exists in some amount. To measure it is simply to know its varying amounts" (p. 282). In psychology this meant mental measurement and intelligence testing. The human science of education means this much and more.

Thorndike preferred to induce connectionist stimulus-response laws of human behavior from precise measures of human performance, a pattern already implicit in the "curves of progress" found in his famous dissertation on *Animal Intelligence:* "It is . . . more scientific and more useful to think of human individuals as all measured upon the same series of scales" (Joncich, 1968, p. 285). In his *Education,* Thorndike attempts to explain this need to teachers. He says, "So scales to measure such educational forces as the teacher's interest . . . and such products as knowledge . . . are much needed" (Joncich, 1968, p. 280). Such statements set a research program that continues to dominate much of contemporary educational research.

If we look at the field of education in most modern Enlightenment democracies, we find the general model of the Panopticon defining power relations in the everyday life of students, teachers, principals, superintendents, and school boards. It is the kind of thinking that guided the first wave of educational reform in the 1980s. If the past is any clue to the future, it is likely to lead us into the 1990s.

Foucault's discussion of the ideas underlying the utilitarian technology of the Panopticon are only a part of his larger critique of instrumentalist-functionalist technical rationality. The most extended effort in this direction is Jean-François Lyotard's *The Postmodern Condition: A Report of Knowledge* (1984). The results of these critiques are so much a part of how we manage our schools that instead of discussing the results of the postmodern critique in postmodern terms we will simply report them in terms of the well known, the everyday lived institutional reality of American educational administration.

TECHNOCRATIC EDUCATION

Early in the twentieth century, technocratic modernism emerged in the form of "scientific management" or "Taylorism," named after Frederick Taylor, the author of the immensely influential *The Principles of Scientific Management* (1911). As its very title suggests, Frederick Taylor's *Principles* was meant to do for the combined forces of machine production what Newton's *Principia* had done for the forces that drove the machine of physical nature. Just as in physical nature there is one most efficient, most economical way for things to move about, so too, there was for Taylor "always one method and one implement which is quicker and better than any of the rest," the one best system, and "this one best method and best implement can only be discovered or developed through a scientific study and analysis of all of the methods and implements in use" (1911, p. 25).

Scientific analysis here meant Taylor's famous time-motion studies. For the sake of analysis, work was atomized so that each individual was "confined to the performance of a single leading function" (Taylor, 1911, p. 99), the leading activities that constituted the human life of machine production. From these analyses Taylor induced the most efficient way to perform the given task. A mechanic working under Taylor once reported that Taylor told him he was "not supposed to think; there are other people paid for thinking around here" (Callahan, 1962, p. 28).

Arthur Wirth (1983) looks on this statement as an example of the degradation of work "where thinking, conceptualizing, intellectualizing about the work process was made a prerogative of management, while people at work were limited to execution of prescribed, limited tasks under the scrutiny and control of supervision" (p. 12). Raymond Callahan (1962) in his *Education and the Cult of Efficiency* shows how public education over the decades of the 1920s, 1930s, and 1940s became dominated by the principles of scientific management. Since then C. A. Bowers (1977) observed that technocratic efficiency was expressed in the form of "teacher accountability and competency-based instruction."

In the 1950s, technocratic expert systems analysis models of management and accountability began to emerge. Ernest House (1978) in his "Evaluation as Scientific Management in U.S. School Reform" provides a historical critique of the introduction of cost/benefit accounting techniques into federal educational legislation in the 1960s, while Arthur E. Wise in his *Legislated Learning:*

The Bureaucratization of the American Classroom (1979) elaborates the "hyper-rationalization of American Schooling by legislative and judicial procedures." The fundamental idea is to maximize the "production function" by minimizing input costs and maximizing output benefits.

Robert MacNamara brought expert system analysis from Ford Motor Company to the Department of Defense where it was used to run the war in Vietnam. Alice Rivlin in turn brought it from the Department of Defense to the Department of Health, Education and Welfare where it was used by the Office of Education to administer and evaluate the impact of Title I (see House, 1978). This management model emphasizes measuring educational "outputs" in mathematical cost/benefit relation (the production function) to "inputs." It led quickly to such systems of documentation and accountability as competency based education (CBE), performance based education (PBE), competency based teacher education (CBTE), behavioral objectives, mastery learning, learner verification, federal, state and local assessment, and criterion norm-referenced testing. Output oriented educational legislation spread quickly to the states.

During the 1980s, new versions of scientific management for American schools emerged. Wise (1988) documents that concern over teacher methods and teacher performance led many states to mandate uniform approaches to teacher evaluation. Evaluators (usually administrators) use a checklist of approved teacher behaviors that has been developed or purchased from educational research tanks by the state. The behaviors are meant to be scientifically derived from the research on "effective teachers" (McNeil, 1988). In one state the assessment instrument derived from the language of classroom management and the narrowest applications of cognitive psychology, lists 45 behaviors that assessors look for (McNeil, 1988). These behaviors are supposed to produce increased student achievement scores on standardized tests of basic skills. Wise (1988) argues that the process by which narrow research findings are translated into general prescriptions for teacher performance is conceptually wrong and empirically indefensible. But these facts are no barrier to state bureaucrats in their use of "science" to legitimate their authority. Examination is a central component in a "disciplinary technology." During the 1980s, teaching became teacher-proof through the conditioning of teachers to comply with state-accepted and mandated behaviors and techniques. Teachers lost even more professional autonomy during the 1980s. The way bureaucratic *power* is transformed through "scientific" *knowledge* into policies of discipline and control of the teacher is a fine example of what Foucault means by power/knowledge.

Another scientific management offspring of the 1980s was curriculum alignment. According to Wise (1988), the fear that teachers will "teach to the test" has been realized in "curriculum alignment—that is, making sure that what is tested has been taught and insuring congruence among objectives, textbooks, and tests" (p. 331). By realigning their curricula, districts can improve students' scores on state achievement tests. Again, attention is focused on outcomes obtained, in part, by state controls on curriculum.

Tyack (1990) sums up the decade of the 1980s when he says "policymakers came to regard tests as the chief measure of accountability" (p. 181). The decade of the 1980s will be remembered as carrying forth the pattern of scientific management by adding new structures that contribute to refining the "disciplinary technology" of schooling. The decade of the 1990s has not brought us anything truly new. Corbett and Wilson (1992) investigated the effects of statewide testing policies on local school districts. Among other things, they found that schools were altering and narrowing their curricula in order to improve test scores at the cost of emphasizing learning. Teachers felt more stress as school administrators and policy makers emphasized improved standardized test scores.

CONCLUSION

We think that technocratic accountability measures of productivity are the new and improved Panopticon. Ultimately the object is to maintain control and maximize "efficiency" by constraining the individual production function. Robert MacNamara demanded the "biggest bang for the buck"; a demand echoed at countless school board meetings throughout America. In order to maximize production, to obtain the biggest bang, it is necessary to minimize the cost of input variables, for example, human capital, while maximizing outputs, for instance, test scores. Expert technocratic systems assume that everything important to production can be reduced to something measurable, otherwise how could you write a production function or a cost/benefit equation. Accountability is obtained at the bottom line by measuring productivity or output. Measures of output became a bit of a problem in Vietnam, so MacNamara counted dead bodies. An enigma, a comedy, or a tragedy?

As we said earlier, when the first wave of educational reform of the 1980s broke over American education, it stressed accountability and reaffirmed the familiar structuralist strategies of technocratic rationality, for example, standardization, hierarchy, testing, centralization, formalized procedures aimed at administrative management for maximum efficiency and productivity. The second wave emphasizing teacher empowerment, decentralized site-based management, and professionalism tends to cancel out rather than resonate with the first wave; the result is the kind of turbulence characteristic of two weather fronts colliding and is about as predictable. Dispensing with the metaphor, the institutional result is the kind of turbulence and unpredictability characteristic of an organized anarchy. It is into this turbulence that the third wave washes. As we said in the introduction, there are no clear images of what the third wave of administrative alternatives may look like. Our suggested image is, needless to say, poststructuralist and postmodern. For instance, postmodern garbage-can models allow us to play with the possibilities of site-based management. Site-based management could decentralize educational administration from the state or county central office only to replicate a technocratic-instrumentalist structure of rationality in the individual building. If so it will fail. On the other hand, if it actually empowers the teachers, support personnel, *and* administrators, it could succeed. For this to happen, *all* participants would have to participate in garbage-can kinds of action.

1. *Problems* would need to be defined collectively within the specific context of the school's culture and within the common language of the participants. The choice of "relevant" variables and their relations to one another would tend to be internal and local. We would see much more practitioner-instituted and institutionally restricted "action research."
2. *Solutions* would tend to be a collective product arrived at through collegial participation. Commonly it could be a resolve to do what they can do well, to solve what they are most able and confident to do.
3. *Participants* would, of course, come to and go from the institution. Within the institution, alignments would be along the lines of shared interests, common cares, and natural social connection and less by administrative mandates. Participation in a common dialogue rather than the soliloquy of hierarchical administration, where those at the top often literally talk down to those at the bottom, would become commonplace.
4. *Choice opportunities* would call for organization-wide participation in the cultural-linguistic and legitimating roles played by accounting systems. There would be shared rituals, perhaps mystical and cosmological, perhaps merely mundane and practically wise. Coercion would of course occur, but its power would be decentered and more collegial.

We have no desire to be particularly specific; rather we invite the reader to playfully imagine their own alternatives for the places where they work. The serious question for the third wave of educational reform is this: Are educational administrators and their expert research associates really interested in improving public education, or are they merely interested in preserving domination and control in the name of accountability?

Finally, while we think garbage-can models are capable of improving administration, accounting, and decision making in educational administration, we do not want to be taken too seriously. Ours is a playful proposal. As March and Olsen (1986) themselves say, "such ideas are only a part of a collection of ideas about decision making, all of which are required for a full appreciation of the phenomenon" (p. 28). An important part of poststructuralism is its rejection of totalizing world-views or "metanarratives" as Lyotard (1984) calls them. What we like about the garbage-can model is that it is almost impossible to take it *too* seriously. In Derrida's language, it is a narrative that deliberately deconstructs itself and, therefore, is not readily able to become another disabling and disempowering dogma.

6

Education Administration in a Postmodern Society: Implications for Moral Practice

Charles J. Fazzaro, James E. Walter, and K. Kelly McKerrow

> It seems to me that the real political task in a society such as ours is to criticize the workings of institutions which appear to be both neutral and independent; to criticize them in such a manner that the political violence which has always exercised itself obscurely through them will be unmasked, so that one can fight them.[1]
>
> —Michel Foucault

In the United States, at least, schools have, at base, the responsibility of transmitting to the masses the knowledge and skills necessary to fulfill simultaneously both individual needs and wants and the sociopolitical good. The individual needs and wants are those that individuals value for their subjective selves. Included among these needs and wants would be access to the broader society sufficiently prepared academically to seek a valued future. In terms of the social good, the original theoretical purpose of universal public education in America included the perpetuation of the democratic ideals upon which the republic was founded.

The decision domains of both subjective needs and wants and the sociopolitical good are value domains. Because of constitutional prohibitions against government intrusion into promoting one value over another, decisions within these domains necessarily have no transcendental, fixed reference. The decision domains should not be conditioned by government sponsored orthodoxy.[2] In this regard, the task for educators is to fashion schools that will best fulfill the historical purposes of education without promoting a particular future for students by restricting their value preferences. Schools expand or restrict the value choices of students through both the formal curriculum and the informal or "hidden" curriculum.

Restrictions in the formal curriculum are relatively easy to detect, but restrictions imposed by the hidden curriculum are not. For example, the way schools are organized and operated have a significant disciplinary effect on students. The symmetry of class schedules, the physical arrangement of classrooms, and norm referenced grading practices codes are examples of practices that privilege regimentation and order over individuality. What fundamental view of reality conditions these organizational practices, and what makes these practices seem so right to educators? The answers to such questions are rooted in the technoscience ideology that is the foundation of both *modernism* and *structuralism*.[3]

This chapter is a critique of technoscience ideology and how it particularly affects education administration as an ethical practice. The critique is from a postmodern/poststructural perspective and divided into six parts. The first part establishes the decision domains of educational practice. The second part is a discussion of structuralism and how it has influenced organizational practice and ways of understanding that practice. The third part is a critique of structuralism and its technoscience rationality. The fourth part is a discussion of the implications of structuralism for education. Part five considers some implications of postmodern/poststructural thought for education administration. The chapter concludes with consideration of moral administrative practice in a postmodern society.

THE DOMAIN OF EDUCATION THEORY AND PRACTICE

The practice of education is conditioned by choices within two primary decision-action (policy) domains—the *knowledge* domain and the *recommending* domain.[4] The knowledge domain includes policies that address the question: What counts as knowledge (*qua* "truth")? In the ideal, the knowledge domain includes everything that is known or can be known. The recommending domain includes policies that address such questions as: What knowledge is transmitted? Who transmits the knowledge? To whom? Through what medium? In what form? and With what effect?[5] The questions in each policy domain require choices from a wide, if not infinite, range of alternatives. The choices become particularly significant when they have an effect on sociopolitical structures.

Regarding such choices, Cleo Cherryholmes noted that, "Choices cannot be made without reference to a value, set of values, criteria(on), or interests . . . [which] are sedimented . . . in the constitutive rules of practice [of a social order]."[6] The answers to policy questions in both the knowledge and recommending domains necessarily would be grounded in values. Because the allocation of values is the heart of politics, it is at this point that public education policy becomes political. But to be legitimate in a democratic society, any policies that allocate core values requires, at least, normative political acceptance that the policies are "true and valid."[7] That is, the legitimacy of the substance of policy issues and their concomitant practices must be an expression of normative political will.

But in twentieth-century America the *substance* of social policies is masked by the hegemony of their technical knowledge which is *process* knowledge. Technology is characterized by its distinction between efficient and inefficient criterion of the acceptability of what is true, false, just, and unjust. Consequently, the legitimacy of public policies through "performativity" of process(es) has replaced legitimacy through "normativity" of substance and practice. In twentieth-century American education, the performativity of process has been the foundation of many pervasive educational practices including, for example, "Tylerism" in the 1950s and 1960s and "Hunterism" in the 1970s and 1980s.

The acceptance of performativity of process is understandable because America is part of the broader Western culture that has allowed process to dominate virtually all forms of inquiry. Process inquiry is the epistemological method of science. At least since 1650, science has been broadly promoted in Western societies as the only legitimate "truth" seeking rationality. Science, the foundation of modern technological knowledge, manifests itself in linguistics and the social sciences as *structuralism*.

STRUCTURALISM AND ATTEMPTS TO UNDERSTAND IT

Structuralism has several variants, each of which would require considerable space to explicate fully. This discussion is not intended to inform the reader of all aspects of structuralism. Presented here are only brief descriptions of its fundamental characteristics and the criticisms offered by the poststructuralists/postmodernists.

The logic of structuralism is grounded in the belief that individual human reasoning, conditioned by values, is fundamentally inconsistent with the idea of a rational self-regulating world. Structuralists believe that human reasoning alone is inefficient in resolving the issues inherent in the problematics of political, economic, and other social institutions.[8] To improve the efficiency of social institutions, structuralism replaces value-based reasoning with highly rationalized "scientific reasoning." John Murphy noted that this mode of thinking has spawned "the belief that human action is the source of the chaos that threatens social order. Therefore, methodologies and organizational structures are invented to preserve reason and the common weal."[9] In a social order structured on objective, value-neutral knowledge the subjective human is submerged within the objective group. Social order and symmetry are privileged over the desires of the individual.

Thus defined, structuralism places the group (organization) as the center of social agency. Being the central focus, organizations take on lives of their own. In the United States, at least, in many circumstances organizations are even given equal legal status with humans. For example, organizations can own property, enter into contracts, and sue and be sued.

Contemporarily, analytical frames to explain structuralism were derived by sociologists such as Talcott Parsons and his view that organizations are like organisms. Later, some anthropologists and linguists eventually challenged this organismic view. One of the most noted among this group is Claude Levi-Strauss. He suggested that organizations are like languages; therefore, they can best be fully understood as one would understand a language.[10] This language view of organizations eventually led to criticisms from contemporary French philosophers/linguists such as Michel Foucault, Jacques Derrida, and Jean-François Lyotard. They argued that social theory and practice are discursive because at base they are sign systems; therefore, they are pregnant with values. To understand this point one must first understand the essentials of structural linguistics.

The historical roots of structural linguistics is described succinctly by David Robey in the following:

> In the *Theses,* presented collectively by members of the Prague Linguistic Circle to the First International Congress of Slavic Philologists held in Prague in 1929, *structure* is the structure of the system, the manner in which the individual elements of a particular language are arranged for this purpose in relations of mutual dependence. Since this differs from one language to another, it follows that the separate components of a system can only be understood in light of the system as a whole, and therefore that the primary object of linguistic study must be the structure of the system itself rather than the individual linguistic fact.[11]

The best known proponent of structural linguistics is Levi-Strauss. Robey described Levi-Strauss's linguistic view of structural analysis as growing out of:

> the supposition that the theories and methods of structural linguistics are directly or indirectly applicable to the analysis of all aspects of human culture, in so far as all these, like language, may be interpreted as systems of signs.[12]

Those who ascribe to this perspective on structures take the view that essentially there are no distinctive differences between discourses and practices. That is, "discourse, a more or less orderly exchange of ideas, is a particular kind of practice, and practice is, at least in part, discursive."[13] Thus, both discourses and practices are part of the grammar of the language that controls the character of a structure.

More recently, in music, art, architecture, philosophy, and the general area of social theory, criticisms of both structuralism, and its correlative modernism, have gained considerable attention in both Europe and the United States. Both *poststructuralism* and *postmodernism* are attacks on "totality," the foundation of both structuralism and modernism. The concept of totality is rooted in the ideology of science and its search for the ultimate "reality" through both objectification and quantification of all things, including the human subject.[14]

In structural social anthropology and linguistics, the search for the ultimate social reality is a search for the "metanarrative." Metanarratives are explanations of the narratives embedded in the "texts" of discourses-practices. It is through both discourses and practices that social structures are created and maintained. As Edmund Leach has noted, the idea that metanarratives exist is based on the assumption that, "If we recognize that we exist in one world rather than many, it must be because we can recognize that messages that reach us through different senses simultaneously share a common structure."[15] Lyotard succinctly defines postmodernism, and its collateral poststructuralism, as "incredulity toward meta-narratives."[16]

THE POSTSTRUCTURAL/POSTMODERN PERSPECTIVE

Cleo Cherryholmes describes the character of structuralism as emphasizing "order, accountability, structure, systematization, rationalization, expertise, specialization, linear development, and control."[17] The result is that the subjective individual is decentered as the focus of social agency. Murphy noted, "As the social system comes to be understood as the locus of order, persons become dominated by their own creation."[18]

Likewise, structuralism does not promote change, unless it is in the interest of the power elites in the organization. Because it resists change, structuralism promotes the status quo. This is important for education because education is socially and politically strategic. In the ideal democratic state, education should promote social criticism, not reinforce, for example, any elitist, racist, or sexist practices that might exist.

A convenient way of understanding the expanding critique of structuralism is through Lyotard's theory of language games. Although Lyotard recognizes that there are many varieties, he defines three types of language games: *denotative* (descriptive), *prescriptive,* and *technical.* In the denotative game what is relevant is the true/false distinction. In the prescriptive game the just/unjust distinction pertains. In the technical game the criterion is the efficient/inefficient distinction.[19] Lyotard argues that in modern societies the technical language game is dominant. Because it goes almost unchallenged, it is normative. As such, power resides with those most skilled at both the technical language game and acquiring and controlling of resources.[20]

Lyotard claims that within modernism (structuralism) legitimation depends on *performativity* — "the optimization of the global relationship between inputs and outputs."[21] As such, performativity increases the ability of the technical language game to produce proof; thus, increasing its ability to be "right" (*qua* "true"). The reliance on performativity denigrates the value of the *denotative* language game. Likewise, lawful actions acquire their legitimation through their normative acceptance by those within a social system.[22] Once having adopted the rationality of the technical language game, Lyotard notes that:

By reinforcing technology, one "reinforces" reality, and one's chances of being just and right increases accordingly. Reciprocally, technology is reinforced all the more effectively if one has access to scientific knowledge and decision-making authority.

This is how legitimation by power takes shape. Power is not only good performativity, but also effective verification and good verdicts. It legitimates science and the law on the basis of their *efficiency* [emphasis added], and legitimates this efficiency on the basis of science and law. It is self legitimating.[23]

Consequently, in highly technical societies laws find their legitimacy not in their normativity of acceptance based on validation of *prescriptive* arguments but in their performativity of procedures.[24]

The poststructuralists/postmodernists criticize the fundamental nature of the policy language and the effects it has on the character of the structures in postindustrial societies. Essentially, their argument is that the technical language game dominates, making technical knowledge the knowledge of legitimation.

IMPLICATIONS FOR EDUCATION

Technoscience discourse, which emphasizes process, method, and procedure over value-dependent substance, is located in the technical language game, with its efficient/inefficient distinction the criterion for legitimacy. Because of its normative nature within the broader society, the technical language game displaces the prescriptive language game—in which the criterion for legitimacy is the just/unjust distinction—from the discourses of value-dependent social institutions. In postindustrial societies, at least, this displacement of value-dependent language games has manifold implications for educational practice. This is so because contemporary education discourse-practices[25] are grounded in the technical language game that depends almost exclusively on "performativity"[26] for legitimacy. A major reason that the technical language game displaced the prescriptive language game in education is situated historically in the discourse of education administration.

The technical language game has shaped education practice at least since its infusion into the discourse of education from the time of the scientific management movement of the first quarter of the twentieth century. Faced with exploding enrollments and limited resources, public education was pressured to be more efficient. Spurred by both the pervasive influence of behaviorism in psychology and the popular rationalistic views of management in business and industry, education administration responded by adopting organizational and supervisory practices commonly found in factories.

Franklin Bobbitt, a highly successful and well-known educator around the turn of the twentieth century, was a strong advocate of scientific management and recommended its application in the schools.[27] Bobbitt argued vigorously for more quantitative approaches to administration. He believed strongly in quantifying almost everything related to schooling, from the number of students per teacher to measurements of intellectual ability. In 1913 he proposed a set of principles of scientific management to be instituted in the schools. One such principle was

Where material is acted upon by the labor processes, and passed through a number of progressive stages on its way from the raw material to the final product, qualitative and quantitative standards must be determined for the product at each of these stages.[28]

Bobbitt's objectification of the students as "material" and his qualification of teaching as a "labor process" explains the behavioristic and mechanistic character of his recommendations for schooling practices. To be efficient, this view necessarily displaces the subjective individual from the center of social agency. In doing so, value-independent process is privileged over value-dependent substance.

The ideology of scientific management is still very much present in schools today. This is testimony to how deeply technoscience knowledge has been institutionalized within the broad American culture. Scientific management has survived and prospered as a practice in education even though the study of education administration went through several other phases. The broader public has grown increasingly skeptical of the claims made by the proponents of technoscience knowledge. That technical adjustments can actually improve education practice is now more widely doubted.

Postmodern America is faced with the question, "What should be the foundation of the discourse-practices of American education now that technoscience is being rejected as the 'metanarrative' upon which educational policy is justified?" Assuming that the subjective individual will be centered, then the answer to this question must be found in the humanities, beginning with philosophy and, in particular, its derivative morals.

EDUCATION ADMINISTRATION AND MORAL PRACTICE

Education administration is a practice conditioned by many factors, including the study of and speculation about the practice itself. It is a practice that requires decisions and actions at various levels of importance and along a time continuum from indefinite to immediate. At the purely technical level, for example, the school administrator must insure that teachers will have the necessary space, materials, and time to conduct their classes. This is so regardless of the state of the economy, world affairs, the weather on any particular day, or on the outcome of any philosophical debates taking place in the academy about the nature of the practice of school administration itself. But the practice of school administration concerns educational issues far more important and complicated than those that require only a managerial (*qua* technical) response.

Practices, according to Cherryholmes, are "activities performed on a regular basis . . . [and] constituted by connected and overlapping sets of rules that organize and give them [practices] coherence."[29] Besides technical and managerial practices, the domain of administrative practice in schools must necessarily concern itself with all aspects within the *problematic* of education.[30] The problematic feature of education includes issues of epistemology and transmission, which are concerned with true/false and just/unjust criteria.

Bates describes the problematic of education as issues related to the following six questions: (1) What counts as knowledge? (2) How is what counts as knowledge organized? (3) How is what counts as knowledge transmitted? (4) How is access to what counts as knowledge determined? (5) What are the processes of control? (6) What ideological appeal justifies the system?[31] These are questions about values; therefore, the technical language game is inadequate when it comes to legitimating the policies and practices associated with their resolution. Likewise, the technical language game frustrates critical social change because it excludes debate about value systems.

Many popular schooling practices, such as "outcomes based education," are presently shaped by the technical language game. The effects of the technical language game on the problematics of education can be minimized through the moral discourse-practices of school administrators. But school administrators must look beyond the physical boundaries of the school in order to have a fuller understanding of what influences the problematics of education.

American public education is not an island unto itself in a dynamic social sea. It is an institution. Organizations become institutions whenever their structures (discourse-practices) are isomorphic with the values of the society within which they exist.[32] Research has shown that the structures of schools tend to be isomorphic with the expectations of the communities within which they function.[33] These expectations are conditioned by values; thus, the discourse-practices that constitute schools have implication for both *private* and *public* knowledge. It is the domain of public knowledge that most concerns itself with the moral dimensions of the discourse-practices of schooling, in particular the discourse practices of school administration.

School administrators have always been faced with making moral judgments, but due to the influence of structuralism and its technoscience rationality for legitimation, school administrators have been disguising moral judgments as "management" decisions (for example, Canter's approach to discipline). Because American K–12 education is essentially a public function—a public experience— the moral choices must be grounded in public knowledge. Public education has the obligation to provide a forum within which a society can identify and give legitimacy to public knowledge. Because school administration is strategically located within the practice of education, school administration must be a moral practice.

But structuralism suggests that the final arbiter of public knowledge should be the school itself. That is, the current discourse-practices of schooling, informed by its technoscience "metanarrative," is legitimized by "expert" opinion informed by "scientific" inquiry. Both poststructural and postmodern inquiry and their incredulity toward metanarratives suggests otherwise. Indeed, such inquiry might reveal, as Michael Polanyi suggests, that "we must accredit our own judgment as the paramount arbiter of all our intellectual performances, and . . . that we are competent to pursue intellectual excellence as a token of a hidden reality."[34] If acceptance of the poststructural and postmodern critique is the direction that education will take, then education administration must anticipate dramatic new changes in the discourse-practices popular in education. These changes could, for example, take place in what Philip Phenix argues is the core of the ideal curriculum.

Phenix suggests that the concept of *meaning* be developed in order to avoid limitations of ideas such as rationality, reason, and mind. Phenix describes meaning as having four dimensions: (1) the experience of the reflective self-consciousness, (2) the logical principles by which the experience is patterned, (3) the selective elaboration of these patterns into productive traditions represented by scholarly disciplines, and (4) the expression of these patterns by means of appropriate symbolic forms.[35] Given that the aim of public education is to promote meaning within the domain of public knowledge where moral choices are grounded, the school administrator is obligated to understand the nature of meanings and to promote that understanding among teachers.

Phenix has identified six realms of meaning that emerge from an analysis of modes of human understanding. They are:

1. *Symbolics,* which comprise language, mathematics, and various nondiscursive symbolic forms such as rituals or gestures;
2. *Empirics,* which include the sciences;
3. *Aesthetics,* such as music, linear art, movement, literature, and those areas concerned with "contemplative perception of particular significant things such as unique objectifications of ideated subjectivities";
4. *Synnoetics,* which includes personal knowledge and Buber's "I-Thou" relational insight and direct awareness;
5. *Ethics,* which includes moral meanings that stand in contrast to science, arts, and personal knowledge and concerns behavior based on free, responsible, deliberate decisions;
6. *Synoptics,* which refers to meanings that are integrated in nature and includes areas of knowledge like history, religion, and philosophy that integrate empirical, aesthetic, and synnoetic meanings.

These realms of meaning all, to varying degrees, inform the structural nature of the discourse-practices of schooling. That is, each realm of meaning proposed by Phenix is included in the philosophy or mission statement of most schools. But the first three realms enjoy most of the attention in the actual discourse-practices of schooling. This should come as no surprise, because it is easier to find legitimacy within a technoscience rationality for the meanings within the first three realms. This explains the widespread acceptance of popular forms of reading, writing, and arithmetic, with their technoscience rationality, as the core (*qua* "basic") elements of school curriculums.

But the seemingly popular acceptance of the emphasis of technical knowledge in the discourse-practices of schooling cannot justify the exclusion of synnoetics, synoptics, and ethics. It is at this point that education administration can anticipate the shift in emphasis mentioned earlier. That is, postmodern school administrators, recognizing the legitimacy of self-reflection through the role of the individual as the arbiter of their own knowledge, might boldly suggest that ethics, synnoetics, and synoptics serve as the core curricular offerings in public education. This would meet the requirements, suggested earlier, that, in order to accommodate changes in the discourse-practices of schooling, school administrators must adjust the fundamental nature of their own discourse-practices. It would further serve the purpose of recentering the subjective individual and placing institutions in the proper perspective of serving, not being served.

NOTES

1. Michel Foucault, "Human Nature: Justice Versus Power," in *Reflexive Water: The Basic Concerns of Mankind,* ed. Fons Elders (London: Souvenir Press, 1974), p. 171.

2. See, among other sources, *West Virginia State Board of Education v. Barnette,* Supreme Court of the United States, 319 U.S. 624, 63 S.Ct. 1178 (1943).

3. Although there are differences between structuralism and modernism and, likewise, poststructuralism and postmodernism, for this chapter those differences are not significant; therefore, the two sets of terms will be used interchangeably.

4. For a discussion of these issues as they relate to a philosophy of education, see Kingsley Price, "What Is a Philosophy of Education," *Educational Theory,* 6 (April, 1954): 86–94.

5. Jean-François Lyotard, *The Postmodern Condition: A Report on Knowledge* (Minneapolis: University of Minnesota Press, 1984), p. 48.

6. Cleo Cherryholmes, *Power and Criticism* (New York: Teachers College Press, 1988), p. 4.

7. Richard Bernstein, *The Restructuring of Social and Political Theory* (Philadelphia: University of Pennsylvania Press, 1978), p. 108.

8. John W. Murphy, "The Political Dimension of Deconstruction," *Review Journal of Philosophy & Social Science,* Vol. XI, No. 1 (1988): 95.

9. Murphy, p. 95.

10. Edmund Leach, "Structuralism in Social Anthropology," in *Structuralism: An Introduction,* ed. David Robey (Oxford: Clarendon Press, 1973), p. 39.

11. David Robey, ed., *Structuralism: An Introduction* (Oxford, England: Clarendon Press, 1973), p. 1.

12. Robey, p. 2.

13. Cherryholmes, p. 9.

14. Eleanor Munro offers an elegant, personal description of modernism in the following: "As a writer I craved to give formal order to my thoughts and experience, believing with the Modernists that content reveals its meaning through the grammar of form. So had my father believed. But he'd gone at the job backward, I now considered. The problem isn't to impose an ideal form on things but to find and express the form in them. A different, stranger form is in the actuality. *Sepere aude,* again." Eleanor Munro, *Memoir of a Modernist's Daughter* (New York: Viking, 1988), p. 266.

15. Leach, p. 42.

16. Lyotard, p. xxiv.

17. Cherryholmes, p. 9.

18. Murphy, p. 95.

19. Lyotard, p. 46.

20. For an excellent discussion of organizational structures see Stewart Ranson, Bob Hinings, and Royston Greenwood, "The Structuring of Organizational Structures," *Administrative Science Quarterly*, 25 (March 1980): 1-17.

21. Lyotard, p. 11.

22. For a complete discussion of the relationship between law, authority, and legitimation, see Carl Joachim Friedrich, *The Philosophy of Law in Historical Perspective*, 2d ed. (Chicago: The University of Chicago Press, 1963), pp. 200-205.

23. Lyotard, p. 47.

24. Niklas Luhmann, *Legitimation durch Verfabren* (Neuweid: Luchterhand, 1969). As cited in Lyotard, p. 46.

25. The term "discourse-practice" is used because both discourse (what is said) and practice (what is done) are value dependent. See Cherryholmes, pp. 1-15.

26. Lyotard, p. 54.

27. Raymond E. Callahan, *Education and the Cult of Efficiency* (Chicago: The University of Chicago Press, 1962), p. 59.

28. Franklin Bobbitt, *Twelfth Yearbook of the National Society for the Study of Education*, Part I, as cited in William F. Kilpatrick, ed., *The Educational Frontier* (New York: D. Appleton-Century, 1933), p. 226.

29. Cherryholmes, pp. 3-4.

30. Lanigan describes a problematic as "a problematical context within which an issue or issues function as a criterion for analysis and judgment of the problem per se." Richard L. Lanigan, "Structuralism and the Human Science Context of Phenomenology and Semiology," *Review Journal of Philosophy & Social Science* 11, no. 1: 56. See also Michael F. D. Young, *Knowledge and Control* (London: Collier-Macmillan, 1971).

31. Richard J. Bates, "The New Sociology of Education: Directions for Theory and Research," *New Zealand Journal of Educational Studies* 13 (1978): 3-21.

32. John W. Meyer and Richard W. Scott, eds., *Organizational Environments: Ritual and Rationality* (Beverly Hills, CA: Sage Publishing Company, 1983).

33. John W. Meyer and Brian Rowan, "The Structure of Educational Organizations" in Meyer and Scott, ibid., pp. 71-97. Also see Janice L. Bailey, "The Correspondence Between Beliefs Within Institutionalized Environments and Structures of School Guidance Programs" (Ed.D. dissertation, University of Missouri-St. Louis, 1989); Mary Ann Governal, "The Correspondence Between Beliefs Within Institutionalized Environments and Structures of Catholic Elementary Schools" (Ed.D. dissertation, University of Missouri-St. Louis, 1989); George E. Frieda, "The Correspondence Between Beliefs Within Institutionalized Environments and Structures of Middle Level Schools" (Ed.D. dissertation, University of Missouri-St. Louis, 1989); and Savannah R. Furman, "The Correspondence Between Environmental Beliefs About Institutionalized Organizations and Structures of School Districts" (Ed.D. dissertation, University of Missouri-St. Louis, 1989).

34. Michael Polanyi, *Personal Knowledge: Toward a Post-Critical Philosophy* (Chicago: The University of Chicago Press, 1958), p. 265.

35. Philip Phenix, *Realism of Meaning: A Philosophy of Curriculum for General Education* (New York: McGraw-Hill, 1964), p. 25.

7
Qualitative Criticism
James D. Swartz

INTRODUCTION

Qualitative criticism is a method of acquiring knowledge to guide decision making based on local knowledge. It is a synthesis of principles from criticism and qualitative research. To explain this synthesis, a short description of criticism will be followed by an explanation of assumptions and methods related to qualitative research. Because the focus or "context" of qualitative criticism is often not explicitly stated, the term *context* will be explained to avoid confusion about the purpose of qualitative criticism.

The function of qualitative criticism is centered within Richard Rorty's theoretical framework of solidarity. George Herbert Mead's description of a generalized other will be used to assist in understanding Rorty's notion of solidarity. I will attempt to sort through a distinction between moral questions and ethical questions and clarify how Rorty's form of pragmatism escapes relativism by focusing on cultural grounding for ethical behavior. By showing that Rorty's pragmatism is not relativistic but grounded in solidarity, I hope to demonstrate that the function of qualitative criticism is to assist in giving shape and cohesion to practice in contentious environments like schools.

The remainder of the discussion will deal with why qualitative criticism is important to critical administrative praxis. Three opposing concepts will be used to illustrate choices available to administrators. They are responsibility versus accountability, pluralism versus homogeneity, and deliberation versus top down management. The three situations represent contexts in which qualitative criticism might be practiced. It is hoped that these examples will clarify how qualitative criticism might be used for administrative praxis.

QUALITATIVE CRITICISM: A DESCRIPTION

What Is Criticism?

To better understand qualitative criticism it is illustrative to briefly describe the nature of criticism.[1] Dewey's (Ratner, 1939) ideas about criticism seem to have been reiterated in one form or another by many writers. For Dewey, criticism is judgment. The material out of which judgment grows is the work, the object, but it is this object as it enters into the experience of the critic by interaction with his or her own sensitivity, knowledge, and funded store from past experiences. As to their content, therefore, judgments will vary with concrete material that evokes them and that must sustain them if criticism is pertinent and valid. Nevertheless, judgments have a common form. These functions are discrimination and unification. Judgment has to evoke a clearer consciousness of constituent parts and to discover how consistently these parts are related to form a whole (Ratner, 1939).

Criticism is the sort of judgment that is greatly influenced by the past experiences of the judge, and criticism is judgment that involves analysis and synthesis. These aspects of Dewey's definition seem common to other thoughtful discussions of critics. For example, Elliot Eisner's (1985) notion of criticism seems to illustrate certain features in common with Dewey.

> Criticism is empirical in the significant sense that the qualities the critique describes or renders must be capable of being located in the subject matter of the criticism. In this sense, the test of criticism is in its instrumental effects on the perception of works of art. It is not abstraction that one understands through criticism but rather qualities and their relationships. (p. 217)

In this quote Eisner directs us to consider the subject matter of criticism and to understand both qualities, constituent parts, and their relationships to a presumed whole. Also, Eisner states that a "test of criticism is in its instrumental effects on the perception of works of art." One way of interpreting this last statement may be to suggest that criticism rests in experience and can change experience. This is somewhat similar to a statement made by Dewey (1934, p. 324) in *Art as Experience*. "The function of criticism is the reeducation of perception of works of art." Criticism of experience through attention to the work or object and through the use of analysis and synthesis appear to be common themes for both Dewey and Eisner.

Eisner (1985), in the same chapter of *The Educational Imagination,* calls the experience of the critic a crucial element of criticism: He calls that element connoisseurship.

> Effective criticism, within the arts or in education, is not an act independent of the powers of perception. The ability to see, to perceive what is subtle, complex, and important, is its first necessary condition. The act of knowledgeable perception is, in the arts, referred to

as connoisseurship. To be a connoisseur is to know how to look, to see, and to appreciate. Connoisseurship, generally defined, is the art of appreciation. It is essential to criticism because without the ability to perceive what is subtle and important, criticism is likely to be superficial or even empty. The major distinction between connoisseurship and criticism is this: connoisseurship is the art of appreciation, criticism is the art of disclosure. Connoisseurship is a private act; it consists of recognizing and appreciating the qualities of a particular, but it does not require either a public statement or a public description of those qualities. (p. 219)

Three aspects of criticism or public disclosure are descriptive, interpretative, and evaluative statements (Eisner, 1985). Educational criticism, it may be argued, has as its aim the characterization, interpretation, and appraisal of educational discourse/practice. Educational materials and settings, teaching practice, student learning, and so on, all may be subject to these three phases of critical inquiry. However, the rather swift and dramatic changes in education make educational criticism difficult. When compared with aesthetic criticism, educational critique finds the objects of educational critique more elusive than objects of art. Curricular matters lend themselves less readily to analysis and synthesis than do paintings and sculptures. And, since education is a value-laden endeavor, the past experience of the judge may be of special and strategic importance to the success of educational criticism. The characteristics of the phenomena of education and the peculiar kinds of experiences brought to these discourse/practices by the critic demand an unusually rigorous and exacting attention to method.

Some of the qualities of criticism mentioned by Dewey, Eisner, and McCutcheon are: Criticism is judgment anchored to a work object or work to be studied; criticism is influenced by the experience of the judge; and criticism involves the analysis of constituent parts through synthesis to a unified whole.

What Is Qualitative Criticism?

Qualitative criticism includes the three qualities of criticism mentioned earlier but adds one more. The additional quality is the values, knowledge, and experience of the creator of the thing or act being evaluated. The purpose of this addition is *not* to leap out of our own values, standards, and experience into the world of another person but rather to come to a better understanding of our own values, standards, and experience by seeing them more completely. An object of criticism is part of our world. The values, standards, and experience of the creator of the object or act being criticized are present in our world by virtue of the presence of the act or thing being criticized by us. In order to better understand the subject of criticism, it seems reasonable to inquire about the values, standards, and experience of the person who created it. How and why we engage in qualitative criticism is the topic at hand. This section will explain assumptions related to qualitative criticism and methods for acquiring information.

Assumptions

The following five assumptions are fundamental to gathering data for the purpose of qualitative criticism. They are taken from *Naturalistic Inquiry* (Lincoln & Guba, 1985). These assumptions do not represent a rejection of statistical research but rather a set of assumptions for qualitative criticism. It is probably accurate to claim that good naturalistic research includes criticism; however, the focus of qualitative criticism is not research but rather criticism. For example, the focus of qualitative research may be an extensive description of something over a period of time (prolonged engagement) while the focus of qualitative criticism could be a specific art object or educational act.

Axiom One: Reality is seen as multiple, constructed, and holistic. Qualitative criticism in education involves an inspection of a complex, subtle context. For example, a high school algebra class might be a subject for qualitative criticism. Test scores in algebra are fairly discrete measures of student achievement. It is easy to point to who achieved the highest score but what if the question was why did a certain student who scored well on a measure that predicts success in algebra do poorly on this test and subsequent tests. We could also conduct a naturalistic research study to determine why some students who scored well on aptitude tests performed poorly in high school algebra courses. The purpose of the naturalistic research study might be to investigate nondiscrete or nonmeasurable data about why students performed poorly. In addition to the test scores, we could interview students who scored poorly even though they scored well on an algebra aptitude test. We could interview the teacher, the student's parents, and classmates. We could observe classroom instruction over a period of time focusing on teacher behaviors and on low achieving, high aptitude student behaviors. The algebra teacher's lesson plans and handouts could be part of the data set as well as student note taking. Student transcripts dating back to grade school might also be of interest. The goal of this research would be an extensive description of a question. Why do some high aptitude algebra students perform poorly in class? The investigation might involve the perspective of teachers, students, and parents each of whom might construe or construct the problem of the algebra student in very different ways. In this example of a naturalistic research study, a picture of the question was derived from multiple viewpoints. An in-depth investigation might try to gain a holistic or comprehensive picture of why the students did not do well in high school algebra when they were predicted to do well. Words comprised the observational and interview data instead of numbers and a description of the problem or question was the primary intent of the study.

While still in the same algebra classroom we could ask a third question. We could conduct a qualitative criticism of an algebra class. The question might be: Does this instruction represent good practice? In fact, principals are asked to perform this task quite frequently. The focus of the qualitative criticism is one class session. The intent is to describe, interpret, and evaluate instruction taking place. The focus is narrow and specific and so is the intent of qualitative criticism. Three general considerations are relevant to the criticism. The values and standards of the critic that McCutcheon suggests are important enough to be made public. A clear description and appraisal of the class session might include an account of teacher and student behavior and documents like handouts and homework. A third factor might be the values and standards of the teacher. For instance, the teacher could comment about his or her lesson plan before the class session and give a personal interview about how well he or she thought the class went after it was over. The critic's view, the event being criticized, and the teacher's view should be part of qualitative criticism. Students might also be interviewed for their perspective. As with the naturalistic study, multiple perspectives were used. Each participant might construe or construct the class session differently. The purpose of qualitative criticism is to gain a holistic picture of the event and appraise it.

Axiom Two: Knower and known are interactive, inseparable. In naturalistic inquiry (also known as qualitative research, descriptive research, qualitative evaluation, etc.) the researcher is the instrument. He or she does the observing, interviewing, and other data collection. Knower and known interact within the setting; hence, they are connected.

In qualitative criticism the critic is the sole describer, interpreter, and evaluator. His or her experience, knowledge, values, skills, and attitudes are crucial to the credibility of the qualitative criticism. Knower and known are even more interlaced in qualitative criticism because qualitative research usually is more extensive in scope and usually more guarded as a form of interpretation and evaluation. Qualitative criticism is written through the critic's lens. It is his or her description, interpretation, and evaluation of an object or act. It is a personal act of appraisal and a statement of community beliefs as I hope to demonstrate later in the chapter. Knower and known are one within a community of experience, knowledge, skills, values, and attitudes.

Axiom Three: Only time and context bound working hypotheses (ideographic statements) are possible. Context may be described as the people, place, and situation under investigation. People and place are fairly obvious terms, but situation may not be as clear. Situation refers to the hierarchy, activities, goals, tasks, and so forth that people are involved in at a particular time and place. Context is the stuff of qualitative criticism. The object or act being criticized, the designer of the object or the doer of the act, and the critic are all part of the qualitative criticism. The critic becomes part of the context and his or her criticism can be understood or judged in relation to the context. Qualitative criticism is a working hypothesis about the *present state of a context.*

Axiom Four: All entities are in a state of mutual simultaneous shaping, so that it is impossible to distinguish causes from effects. A quantitative researcher has the benefit of experimental design to control for internal and external threats to validity. The naturalistic researcher and qualitative critic do not have the benefit of a controlled environment because it is their task to describe and report an uncontrolled, subtle, and frequently contradictory context or setting. Social interaction within a given context may be so complex that causes and effects cannot be sorted out. In the example of the algebra student, a case study of several students might yield valuable information about why high aptitude students perform poorly in an algebra course but it would not be able to identify cause and effect relationships. Such a case study would describe a specific set of events, in a specific time, a specific place, and a specific situation. Many interacting factors would probably be occurring simultaneously in the lives of the algebra students. While it might be fair to say some factors or occurrences were significant, it would be impossible to control for unknown intervening occurrences that might fall outside of the investigation. It would be impossible to distinguish causes from effects. For the qualitative critic, an evaluation does not involve cause and effect. Instead the appraisal requires a grounding in the act or object being criticized, and it requires the experience, knowledge, skills, and attitudes of the critic and the criticized.

Axiom Five: Inquiry is value bound. This is a rather obvious assumption for the qualitative critic. The criticism is bound to the values found within the context and to the experience, knowledge, values, skills, and attitudes of the critic, the object of criticism, and the creator/designer/doer of the object or act under criticism.

Solidarity as a Framework for Qualitative Criticism

The intent of the short discussion of Lincoln and Guba's (1985) five axioms related to naturalistic inquiry was to illustrate the synthesis of criticism and naturalistic inquiry. Hopefully, good naturalistic inquiry contains some qualitative criticism but qualitative criticism has its own scope and purpose. The difference between criticism and qualitative criticism is not merely the addition of the perspective of the doer/designer/producer of the thing or act being criticized but more importantly the five axioms or assumptions of naturalistic inquiry are emphasized in qualitative criticism. These five axioms point toward a larger framework that extends the notion of qualitative criticism. This larger framework for qualitative criticism indicates a social underpinning and role. In brief that role is to give shape and cohesion to practice in contentious environments like schools by providing an exchange between the critic and his or her context. The larger framework is Richard Rorty's concept of solidarity.

George Herbert Mead's framework for understanding social interaction may relate to an understanding of solidarity. The expectation that this unique viewpoint concerning social interaction may aid in studying solidarity is the point of the following short section about Mead's ideas.

George Herbert Mead was committed to a social idea of self. For him, the social act was the unit of social existence. It consisted of stimulus, manipulation, and response (Miller, 1973). Manipulation was the focus of an act. For Mead, manipulation was what makes us human. Manipulation meant to rehearse action in terms of an anticipated response of others before engaging in an act. This rehearsal included three tenses: the past, present, and future. The past represented our reservoir of experience that was the product of tradition or a generalized other, the present was the present context or circumstance, and the future was the anticipated response of some person or persons to our action.

Manipulation was how a concept of self was formed. According to Mead, by rehearsing the reaction of other people to our own actions we form a concept of self. In order to understand manipulation more clearly, some other terms should probably be introduced and explained. Among them, "experience" and "adjustment" might contribute to clarifying how Mead viewed the formation of self. "The environment of living organisms is constantly changing, it is constantly invaded with other and different things. The assimilation of what occurs and that which recurs with what is elapsing and what has elapsed is called experience" (Miller, 1973, p. 37). This is a process of taking what occurs via the senses into a system of awareness about what is happening and remembrances about what has happened.

The validity of what occurs depends on practical outcomes in terms of adjustment. "The process of adjustment is therefore a case in which items in the old system must adjust to the emergent and it to them, and the adjustment has definite implications for the future" (Miller, 1973, p. 23). Mead's notion of the social act is grounded in experience. The most primitive sort of experience is the nonsocial act. "A nonsocial act is an ongoing event that consists of stimulation and response and the results of that response" (Miller, 1973, p. 31). The response leads to some sort of adjustment. In contrast, during the social act there is a manipulatory phase that might be referred to as reflexiveness. "By reflexiveness Mead meant, '. . . the turning-back of experience of the individual upon himself' " (Franklin, 1975, p. 6). During the social act there is a manipulatory phase in which incoming stimuli are subjected to reflexiveness before consummation (response) occurs. The manipulatory phase is the social phase because objects or symbols are "reflected upon" in terms of a social perspective. "A perspective, then, requires the selection of that which is necessary for the adjustment of the organism, an adjustment made by completing the act" (Miller, 1973, p. 32). Social acts seem to require a shared perspective for adjustment. Shared perspective may be understood through the following:

Taking the role of another happens when the individual is able to evoke in himself by his own behavior (gesture) the same response (a functionally identical response) that his behavior evokes in another . . . The role which is shared by the other is the role manipulation fundamentally in that all shared experiences derive from it. (Miller, 1973, pp. 33–34)

Thus, individuals look at their own response in terms of a perspective shared by others. They manipulate objects and symbols by internalization of the knowledge of the community. The connection between language and the development of self is direct. "Communication is a relationship between one part of the social act, the gesture, and the response of adjustment by a second form to that gesture" (Miller, 1973, p. 47). A gesture is part of a social act which requires manipulation by another. "Language gestures are the means by which functionally identical responses are evoked in both the speaker and the other to whom the gesture is addressed" (Miller, 1973, p. 48). Communication through language is a method of development of self for individuals and the common community in which individuals participate. Common or shared attitudes may be formed through this process. An attitude is defined as "a readiness to respond in a certain way when a particular that will fulfill or aid in completing the act is present" (Miller, 1973, p. 82). ("Particular" refers to a specific object or symbol belonging to a class that elicits a functionally similar response as it would from other members of the same class.) "The organized set of attitudes, and their corresponding responses which are common to the group, is the generalized other" (Miller, 1973, p. 49). It is the generalized other as the self views it. The generalized other appears to be the shared moral that the community carries in its traditions (Miller, 1973). Duality of generalized other and self seems to be a constant interlocking, mutually formative process. The duality can be seen in Mead's comments about self (Franklin, 1975).

The fully developed self for Mead had two phases, which he called the "I" and the "me." The "me" represented the attitudes called for by the generalized other, that is, society. The "I" constituted the response of the individual to these attitudes. "I" then represented the individual's particular and unique identity within social life. As such, self for Mead was not a physical object, such as the brain or the body. The self was reflexive, which an object, such as the body was not. (p. 6)

Mead's notions about the formation of self through symbolic interaction with a generalized other are important for several reasons. First, symbolic interaction outlines a specific version of how an individual is related to community-based knowledge. Although my presentation of Mead's theory of symbolic interaction is adumbrated, enough elements may be present for the reader to comprehend that a relationship exists between the formation of an individual self and a larger knowledge consisting of shared perspectives and attitudes related to social activity. Within the parameters of Mead's ideas, knowledge might be construed to mean a shared framework of ideas about words, objects, and other symbols that inform the social act. Knowledge may be dependent on the shared perspectives, attitudes, and communication that the individual perceives as a generalized other. A generalized other may be understood to be "the organized set of attitudes and their corresponding responses which are common to the group" (Miller, 1973, p. 49). The size of the group may be as small as a family or as large as the social acts of the group extend. Group based knowledge may be understood, in Mead's terms, as symbolic; therefore, a shared framework of ideas about words, objects, and other symbols that inform social acts seems to be a conception of knowledge appropriate to this viewpoint.

Mead's description of a generalized other or normative community is one of the ideas that lies at the center of pragmatism. Since Rorty refers to pragmatism, Mead's explanation seemed particularly appropriate. For practical purposes the concept of a generalized other can be substituted for solidarity. Richard Rorty's *Objectivity, Relativism, and Truth* (1991) aids in our description of solidarity and pragmatism. For Rorty, one of the ways reflective humans seek to give meaning to their lives is by telling the story of their contribution to a community (p. 21). Another way that a person may be defined is through the community's contribution to him or her. For Rorty, there is a mutual shaping between community (solidarity) and individuals (p. 21).

In his rejection of the relativist label, Rorty discusses the ethical nature of truth as it comes to be based in cultural ethnocentricity. It originates from the type of exchange that Mead described as "manipulation." Rorty tells us that "relativism" is an epithet applied to pragmatism by realists and takes three differing forms of ethnocentrism: The first finds any belief is as good as any other. In the second perspective, the term "truth" is equivocal and has as many meanings as there are justifying procedures. The third view has it that nothing may be stated regarding either truth or rationality apart from describing the familiar procedures of justification that our particular society uses in any domain of inquiry (p. 23).

Pragmatists, Rorty argues, hold to the third view, although without accepting views one and two. The pragmatist believes the pragmatic position is better than the realists', but without thinking his or her perspective corresponds to the nature of things. The term "true" is flexible, functions merely as commendation, and thus operates in the same manner in all cultures. Rorty emphasizes this point when he adds, "the identity of meaning is, of course, compatible with diversity of reference, and with diversity of procedures for assigning the terms" (1991, p. 23).

I believe Rorty draws a line between moral questions and ethical questions. He seems to see a relationship between community definition through cooperative human inquiry and ethical definitions of right and wrong. It is through ethical behavior that we define our community. This is the role that I believe qualitative criticism plays within the educational sector of solidarity. The function of honoring our own solidarity occurs through cooperative human inquiry like qualitative criticism.

Rorty tells us that accepting the value of solidarity, the pragmatic account of the value of cooperative inquiry rests on an ethical, rather than an epistemological or metaphysical base. The pragmatist must, in practice, privilege his or her own group, even though there can be justification for doing so that is not circular. Nothing is immune from criticism; however, this does not mean that we are obliged to justify everything. We must start from where we are, and this assumption means that there are many views that cannot be taken seriously (1991, p. 29).

Establishing community standards may emerge through unforced agreement, such as an exchange of qualitative criticisms. Through such exchanges we can become aware of who we are as a community.

Rorty calls for a "new fuzziness," or effort to blur precisely the distinctions between the objective/subjective and between fact/value that are the legacy of rationalism. Rather than adopt the traditional "objectivity" of science, Rorty proposes we "fuzzies" substitute the idea of "unforced agreement" (1991, p. 38).

In his description of a utopia of reciprocal loyalty, Rorty sees the preservation and self-improvement of community as essential to its survival. Qualitative criticism is an attempt to describe how Rorty's community might work. Qualitative criticism is an exchange within the community that expresses individual and community standards by including multiple perspectives of community standards through individuals experienced with the generalized other or solidarity.

Again, borrowing from Rorty, one's first and ultimate loyalty would be to the larger community that permitted and encouraged freedom and the lack of concern for irrelevancies. Such a community would have as its goal its own preservation and self-improvement as well as the preservation and enhancement of civilization. Rationality would come to be defined in terms of these efforts rather than with the goal of objectivity. Out of this arrangement would be found, at base, reciprocal loyalty (1991, p. 45).

Why Is Qualitative Criticism Important to Administrative Praxis?

In this final section of the chapter, three opposing concepts will be used to illustrate the choices available to administrators. They are responsibility versus accountability, pluralism versus homogeneity, and deliberation versus top down management. The role of qualitative criticism is to lay out reasons for choices so that individuals and communities can learn and grow from well-reasoned public discussion. Qualitative criticism combines the community knowledge of criticism and the axioms of naturalistic inquiry to assure its connection to a generalized other. It is intended to be a method for the discussion of a particular solidarity at a specific time and context. Policy making about the three types of decisions mentioned here could be guided, in part, by an exchange of qualitative criticism about problematic topics. If the idea of praxis is theory driven action, then the pragmatic theories of the community must be exposed through some sort of reflexive, thoughtful, community based theories found through disciplined discussion.

Responsibility Versus Accountability

Responsibility and accountability (Taylor & Johnsen, 1986) are opposing concepts. Responsibility originates from the community fund of experience, knowledge, skills, values, and attitudes. It is the product of an open conversation within the community that is the very heart of Rorty's solidarity. Responsibility coexists and interacts with the mutual and simultaneous change noted in axiom four of the naturalistic paradigm.

Responsibility presumes that humans have the potential to act as free moral agents guided by deliberation and internal sanctions, in choosing their acts in the light of the consequences. Responsible action can be intense but it is never mindless. Accountability, on the other hand, means being subject to giving an account to an external agent who has prespecified a minimum standard to be achieved. Accordingly, accountable action can be intense but is often mindless. Responsibility requires freedom to make choices; accountability requires constant surveillance. The two are opposing concepts. (p. 16)

Accountability results when a conversation about community experience, knowledge, values, skills, and attitudes ends. Rorty, quoted in Bernstein (1983), cautions about closing the conversation.

We must appreciate the extent to which our sense of community is threatened not only by material conditions but by the faulty epistemological doctrines that fill our heads. The moral task of the social philosopher or social critic is to defend the openness of human conversation against all those temptations and real threats that seek closure. (pp. 204–205)

As administrators, it is all too easy to fall into a trap of closure in order to expedite the day-to-day activities of schools. It seems reasonable that one way to guard against the pressure to run a well-ordered organization would be to encourage qualitative criticism by administrators, teachers, staff, and even students. Those who are within the context may have the kind of expertise that Dewey, McCutcheon, and Eisner advocate. The five axioms devised by Lincoln and Guba suggest the type of research paradigm appropriate to studying issues related to responsibility versus accountability. The combination of criticism and qualitative research techniques seems well suited to avoiding opinion and revealing thoughtful, informed qualitative criticism. If the idea of praxis means theory governed behavior, it would seem desirable that praxis originate from within the generalized other (community and solidarity express the same concept as generalized other). This is why Rorty's pragmatism and sense of community is so important. If we are to honor our own ethnocentrism as a standard for action as Rorty suggests, we do have right and wrong answers about problems that are specific to a definable time and context.

The subject of criticism might be rules for classroom behavior. Should dress codes, special programs, or evaluation programs be imposed from an external source or should these standards be generated from within the community? Specific answers might be generated for problematic situations by requesting that those who have something at stake (administrators, teachers, staff, students) engage in a qualitative criticism of a specific existing practice. The advantage of qualitative criticism is that it employs techniques like observation, interview, and document collection to question social assumptions about the people, place, and situation that presently exist. Qualitative criticism requires questioning a specific, concrete practice over a short period of time while considering information related to the critic, the object, or act under scrutiny, and the designer/producer/originator of the object or act being criticized.

The question of responsibility seems to offer some productive problems for the qualitative critic.

Pluralism Versus Homogeneity

For the purposes of this chapter, *social* diversity, or pluralism, is a theory that reality is composed of a variety of constructed realities and that members of diverse ethnic, racial, religious, or social groups can autonomously participate in the development of their traditional culture or special interests while contributing to a common cultural reality. If culture is understood as the sum total of what people do together, then a cultural reality can, at the same time, be diverse and recognizable.

Often, pluralism is referred to simply as a theory that society is diverse in its makeup. However, diversity may constitute an incomplete idea of pluralism. Bernstein (1983) described Arendt's version of plurality:

> By plurality, Arendt does not merely mean that there is "otherness," that there are individuals who oppose or thwart my desires, passions, interests, and ambitions. Rather, it means that there is a unique distinctiveness about each and every individual, rooted in human natality, the capacity to begin, to initiate, to act. Plurality is not so much a permanent state of being as an achievement realized only when individuals act. "To act, in the most general sense, means to take an initiative, to begin . . . to set something in motion. A life without speech and without action . . . is literally dead to the world; it has ceased to be a human life because it is no longer lived among men." Human plurality is the basic condition of action and speech because action and speech take place between men in their singularity and plurality. Action then is, intrinsically, political activity requiring the existence of that public space or polis within which individuals can encounter others and reveal who they are. (p. 208)

It has been suggested that education may be such a public place. Greene (1976) encouraged teachers to use their own voices to shape the school environment and "to create the kinds of spaces where dialogue can take place and freedom can appear" (Greene, 1986, p. 73). Greene's admonition seemed to be about teachers taking an active role in creating a diverse environment for assisting student learning.

One major problem for administrators who are sensitive to pluralism is defining whose knowledge is to count as knowledge in schools. One dramatic example was the problem of French Canadian children and their local schools. Even though a great many French speaking children attended schools in Quebec province, instruction was in English. Very few French symbols were present in school for children to identify with such as flags, signs in French, or audio visual materials about French speaking Quebec. This problem, which was also widespread outside of schools, eventually caused a serious move to establish an independent French state. In the United States, we face similar problems with English as the language of instruction for Spanish speaking Americans. There is also a problem about language based standardized testing that may be unfair to some inner city elementary and secondary students who do not use standard English. Fundamentalist religious groups, feminists, environmentalists, and people of color may and have objected to classroom media that offends their community knowledge base. I view qualitative criticism as providing a conceptual space for informed dialogue about these very contentious issues for all those who have a stake in schools. Qualitative criticism is a method of bringing community based experience, knowledge, skills, values, and attitudes to the forefront to formulate community based theory to guide practice about issues concerning pluralism.

Deliberation Versus Top Down Management

The larger issue here is that of deliberation in general. How can administrators convert practice into praxis? How can solutions to practical problems become theory directed? Obviously the choice of qualitative criticism would depend on the nature of the problem. Many everyday problems and not so everyday problems can be guided by rule governed theory generated from statistical research, which I might argue can be similar to qualitative criticism. Statistical research may share many characteristics with qualitative criticism when that research is done from within the community in order to address a specific problem in a specific context at a specific point in time. However, many common problems are too vague to be addressed by quantitative measures. For example, what standards are used to evaluate teachers may be both a qualitative and a quantitative problem.

The method by which most everyday practical problems get solved has been variously called "deliberation" or "practical reasoning." It is an intricate and skilled intellectual and social process whereby, individually or collectively, we identify the questions to which we must respond, establish ground for deciding on answers, and then choose among the available solutions (Reid, 1979). Reid (1979) listed seven features of deliberative questions:

1. Unlike theoretical or academic questions, practical questions, which are the subject of deliberation, must be answered. In fact, to do nothing is an answer to a practical question.
2. The grounds on which decisions should be made are uncertain.
3. In answering practical questions, we always take some existing state into account.

4. Each question is in some way unique, belonging to a specific time and context, the particulars of which we can never exhaustively describe.
5. Our question will certainly compel us to adjudicate between competing goals and values.
6. We can never predict the outcome of the particular solution we choose, still less know what outcome would have been had we made a different choice.
7. The grounds on which we decide to answer a practical question in a particular way are not grounds that point to desirability of the action chosen as an act in itself, but grounds that lead us to suppose that the action will result in some desirable state of affairs (pp. 188–89).

Reid lists uncertain grounds, a current existing state, uniqueness of time and context, particulars that can never be exhaustively described, competing goals and values, unpredictable outcomes, and an emphasis on intent as qualities of deliberative questions. Qualitative criticism seems like a wonderful method to establish dialogue about how teachers plan and how curriculum should be structured based on knowledge about teacher planning. Such a dialogue might lead to a community based praxis about teacher planning. These themes become clearer when Reid's features of deliberative questions are compared to questions asked in teacher thinking planning. Questions about how teachers plan (Yinger, 1979), how they make decisions, and how they form theories and beliefs (Sanders & McCutcheon, 1986) in uncertain and changing circumstances, seem to share the qualities of deliberative or practical questions. In contrast to the prescriptive approach, or what I refer to as top down management, teacher planning seems to share many of the features of deliberative questions. However, the main qualm teacher thinking writers appear to have is not the existence of the prescriptive model, but rather its dominance. Van Manen (1977) has commented on the technical approach that examines questions in terms of quantification, for the purpose of prediction and control: "The point is not that these are bad questions, but that there are other questions to be asked" (p. 210). As a dominant approach, prescriptive or technical questions are probably not the focus of teacher thinking planning because there often are other questions to be asked. Surveys of teacher thinking planning (Pape, 1988; Clark, 1988) reflect practical or deliberative questions more often than technical questions.

Sanders and McCutcheon's (1986) definition of practical theories of teaching seems to imply such a connection. "Practical theories of teaching are the conceptual structures and visions that provide teachers with reasons for acting as they do, and for choosing the teaching activities and curriculum materials they choose in order to be effective" (p. 54). Practical theories of teaching are not scientific because they are "particularistic" and "individualistic" (Sanders & McCutcheon, 1986, p. 63). They are particularistic because practical theories are centered in a singular value-laden context. Teachers are concerned with whether their theories are valid in the present with the children they are trying to educate rather than whether their theories can generalize to all instances of a given kind. Practical theories are individualistic since they are specific to an individual teacher's skills and knowledge. An example of how the particularistic and individualistic character of practical theories of teaching may influence teacher selection of curriculum materials (print and nonprint media for classroom use) and classroom activities may be found in McCutcheon's (1981) research on teacher planning. When teachers discovered errors in media they adjusted their plans based on their own knowledge and skills.

Teachers' skills and knowledge, then, influenced the nature of planning and topics to be addressed. Plans frequently transformed a program's intentions into a lesson the teacher felt more able to engineer in a classroom than a plan suggested in a manual accompanying a program (p. 55). It would seem that practical decisions about the nature of teacher planning and topics related to teacher planning would be an excellent context for qualitative criticism. This seems plausible because Reid lists uncertain grounds, a current existing state, uniqueness of time and context, particulars that can never be exhaustively described, competing goals and values, unpredictable outcomes and an emphasis on intent as qualities of deliberative questions. These qualities describe a context consistent with the idea of qualitative criticism (e.g., Lincoln and Guba's axioms).

It seems reasonable to speculate that practical theories of teaching as described by Sanders and McCutcheon might have an influence on the acceptance or rejection of daily deliberative educational practice as described by Reid. Doesn't it seem counterproductive and wasteful not to have knowledge of the practical theories of teaching held by teachers, administrators, staff, and students? To not have this knowledge means that administrative practice will probably not be governed by community based knowledge. Practice will remain practice and not praxis. It is difficult to conceive how practice can be converted to community based praxis with a community based fund or store of knowledge about practical theories of teaching. If praxis is theory based practice, then practice without knowledge can seldom lead to praxis.

CONCLUSION

The function of qualitative criticism is to enrich a local community of knowledge by enriching its knowledge base. The critic learns more about him- or herself by a disciplined examination of his or her own community. The person who produced/designed/created the act or object of criticism learns more about his or her own participation or contribution to the community. And the community gains new knowledge to add to its fund or store of knowledge that may help it to sustain or improve itself. The axioms that describe qualitative criticism are consistent with Rorty's notion of community in which we trade objectivity for unforced agreement.

NOTE

1. I want to acknowledge the contributions of Dr. Bruce Smith to the formation of ideas about qualitative criticism. We have had extensive conversations about it. At this point in time it is difficult to separate his ideas from my own. I am grateful to have such a creative friend and colleague.

PART III
Postmodern Organization

8

Educational Administration in the Postmodern Age

Bill J. Johnston

The decade of the 1980s witnessed successive "waves" of educational reform. The first was heralded by such national reports as *A Nation at Risk, Action for Excellence, Making the Grade,* and *Academic Preparation for College.* The problem was identified as an economic crisis and the solution was to emphasize academic standards, accountability, standardization, and leadership. The logic of reform was grounded in structural-functionalism and held the promise that if only schools would do more and better than what they have traditionally done, the United States could regain its rightful place within the world economic community. State legislators responded to the challenge of reform by mandating performance standards, curriculum, and pedagogy, and by "ensuring" student and teacher accountability through testing.

This represented intensification of the familiar strategy of top-down, bureaucratic control (Kirst, 1988; Hawley, 1988), now grounded in the rhetoric of "effective" teaching and schooling (Brookover, 1982; Edmonds, 1986; Brophy & Good, 1986; Presseisen, 1986). Within the logic of bureaucratic control, education administrators were considered pivotal to the reform process and were directed to adopt strategies of "assertive leadership" relative to the development of school vision and instructional strategy. Hawley (1988), while critical of some school reform efforts, suggests that first wave reform efforts have been more successful in the 1980s than education critics may have yet recognized. True indeed, and if "first wave" types of improvement continue we may yet achieve the schools envisioned in 1957 following the launch of Sputnik and passage of the National Defense Education Act; schools characterized by standardized national curriculum and teachers treated as technicians.

Second wave reforms were ushered in by the Carnegie Task Force (1986) and the Holmes Group (1986) reports in recognition that not only better but different forms of schooling were needed. The problem was still located in the economy, but there was growing recognition that the structure of the economy had undergone profound change. The solution remained located in education, but issues of teacher empowerment, site-based management, and professionalism became central. These are reform strategies that serve to alter the social relations of work and the technical division of labor.

Second wave reforms still rely on the logic of structural-functionalism but are now used within a framework of recognition of structural discontinuity between institutional sectors of the social formation. The "restructuring" turn of educational reform is offered as a means to reduce discontinuity. One significant effect of these reforms has been to subordinate building level administration to faculty leadership in the name of teacher empowerment (McNeil, 1990). The redistribution of school authority may be appropriate, but it is not simply a value-neutral, technical-rational exercise. It is also a political act. Bureaucratic and professional strategies of organization are combined in a rather arbitrary and contradictory manner in response to shifting political pressures.

The success of second wave reforms will be dependent on the ability of educators to develop alternative school structures and leadership styles (Firestone, 1989) and their ability to influence the logic and rhetoric of school purpose and process. This is likely to be a difficult undertaking. Teachers and administrators, parents and policy makers have been conditioned for decades by prevailing bureaucratic forms of schooling. To paraphrase Michels' "Iron Law of Oligarchy," It is difficult even to imagine alternative organizational possibilities or the leadership styles necessary to achieve them (Jacoby, 1973). Even ideologically popular concepts such as "professionalism" have tended to be associated more with the attributes of persons (referring to the skilled execution of assigned tasks) than to organizational structure and process.

Emerging third wave reforms directly address the issue of administrative leadership. Led by the Danforth Foundation and the University Council for Educational Administration (UCEA) the initial call has been to reform administrator training. Two central problems of extant training programs have been identified. One is that typically part-time, drive-in students participate in piecemeal, "courses and credits" programs. The recommendation is to improve academic programs to make them more coherent and integrated. In this regard UCEA calls for return to a "classic model" of extended study; the Danforth Foundation has adopted a strategy of funding university experiments with program design.

A second problem is that the models of administration typically offered in the university are grounded in rational, bureaucratic approaches to organization and fail to meet the emerging needs of practicing administrators. Training in rational management strategies may be necessary, but it has not proven to be sufficient to prepare administrators to adopt roles of transformative leadership consistent with the needs of restructured schools. Moreover, past attempts to obtain more relevant administrator training have generally contained an implicit antitheory bias.

The academic response has been to codify existing practices and then "align" program curricula so as to convey those practices to students. This is an appropriate strategy to the extent that we wish to perpetuate extant practices (and malpractices). Administration reform efforts, however, demand development of new theories to guide interpretation, design, and implementation of restructured schools. These efforts recognize that to create educational organizations different from what we have requires new ways of thinking and acting. In this regard development of new theoretical perspectives is central to developing effective practice.

In developing new theoretical frameworks to guide school administrators, it is necessary to locate schooling within the broader framework of institutional relations of the social formation (Carnoy & Levin, 1976; 1985; Apple, 1979). Many scholars recognize that economic institutions have experienced profound change in the past twenty-five years associated with deindustrialization; that political institutions have had to adapt to the management of decline and the legitimation of inequality; that social relations have been altered by relative decline in the middle class and expansion of the under classes, and that all of these changes influence school structure and practice. In responding to these political, economic, and social forces, second wave reform efforts have been significant in redirecting attention toward the need to create fundamentally different school structures. There is a persistent tendency, however, to treat schools as simple technical-rational systems that lend themselves to managerial manipulation. This approach tends to ignore the changing cultural context within which schools exist; the systems of value and belief through which organizational structures and relationships are imbued with meaning (Greenfield, 1973; Sergiovanni, 1986).

Considering school restructuring to be a cultural as well as structural phenomena necessitates investigation of the cultural context and epistemic grounding of school organization and administration. Postmodernism may be interpreted as a general cultural sensibility, incorporating poststructural and postpositivist movements, reflecting the transformation of social life in a postindustrial social formation. To the extent that postmodernism does represent an ascending general cultural sensibility, one may expect that postmodernist themes may be reflected in the organization and structure of public schooling. The remainder of this chapter will examine the rise of postmodernism as it relates to the development of educational administration theory and practice. Postmodernism is grounded in phenomenological and critical approaches to the interpretation of social life. As a symbolic theory, postmodernism serves to provide alternative conceptual and strategic orientations to organizational development and change than are offered by structuralist theories.

CONTEXT OF POSTMODERNISM

The social and intellectual context of postmodernism may be traced to the 1960s and is associated with (1) the changing structure of the economy and (2) the challenge to the foundational principles of modernist and Enlightenment ideologies. While the rise of postmodernism reflects social uncertainty associated with postindustrial capitalist development, this is not to suggest that postmodernism is the dominant cultural representation of advanced capitalism. Rather, postmodernism is considered to constitute just one alternative interpretive system through which individuals articulate and construct their lives in a changing social formation. Movements of conservative restoration (Shor, 1986) or critical application of modernist cultural beliefs (Bowers, 1987), which locate reform within authoritative belief structures, are also more visible. Without adopting economistic epistemology, it is reasonable to propose that economic restructuring has stimulated cultural critique and reformulation, which is being reflected more directly in postmodern problematics than those associated with more traditional perspectives.

Economic Deindustrialization

From 1960 to 1985 the absolute number of persons employed in the industrial sector has remained relatively stable (Kutscher & Personick, 1986). General population growth and increased female participation has led, however, to considerable expansion of the labor force, and that expansion has occurred largely in the service sector (Shank, 1988; Jones & Rosenfeld, 1989). The proportion of persons employed in the industrial sector has declined from approximately 73 to 23 percent of the total labor force (Kutscher & Personick, 1986). Personick (1987) predicts that in the year 2000, 80 percent of all wage and salary jobs will be in the service-producing sector. This is a rather dramatic demographic change.

As "restructuring" from an industrial to a service economy has occurred, the class structure has also been transformed. Changes in class structure are associated with the distribution of income and the nature of work. Approximately half of the new (service economy) jobs created in the past quarter-century are associated with minimum wage. Moreover, the real value of the minimum wage shows considerable variation over time as a consequence of variation in prices and non-minimum wage rates. The value of the minimum wage is at the lowest level since the mid-1950s (Smith & Vavrichek, 1987). One consequence of these income dynamics is the rise of a "dual economy" (high versus low wage jobs) within the service sector; there is a growing income bi-polarization, both absolute and relative, and a decline in the size of the middle class (McMahon & Tschetter, 1986; Horrigan & Haugen, 1988).

Quite apart from income distributions, the nature of work is undergoing change. Words like "postindustrial," "knowledge society," and the "technological era" have been used to describe these changes (Peters, 1989). The referent is to the expansion of jobs requiring the manipulation and processing of information. The technology of postindustrial work requires that one make nonroutine decisions and engage in problem solving. While the nature of decisions will vary by job level, the fact of being faced with decisional situations remains at all levels— and in forms different from those historically faced by labor.

As the technology of work changes, so too do the social relations associated with coordination and control over the work process. No longer may one depend on the "discipline of the machine" nor even on bureaucratic rules to maintain control (Edwards, 1979). Rather the effective execution of "knowledge-work" tasks demands that each person be able to conceptualize the superordinate purposes and practices driving the work process. Without such conceptual understanding it is impossible to develop shared and meaningful assumptions and criteria to guide the decisional process. The historical strategy of maintaining control by separating conceptualization from the execution of tasks and centering "mental" labor in management (Braverman, 1974), is simply ineffective in a postindustrial work environment. Likewise bureaucratic control strategies, which are grounded on the premise that one will "work to the rule," are only suitable for those organizations in which the nature of decisional situations are relatively stable, routine, and prescriptive (Perrow, 1970).

I think few people would characterize the current political economy as one of stability, nor knowledge-work organizations as typically engaged in routine decision making. Indeed, business organization and management strategies have begun to emphasize such concepts as shared vision, participatory decision making, site-based management, and quality circles—all of which recognize the importance of labor's conceptual participation in the work process. The educational need expressed by the business community is for all members of the labor force to acquire "higher order" cognitive skills (Carnegie Task Force, 1986; American Society for Training and Development, 1988; Levin, 1990). The message to schools is that fundamentally different attitudes and skills are required from today's students. To the extent that goal reorientation may require the adoption of new forms of facilitating organizational structure, development of a new logic of organization guiding administrative leadership and social relationship within schools may be considered the central problem of reform.

Critique of Modernist Management Ideology

The development of modernism as a cultural phenomenon is associated in the United States with the late nineteenth century. Brown (1976, p. 5) suggests that modernization became the secular counterpart of salvation and was inseparable from ideas of industrialism and progress. Basic components of modernist belief structure include mastery over nature, progress and change, rationality, efficiency, and impersonal communication. The quintessential form of modernist organization is bureaucracy, and within bureaucracy, rational administration is the central and primary mechanism for social and organizational development.

The modernists believed that mastery over nature and society could be achieved through technological development and rational administration. In order to achieve such mastery, however, it was first necessary to relativize traditional forms of cultural authority (Bowers, 1987). The relativizing of traditional authority demanded creation of new principles governing social behavior. These principles were located in equality, rationality, impersonality, and atomistic individualism. One consequence of relativizing traditional authority and relocating authority within rational individuals was the politization of everyday life. Social interaction was understood as a "constructivist" enterprise (Berger & Luckmann, 1967), and the modernist task became the search for balance between the demands for individual autonomy and equality, on the one hand, and social order and stability on the other.

The balance achieved was never particularly stable, equitable, or unifying. Modern consciousness during the twentieth century became clearly ideological in privileging problem identification and solutions consistent with bureaucratic organization, technical control, and protection of private property (Jacoby, 1973). That is, an organizational strategy began to determine the selection of problems and solutions.

Social change, now represented as progress rather than the outcome of historical conflicts between racial, religious, class, or gendered social groups struggling for power, also became an essential feature of modern consciousness. The notion of change, however, has remained problematic. For classic liberal ideology to gain ascendancy, it was necessary to separate legitimacy claims from the apparent ideological interests of powerful social groups or from social tradition itself. Positivism, coupled with empiricism, became accepted as the epistemic basis for truth claims and gave rise to a view of science as detached and objective. The consequence for development of modernism was belief in the power of rational/empirical science to control the natural and social world. This belief has evolved into expressions of hegemony of technical-rational thought structures. Change governed by technical-rational patterns of thought became privileged as natural and progressive, while change grounded in alternative logic structures was depreciated as unnatural, irrational, and reactionary.

Modernism may be considered then to represent a particular ideological version of scientism, positivism, and empiricism, and to legitimate continual social change and challenge to traditional structures of authority insomuch as change and challenge is consistent with technical-rational discourse. But modernism also incorporates rhetorical belief in the centrality of the atomistic individual exercising technical-rationality. This creates something of a social dilemma between the competing interests of rational individuals, on the one hand, and extant institutional formations, considered to represent the collective expression of technical-rationality, on the other. The individual is placed in relationship with, and is confronted by, new traditions in the form of a hegemonic discourse of reason and a derivative institutional structure.

The modernist mistake was the rather narrow manner in which the classic liberal view of rationality came to be interpreted. The distinction to be made by Weber (Gerth & Mills, 1948) between instrumental and substantive rational authority and the tendency of the instrumental-rational to degenerate into antidemocratic organizational formations, on the one hand, and vulgar technical-rationalism, on the other, was largely ignored in the institutionalization of rationality during the industrial period (Marcuse, 1960; Habermas, 1971). A form of hegemonic rationality prevailed that encouraged the reification of social relations and suppressed integration of the instrumental and the normative. The general consequence was to privilege patterns of epistemic dogmatism in science, of structured social inequality in institutional relations, and of denial of the normative and emotional components of human subjectivity. The rational individual became defined as one who accepted the dominant discourse and derivative institutional relations.

DEVELOPMENT OF POSTMODERNISM

Throughout the industrial period, the ideologies of modernism, positivism, and structuralism were considered to have served the society well. Political democracy, industrial development, even the struggle for social equality, were considered to be grounded in the legitimate expression of these ideological formations. But by the late twentieth century a voice of discontent was being raised. Within the ideology of modernism, the reasoning individual was granted a central location, yet it was the structure of reason itself, rather than the individual that was most valued. Critique of the hegemony of technical-rationality became a central feature of postmodern consciousness, as was investigation of patterns of subject formation and the relationship of knowing subjects to established structures of discourse. Critique, resistance to conventional meaning, and the transformative potential of discourse structures emerged as central postmodernist concerns.

In this shift of organizing problematics, postmodernism represents not so much a break with the analytic categories of the past, as it does a "deconstructive" move of substitution of one center for another (Jauss, 1988-1989). Whereas in its evolution modernism centered the structure of reason over the individual and the privileged examination of issues of unity, coherence, and certainty, postmodernism inverts the center and examines moments of uncertainty and ambiguity. Such a move facilitates both critique of reason and incorporation of issues of power and ideology within that critique.

The historical analytic neglect of normative expressions of power are understood to both privilege and reify extant social formations while blocking the expression of alternative logics expressed by disenfranchised groups and reflective individuals. Postmodernism attempts to overcome these limitations through social and structural critique, by reducing the categorical distinctions between objectivity and intersubjectivity, and by focusing on symbolic action represented through "texts," broadly conceived, while maintaining a posture of textual indeterminacy and semiotic ambiguity of phenomena.

Postmodernist Variations

Two strands of postmodernist development may be identified (Huyssen, 1986). The first, prior to 1970, was characterized by a revival of avantgardism, a rather uncritical attempt to validate popular culture, and a sense of discontinuity between ideological formations and extant conditions, and yet optimism about constructing a new future. After the 1970s a more critical and politically engaged form of postmodernism emerged. Central themes of later postmodernism include a growing sense of disillusionment, a partial abandonment of hope regarding the ability to reform the social formation, a sense that "nothing works anymore" that led to a sense of individual fragmentation, and attempts to incorporate historically marginalized voices in opposition to the perceived reemergence of neoconservatism.

Throughout the 1980s postmodernism has developed as a form of cultural politics in revolt against modernist reason and institutions. The Enlightenment promise of liberty, equality, and fraternity is perceived to be hollow as it has been expressed in modernist ideology, thus development of new social ideologies is considered necessary. Postindustrialism, postpositivism, and poststructuralism each represent separate intellectual traditions challenging modernism, yet these traditions remain interreferential. Adopting for the moment an essentialist posture, one may identify the contribution of each tradition to an ascending postmodernist "spirit of the age."

Postpositivist Contributions

Positivism emerged historically to counter the "negative philosophy" of the Enlightenment by providing the epistemic grounding for developing positive knowledge of nature and society. By posing categorical distinctions among the empirical, interpretive, and theoretical, however, positivism separated knowledge from social action. Postpositivism emerged to challenge the taken-for-granted assumptions regarding the centrality of scientific knowledge, objectivity, and detachment. Fleck (1979) and Kuhn (1970) succeeded in relativizing and politicizing the dominant paradigms of "normal science" discourse through examination of the social dynamics attending the emergence of scientific revolutions. Others contributed to the relativization of scientific dogma through identifying the importance of "irrational methods" and "analytic anarchy" in scientific discovery (Feyerabend, 1978), and through locating acts of comprehension in a "fusion of the personal and the objective" as personal knowledge (Polanyi, 1962). The consequence was both to challenge the hegemony of conventional structures of scientific thought and derivative institutional formations, while simultaneously legitimating personal knowledge and critical discourse. In essence the "clockwork universe" imagery of modernism, which had guided natural and social science throughout the industrial period, was being modified.

Indirectly, postpositivism rendered problematic the relationship between scientific knowledge and the social order. Lyotard (1984), for example, argues that the language game of science is but one of two archetypes of social legitimation, the other being narrative, which have served historically to maintain social cohesion. In narrative, humanity is the hero of liberty; legitimate knowledge is that which contributes to the heroes' progress in the face of opposition by nature, the state, or fate. Knowledge is functional; legitimation is determined by analysis of its consequence. Thus the criteria for determination of knowledge utility is contained within the social occasion, the narrative, within which it is used. This represents an image of discourse resting upon substantive rationality and social organization freed from prescriptive procedure.

In the language game of science, the people (as abstract category) are served by knowledge (codified into disciplines and systems of belief) but remain separate and distinct from knowledge itself. Legitimation of knowledge is determined by the self-referential rules of the game of knowledge production: derivation of assertions from original principles and verification or falsifiability. Knowledge is thus considered to represent a speculative unity with its own history and trajectory. This represents knowledge production without immediate purpose. Purpose, to serve the people, is obtained through the synthesis (by experts, the state) of categorical subjects' needs and available knowledge. Knowledge itself remains legitimated only through its own discourse. Thus scientific knowledge becomes directly separated from the social occasion of its use, except to the degree that the formation of social institutions may be derived from the application of scientific language games. The difficulty created by such indirect social engagement is that only the "certified" class is vested with legitimacy to utter "true" statements and thus direct the social formation. This creates agonistic social relations among various members of the social formation, a condition Lyotard describes as "mutual exteriority," which in turn increases the perceived need for the imposition of structural unity, order, and control.

Both versions of knowledge legitimation are constituted as metanarratives. The technological and informational revolution that has characterized postindustrial societies serves, however, to challenge these grand narratives. First, the technological revolution serves to shift attention from goals to means. This has two contradictory consequences. One is renewed interest in narrative forms of legitimation relative to the liberatory potential of technology. The other, however, given the cultural dominance of science, is to release technology from the responsibility of purpose; technology for its own sake, technology run amok.

The information explosion also creates contradictory moments. One is that heroic/liberatory action becomes theoretically overdetermined. Choices become so plentiful that one may become incapacitated by indecision or arbitrary in selection. There increases, in either event, a sense of atomistic individualism and social fragmentation. Alternatively, and as the medium of knowledge transmission becomes subject to technological advance, those who control the machine have the power to control the categorical other. The former is a situation characterized by both liberatory and anomic potentials, the latter by totalitarianism and alienation.

Within the context of a postindustrial social formation these cultural contradictions are expressed through postmodernism. As a condition of social existence, postmodernism is characterized by mistrust/rejection of grand narratives, renewed interest in examination of language as the medium of expression, and privileging of private narrative as authentic, substantive expression. The objective of private narrative is considered to be reassertion of the social bond in the face of an agonistic social formation attempting to impose a totalizing structural unity.

Poststructural Contributions

Structuralism emphasizes the stability of structure, the connectedness of constituent parts, and the conventions of institutionalized meanings (Giddens, 1987; Cherryholmes, 1988). These elements constitute transcendent principles from which all other meanings are derived; within science, for example, principles of objectivity and empiricism determining problem selection and methodology, or within modernism, principles of unity, order, and control determining institutional relationships. Structuralism thus contains both a metaphysical and epistemic moment. It tends to privilege analytic investigation of extant structures. If within modernism, forms of technical-rationality dominate, then structuralism becomes the technical-rational analysis of derivative institutional formations. Formation of structuralist problematics may only be grounded in the institutional structures and conventions that are also the object of investigation. It becomes most difficult, then, to employ structuralist analysis for transformative purposes or to explain historical transformations of institutional relationships.

Poststructuralism challenges the centrality of stability, connectedness, and convention constituting the "Symbolic Order" (Lacan, 1977). If the structures of discourse governing social formation and knowing are grounded in forms of personal knowledge, then meaning becomes "dispersed" and the search for transcendent principles becomes illusory (Derrida, 1982). The dispersal of meaning makes problematic issues of social goal and purpose. Where meaning is no longer considered located in canonical texts and exemplary institutions, then it must be interpreted and negotiated by social actors. Collective interpretation and negotiation necessarily introduces a political element to determination of truth claims; individual interpretation of meaning becomes, then, a political act.

Moreover, historically situated issues of power giving rise to particular discourse practices become "centered," not in the sense of transcendent principles, but rather as the shifting dynamic of social formation. Foucault (1980) provides analysis of power, considered not as a commodity, but rather as something exercised in a social relationship. He rejects the Weberian association of power with authority/domination; power is considered as a "strategy," a cluster of relations, rather than a property of institutional position. To conceptualize power as a strategy suggests that discourse is central to its exercise. To analyze power thus requires the investigation of structures of discourse and the manifest and latent consequences of that discourse relative to the interpretation of meaning and the social construction of reality. Moreover, if one assumes that social consciousness will be determined in part by the structures of discourse that convey knowledge, then power and knowledge are inseparable in the form power/knowledge.

Postmodern Conceptions of Power and Agency

To exercise power is to engage in a knowledgeable discourse; it is to pose a particular vision of reality as discursively true and imbued with the obligation to obey. We all exercise such power, and to exercise our power it is necessary to invite others also to exercise theirs. As they do it becomes apparent that no single "regime of truth" exists to direct our collective behavior. The exercise of power thus always invites dissension and resistance, if only (but significantly) in the form of the multiplicity of possible interpretations of truth and obligation. Postmodernism, in rejecting the "grand narrative" of totalizing discourse, suggests that the exercise of power unavoidably leads to the politicization and relativizing of social life.

While Foucault tends to locate the individual in a position of dependency relative to extant discourse traditions ("regimes of truth"), he also recognizes the role of the reflective individual in producing and reproducing counter-hegemonic discourse practices, that is, of engaging in a "politics of truth." Thus the issue of human subjectivity in the exercise of power becomes central within the postmodernist problematic.

The sociological concept of subjectivity tends to imply a determinate relationship of extant discourse traditions upon social identity formation. To the extent that such determination in fact occurs it becomes difficult to identify the basis for social resistance. The concept agency implies a relationship of mediated determinacy between discourse structures and social identity formation. The difficulty here is that the formation of human agency tends to be located only through reference of opposition to extant structural relations of modernism.

Sarup (1989) finds postmodernism reflecting a generalized crisis of meaning of the individual that leads to the fragmentation of the subject. Such crisis is associated with rejection of the grand narrative of modernism, and with such rejection, loss of the unifying bond of social integration. One is then left with an image of the individual as atomistic and alienated. Likewise, Habermas (1981) argues that in the revolt against reason, postmodernism denies the liberatory potential of Enlightenment ideology, and thereby furthers the emergence of reactionary and conservative agendas. Habermas thus defends a particular version of critical modernism against what he considers conservative and romantic forms of the postmodern.

Lyotard (1984), however, considers the rhetoric of social and individual crisis attending the postmodern to be unwarranted. Rather, the individual is forced to participate self-consciously in a variety of "language games" the effect of which is to continuously reaffrrm the social bond. While there may be institutional limitations on possible discourse (e.g., acceptable forms and content of utterance), there remains considerable opportunity to participate in the positive social reconstruction of meaning and identity. Postmodernism captures this sense of indeterminacy of traditional narratives to provide the basis for identity formation and highlights the process of individuals participating in the analysis and reproduction of ongoing social reality. A similar theme is echoed by Bowers (1987), who while defending critical modernism notes that in contemporary society those individuals lacking "linguistic competence" will be unable to fully participate in social reconstruction.

In no small part then postmodernism represents a relational and individually centered modernism: a modernism of "mediated agency" with emphasis on themes of liberty, equality, and fraternity while rejecting patterns of bureaucratic expansion and institutional reification. Such partial selection of modernist themes occurs, as Derrida (1982) notes, because no rhetoric may escape its culture of reference. A significant part of the culture of reference of postmodern thought is the institutional structuring of experience (Wexler, 1987). While one may wish to "decenter," to transform human subjectivity, to avoid privileging transcendental signifieds and origins, the concepts center, subject, and signified remain part of the postmodern rhetoric.

Textualism within Postmodernism

As a form of cultural politics the objective of postmodernist critique is to uncover symbolic relations of meaning. Since meaning is conveyed through discourse and other forms of symbolic action the object of investigation becomes social interaction considered as "text." Within textualism the imagery of cultural performance replaces that of social behaviorism, manipulation, and control. Postmodernist analysis attempts to replace "scientific" analysis of social cause and effect with textual interpretation of the dialectic relationship between meaning and action. Textual interpretation remains particularistic and relational; an inherently antireifying practice. In this regard Wexler (1987, p. 133) notes that "If discourse is a dominant condition of (textual) production, then its dereification becomes the historically appropriate critical practice." To engage in a postmodernist cultural politics requires, then, adoption of a critical attitude relative to established structures of social meaning, discourse, and social action. It is within textualism that the themes of critique, the affirmation of personal knowledge, the rejection of the totalizing narrative of the Symbolic Order, and reconceptualization of power and agency coalesce and give shape to postmodern cultural sensibilities.

Through textualism the mistrust of totalizing narratives becomes transformed into a critique of derivative institutional formations. Moreover, the validation of personal and local knowledge leads to greater emphasis on personal growth and development within the organizational life-world. Organizational participants are becoming less tolerant and willing to submit to organizational demands grounded exclusively in technical-rational thought structures. Technical-rationality becomes perceived as just another ideologically based, arbitrary, and unjustified denial of personal expression and democratic participation. The tide of history is on the side of democracy interpreted as both process and consequence. In Europe the focus is on political democracy; in the United States there is growing interest in democratization of the workplace (Carnoy & Shearer, 1980).

Questioning the "symbolic order" of modernism creates a "legitimacy void" that is filled by reassertion of narrative forms of legitimation. Qualitative and practitioner based research (e.g., ethnography, action research) that combine the "story" of an event with its analysis are often perceived as more legitimate and useful than are traditional forms of quantitative research that maintain separation between knowledge and the social occasion of knowledge use.

Strategies of mobilization for collective action must attend to the symbolic structure of meaning of local participants and include opportunities for participation in the formation as well as the implementation of policy. This in turn lends support for policies of local autonomy and organizational democracy. For an administrator to violate the cultural precepts of autonomy and democracy is to invite resistance and sabotage of policy. Administrators may lament the decline of personal sacrifice and organizational loyalty that marked "corporate man" in the postwar 1950s, but the fact remains that administrators must now create work environments more worthy of loyalty and respect.

DEVELOPMENT OF POSTMODERN EDUCATIONAL ADMINISTRATION

Political support for school restructuring is primarily located in the desire to improve United States economic competitiveness. Most teachers and parents, however, share a more broadly based concern with school purpose, including emphasis upon civic learning and general education (Goodlad, 1984). These interests require reconsideration of school outcome measures and of the social relationships governing schooling. Simply tinkering with the structural dynamics of schools will likely prove insufficient to achieve significant change in either schools or society. Rather the school administrator must address the cultural meanings and purposes organizational participants bring with them to school and that develop as a consequence of participation in the daily routines of the institution. In part the meanings participants bring with them to school are informed by nascent postmodern cultural sensibilities.

The current focus on school restructuring reflects a view of school administration as a managerial activity oriented toward the imposition of a "new" social order. Rather than considering schooling to be an object in need of management, however, one might instead approach schooling as a social text to be engaged in dialogue. The view of schools as text reflects a view of an administration oriented toward facilitating conditions under which transformative educational discourse and practices may emerge; a view in which social order/text is continually written and revised by those who live that order/text. This is a conception of administration as cultural leadership, practiced in an arena of contestation over social meaning and purpose.

The development of transformative administration theories and practices may be advanced through incorporation of postmodern themes and imagery. The general purpose is to develop within members of a social group new "thought styles" (epistemic and paradigmatic structures) governing organizational purpose and process. Central theoretical issues will include consideration of the concepts of power and language, structure and context, and critical pragmatic action.

Administration in a Different Voice: Power and Discourse

It is perhaps axiomatic that administration is about the exercise of power. What remains at issue is how power is to be conceived and to what purpose it is used. Traditional approaches have responded to the question of power through appeal to Weberian sociology. Power is conceived as authority/domination associated with bureaucratic position; the rationale for the exercise of power is located in the desire to maintain efficiency and control of operations.

The Weberian conception of authority/domination contains a number of assumptions about the nature of organizations. One is that organizations are technical systems and that formal description of structure and function is sufficient to account for primary organizational dynamics. Another is that organizational participants should be treated as functionaries both willing and able to subordinate personal and idiosyncratic desires to the demands of the position. Yet another is that through rational task analysis one may predict the appropriate division of labor necessary for goal attainment and may prescribe appropriate role relationships to maintain efficient coordination among persons and units. This is, of course, a vision of organizations as machines existing in a value-neutral institutional environment.

This vision of organization has been frequently challenged but not altered in any fundamental fashion. For example, the human relations movement, and more recently some of the popular management literature (e.g., Peters & Waterman, 1982), attempted to incorporate recognition that organizations are social as well as technical systems. Nevertheless, "humanity" was treated primarily as a mediating variable, or perhaps as a latent variable (reflecting conceptual or measurement error), within a rational system. Within this framework, the management task is to develop strategies to limit the disruptive influence of people on the efficient operations of the rational organization.

Postmodernist conceptualizations of power move away from the Weberian inspired thought style characterized by obsession with technical efficiency and social control. Foucault (1980), for example, suggests that power is exercised through discourse and that the structure of discourse may serve either to silence or give voice to subordinates and marginal members of an organization.

The implication for education administration is that the task ahead is to create the social-political conditions under which others may raise their voice. Teacher empowerment becomes simply the freedom to be heard, to share knowledge/power, and to participate in a discourse community. In a manner parallel with feminist scholarship, postmodernists also have been concerned with the issue of voice. Rejected are patriarchal and modernist assumptions of power as command. In its place is offered an alternative power/knowledge discourse. A discourse centering on issues of care, concern, and connectedness (Martin, 1985); of relationship and attachment (Gilligan, 1982); and rejection of the inherent logocentrism and "methodolatry" (Belenky et al., 1986) of modernist and bureaucratic discourse. This represents use of a metaphor of organization as an organic community rather than a mechanical phenomena, which in the context of educational reform is expressed through the rhetoric of collegiality, shared decision making, and consensus (Bacharach, 1990).

Within the postmodernist orientation, collegiality, shared decision making, and consensus may emerge as a consequence of participation in the organizational life-world but may not be designed in the manner one would use to create a machine. At the center of postmodernist discourse is concern with "right action"; attaining school goals in a manner that respects the growth and integrity of persons. Nurturance of the organizational life-world is raised to equal status with the attainment of school goals. The school text is considered to write itself, to generate its own meanings, quite apart from the authorial hand of the administrator.

Speaking Out in School: Narration and Control

Traditional administration is modernist in the sense that a primary objective is to exercise control over the social and natural world. Within the framework of a symbolic order that privileges technical-rational thought structures, there will also be the tendency to objectify people (e.g., subjects, clients, role actors), as well as procedures, and to perpetuate agonistic social relationships. To the extent that the "language game" of educational reform is based on control and objectification, it will be possible to reconstruct the "commonsense experience of everyday life" (Berger & Luckmann, 1967) characterized by subordination, atomistic individualism, alienation, and fragmentation of self-concept, but it will be much more difficult to participate in the construction of new commonplaces grounded in interconnectedness and engagement.

Narrative, reflecting the "local knowledge" of organization participants, provides a language and structure of discourse to guide administration. To participate in the narrative of the school is to share in the self-conscious construction of social text. This is the true meaning of empowerment. When power is located in position then power becomes a thing, a tool. One may be delegated authority to use the tool, or perhaps denied its use, but one cannot be him- or herself empowered. When power is located in relationship, empowerment is simply a consequence of participation in the social order. One empowers him- or herself and others to the extent one chooses to participate. In relationship, power is neither granted nor seized, it is manifest. And in its expression increases both its presence and its ability to achieve the collective will. Transformative administration is not achieved through sharing the tools of power but rather by harnessing its presence.

In most schools teachers work alone in isolated, self-contained classrooms. There are few opportunities to engage in the collective narrative. The school text, the story of institutional life, becomes then like James Joyce's *Ulysses,* for most of us a fragmented cacophony of discordant accounts, or like Jean-Paul Sartre's *Nausea,* in which the individual is isolated and powerless in the face of institutional fate. A school administrator may facilitate development of a more harmonious voice through critical analysis of the stories teachers tell and by creating opportunities for teachers to recount their story in a public forum. Storytelling serves then to reaffirm collective criteria for judging right action and provides a means to share troubles and solutions. It provides opportunities to participate in the reconstruction of the social order and to reaffirm social bonds.

A school administrator can and should participate in writing the school's story and may be held publicly accountable for the story that emerges, but the story belongs to all the members of the school. Opportunities to share authorship have historically been denied teachers, which results in the cycles of failure that have marked the recent history of school reform. To share authorship does not mean, however, that teachers are invited simply to write a chapter already outlined by the administrator. To the extent that administrators attempt to "overwrite" the story, ownership is denied to teachers and students. Under these conditions the administrator may be able to coerce compliance with the script but should not expect commitment. An alternative strategy is to seek original contributions that may lead the story in unanticipated directions.

Responding in the Present: Transformation and Tradition

School administrators are becoming ever more subject to contradictory demands; there is, on the one hand, state and district level mandates to assert order and control consistent with traditional conceptions of bureaucratic organizational practice and, on the other, the demand to adopt a logic of professional organizational practice for teachers. These represent competing thought styles and visions of what the schools should become. Indeed, the concept of vision has become a central component of organization theory. But more important than the concept of vision is its substantive content. We are experiencing a social and economic revolution brought on by deindustrialization. It is not yet decided how our social institutions will change to maintain cohesion within the social formation, but change they will. We may only hope and work to realize that hope, that the promise of liberty, equality, and fraternity may be achieved for ourselves and others through the institutions we build today.

The practical task is how to proceed in the face of contradiction and constraint. The practical resolution of contradiction is difficult to achieve and impossible to prescribe. One must not simply present an image of utopia and hope for success. Rather one must begin by addressing critical issues within the ongoing stream of social reality. The following is offered as a very simple first step to engaging in transformative administration in the present.

Start with the school. Over the past decade teachers have borne the brunt of public criticism of schooling and reform mandate. They are becoming tired of criticism and wary of melioration. Most teachers do not seek the imposition of yet another authoritative program. They want only a little understanding, perhaps some inspiration and support, and the freedom and flexibility necessary to realize the instructional purpose that drew them to the occupation in the first place. These attitudes are as much a part of the environment of administration as are public demands for instructional leadership or of administrative control and responsibility. Adopt as your mandate then "To serve the Teachers."

Talk with teachers and collect stories and images. Fashion a composite picture of the good school. Share the story that emerges. Invite others to elaborate the story. The objective is to identify relevant issues that can be addressed. Don't be surprised if identified issues appear rather mundane, such as access to a telephone or office space, or for more convenient meeting times. If these are the issues that count in the school, then address them. Don't promise what you can't deliver, but don't ignore possibilities simply because they are untried.

Be willing to take risks and defend the right of failure. Realize that many experiments are unsuccessful the first time out. Don't become impatient and attempt to shortcut the efforts required in drafting a good story. Even those who share the vision will move at different speeds. Not everyone will do what they say they will, but some will do much more. Trust that persons willing to undertake one of the most demanding and stressful occupations known are moved by a sense of commitment to students. Remember also that it takes time to overcome a history of organizational caution and defensiveness, to put away agonistics, and dust off democratic spirit.

As the story of the school takes shape don't become too concerned with the particulars. Expressionism is not only an art movement but is also a necessary component for development of self-concept, ownership, and commitment. Two considerations are important here. One is that the facts of the story are not as important as the interpretation of the facts. Focus your efforts on meaning making. The importance of narrative is not the aesthetic purity of the story that emerges but what occurs to persons during production of the story. Second is the centrality of ownership. To own the story implies responsibility and obligation to act. To the extent that the state has accepted ownership of the problem of school reform, teachers may be considered part of the problem or perhaps agents of alleviation, but teachers' responsibility for problem identification and solution generation is diminished. This affects teachers' attitudes, it creates separation between purpose and practice. An objective of treating school as text with teachers as authors is to reaffirm the centrality of teachers' responsibility in producing solutions.

Analysis of school stories is also a means to uncover the symbolism through which events are mediated and interpreted. The school story represents the collective imagery of the real, the desirable, and the attainable. In this regard the story not only reflects extant perceptions of the boundaries of possibility but may also direct collective perception of new possibilities. Remember that the superordinate goal of transformative administration is to enhance perceptions of possibility to engage in transformative educational practices.

9

Moral Leadership in a Poststructural Era

Louis F. Miron and Richard J. Elliott

Poststructural thought holds great promise for the practice of school leadership as it restores human agency to the center of meaning and history. The development of leadership theory and practice has suffered from a structuralist paradigm where individuals are viewed as objects of fixed organizational structures, which themselves are inherently cohesive and self-regulating. Subjectivity is displaced within this theoretical perspective, and human agency is relegated to passive role as presage of predetermined, ahistorical structures. As Cherryholmes observes, structuralism "puts relationships among the elements and structures at the center and people at the margins" (1988, p. 31). School leaders can now maintain a self-image of actors capable of altering structures and changing schools to benefit their students and the school community.

This chapter will briefly review the literature on poststructuralism/postmodernism and argue that the moral exercise of power—a consequence of these new organizational contexts—permits school leaders to facilitate the positive side of power and politics in school sites (Miron, 1991). This view offers a stark contrast to the widely held perception that power and politics represent the "dark" side of schools as organizations. We assert that the moral use of power helps move schools from organizations to communities.

Many commentators on the theory and philosophy of educational administration have noted that its study and practice is fraught with structural assumptions (Anderson, 1989b; Bates, 1980; Foster, 1989). Callahan's (1962) classic image of schooling as "the cult of efficiency" not only situates the role of the school administrator as structural/technical manager in the context of scientific management, but this image also undergirds contemporary views of the school administrator as instructional leader.

For example, first wave educational reforms following the publication of *A Nation at Risk* in 1983 called for "top down" structural mandates on teaching and learning (Berry & Ginsberg, 1990; CPRE, 1990). Second wave reform measures sought "bottom up" changes aimed at the professionalization of teaching. Regardless of direction, the school administrator's function is the same—to closely monitor the structural features of schooling so as to improve the quality of instruction (Greenfield, 1987; Deal, 1987) and ultimately to increase the levels of student achievement through raising scores on nationally norm-referenced tests. There is agreement that nothing short of a revolution in schooling is needed, with the school administrator providing "competent, skilled, visionary leadership as has never been available before" (National Commission on Excellence in Educational Administration, 1983, p. xvi).

What is missing from both the first and second level reform analyses and recommendations is a thoughtful consideration of power. The school administrator, in his or her capacity as a manager of resources, a creator of school climate and vision, and a "manager of meaning" (Anderson, 1989a) uses power to accomplish the strategic objectives of the school and can either facilitate or hinder change through the symbolic (less obtrusive) control of meaning. The office of the principal in the social structure of the school is characterized by unequal power relations. Thus, the one who is occupying this office has the potential to enhance or undermine many of the goals of the reform movement that have focused on the technical features of schooling. Arguably, the outcome depends on the intentions of affective ability in the school-site administrator that this structural assumption implies.

Our purpose in this chapter is to identify the structural assumptions underlying education administration theory and practice, focusing on the school site. We will distinguish between "surface" structure and "deep" structure and establish that structural assumptions of school administration lead to a flawed analysis of change. Finally, we will examine the implications of school administration from a poststructural perspective, arguing that the role of the administrator is to facilitate the leadership process through the moral use of power. This conception of power accepts the poststructuralist overriding assumption that power is a shifting, inherently unstable expression in various networks and alliances.

STRUCTURAL ASSUMPTIONS OF SCHOOL ADMINISTRATION

Structuralist assumptions of school administration, embedded in positivistic and functionalist paradigms, can best be illustrated by scientific management. According to Foster (1989) the following propositions can be derived from these assumptions:

1. School administration is a quasi-science, employing a natural-science methodology.

2. A systems-based functionalism accounts for the relationships that occur between actors in the school as system.
3. Research will reveal additional systemic regularities and these will lead to predictable avenues of administrative intervention.

Foster's list sets out for the student and practitioner of administration the key theoretical assumptions of a structuralist perspective. According to Cherryholmes (1988, p. 17), "A key assumption about structurally examined phenomena is that they are characterized by an underlying structure, not too surprising, that is defined, in part, by relationships among their constituent elements." Viewed structurally, school administration consists of a one-to-one correspondence between the structural features of schooling (for example, textbooks and teaching methods) and desired outcomes—student achievement. Scientific management, as espoused by Frederick Taylor, assumes a "tight," not a "loose" coupling (Weick, 1976) among school organizational structures, goals, objectives, and outcomes. Put simply, the task of the school administrator is to tightly control school structures so as to achieve the most efficient instructional system. Increasing "time on task," as advocated by school effectiveness and teacher effectiveness proponents (Edmonds, 1979; Teddlie, 1984; Stallings, 1980) is an example of the tight coupling desired by a structuralist-functionalist paradigm.

The focus of the principal's role in promoting increase time on task highlights a key distinction between "surface" and "deep" structure. School effectiveness research took the educational researcher inside the classroom to observe the principal's monitoring of instruction, supervision of teachers, and evaluation of learning. The technical core of education—teaching and learning—would, therefore, represent the school's surface structure and through careful observation of the social organization of the school through ethnography, researchers could begin to disentangle what theorists and scholars have called the "hidden" curriculum (Apple, 1971). These "deep" structural features are clearly distinguished from more surface, organizational characteristics, such as staffing patterns, grade level configurations, and class schedules. Moreover, "deep" structures have been linked to broad macrolevel forces, such as the world's political economy (see Anderson, 1989a; Apple, 1982; Giroux, 1983).

Theoretical and scholarly work on the "deep" structure of the school is an important development here because it marked the investigation of the power relations embedded in the school organization, heretofore empirically and normatively overlooked by most positivistic educational research. As Clegg (1989) argues, power should be viewed not as a relationship between individuals; but rather "as a social relationship mediated by broader economic and historical forces" (in Anderson, 1989a, p. 11), that is, deep structure. The contribution of structuralist thought, in particular the discovery of deep structures, was the acknowledgment in postindustrial societies and bureaucratic settings of the powerful influence of macrolevel economic, political, and social structures on the everyday lives of individuals. Its weakness was that it removed the individual from reality and meaning. As Cherryholmes (1987, p. 19) writes, "Meaning is located in structures, not in individuals." The possibilities of human agency are, therefore, greatly constrained, if not eliminated.

POWER AND POSTSTRUCTURALIST ASSUMPTIONS

Power and Structure

If structuralism assumes a rational, orderly, and systematic progression of organization as an outcome of the presence of fixed, objectively determined structures, then poststructural analysis turns this configuration upside down: Structures are *socially constructed* and meaning derived from discourse and practice results from history and the exercise of power. Within this context, power is defined, following Cherryholmes, as "relations among individuals or groups based on social, political, and material asymmetries by which some people are indulged and rewarded and others negatively sanctioned and deprived" (1987, p. 5). Because structures are never fixed and power is relational, it is dispersed and "decentered" (Wolin, 1988, pp. 179–203).

Foucault's (1978) conception of power is its shifting, inherently unstable expression in networks and alliances. As Clegg (1989, p. 155) suggests, "Rather than the monolithic view of power as a third dimension incorporating subjectivities, the focus is much closer to Machiavelli's strategic concerns or Gramsci's notion of hegemony as a 'war of maneuver,' in which points of resistance and fissure are at the forefront." Because this conception of power is directly related to individual or group expression, language is central to poststructuralism. Meaningful existence is only possible through language, for it sets our limits and gives a sense of ourselves as distinct from other selves. Therefore, discursive practices are critical to the exercise of power for it communicates identity, as identity is always provisional, contingent, and in process.

Clearly, poststructuralist perspectives of power do not emanate from historical sovereign notions of authority, such as the state, nor juridical sources, such as law. Neither is it a commodity to be transferred nor a property right of individuals. For Foucault, power is conceptualized "as exercised, rather than given or exchanged, and as a relation of force" (Smart, 1983, p. 81). A structuralist framework assumes that power is a by-product of sovereignty, with the school site administrator accordingly eligible to receive the transfer of power from the legal authority of the state or the local school board. We will return to the implications of these different conceptions as to the origins of power subsequently.

Power and Knowledge

An important corollary of the previous discussion is the interplay of power and knowledge. The conventional structural view maintains the fact-value dichotomy of scientific management. Not only are structures and power neutral, but knowledge is objective and "value free." However, if discourse results from history and unequal power arrangements, then knowledge, and ultimately "truth," are relational as well and socially constructed. However, what "counts" as meaning in the curriculum, for example, and what textbook authors deem central remains hidden and "invisible" (Anderson, 1989a). The school principal, thus, can control the meaning of learning in the everyday life of the classroom through the use of unobtrusive measures, such as legitimation, myths, and, above all, through the control of language use. At the "micropolitical" (Ball, 1987; Blaise, 1989) level, this involves the strategic exercise of power, a subject we will return to shortly.

Power and Language

Language in any social context is important. When power is "decentered," however, its use and orchestration is paramount. As previously stated, for poststructuralists the central focus of language as the vehicle through which knowledge is reified gives language the effect of power. Through language the administrator, in this case the principal, exercises power through discursive practices: Speech, text, writing, cognition, argumentation, and representation—these define the possibilities of meaningful existence in the school setting. The limitations in discursive practices are directly related to how effective the administrator will be in accomplishing task. Historically, "anonymous" (Foucault, 1980) authors have given rise to discourse and texts and have silenced voices of teachers, students, parents, and community members. Only through human agency can social reality be reconstructed in schools and other traditional institutions that have, knowingly or unknowingly, functioned to marginalize such groups.

Power and Action

Power conceptualized as exercised, rather than given, and the influence of power on the acquisition of knowledge, posits a radically different relationship between power and action. Rather than a passive victim of preimposed structures and apparently binding legal constraints on the actions of principals, the school administrator is, ironically, free to act. Through the exercise of power, the school administrator can coerce subordinated groups, such as teachers, students, and cafeteria workers, or can facilitate the transformation of the school membership into a community of intellectuals (Foster, 1989). In simple terms the choices are two: (1) principals and other school site administrators can work towards the self-regulation of the status quo, a normative goal of structural-functionalist legacies; or (2) can seek to change the inherited history of the school through the leadership process. The principal's identity as a leader is seen as contingent, and provisional, not given. Thus, this leadership identity is always seen as a social process, always subject, problematically, to reproduction or transformation through discursive practices that secure or refuse particular identities.

Foster (1989) defines school leadership as the capacity to instill "reciprocal relationship between leaders and followers oriented towards the achievement of social change" (p. 15). Although prominent poststructuralists, such as Michel

Foucault, have been historically preoccupied with the negative exercise of power, there remains, equally, the possibilities for the transformative and renewalist effects of power. Cherryholmes characterizes such potential as "critical pragmatism." It is to these themes that the remainder of this chapter is devoted.

THE MORAL EXERCISE OF POWER

Foster (1989) proposes a "transformational model of leadership," which, following Burns, he defines as "the enmeshing of goals and values (wherein) both leaders and followers are raised to more principled levels of judgment" (p. 16). He argues that all social action is transformative. Foster's critical approach to the study, preparation, and practices of school administration emphasizes the leader as "transformative intellectual," one who "has an image of a better place, an image guided by certain end values of importance to both her/him and to the society" (p. 16). Moreover, leaders always occupy "transitory" places and are not to be confused with authorities (Burns, 1978). Two dimensions of leadership are prevalent in Foster's view: values and the nature of intellectual leadership.

The exercise of leadership extending beyond the quest for personal and institutional power has the effect for leaders and followers of motivating each to work; therefore, this must involve values and purposes. With respect to school administration, teacher and student empowerment, the democratization of education, and the pursuit of equality and justice "could all strike fires within school-site administrators" (p. 16).

Foster borrows from the work of Habermas (1971) and Langer (1971) whose critical theoretical work on ideas focuses on the power of the "generative idea" as a basis for establishing the intellectual nature of leadership. A generative idea is one that can change practice. We are reminded of Cherryholmes notion of "critical pragmatic strategies." Textual power is an asymmetrical relationship weighted on the side of the reader. If, to the contrary, readers (students, teachers, administrators, or researchers) conceptualize their job as discovering the "definitive meaning of work placed before them, then the asymmetrical relationship between readers and works is weighted on the side of the latter (along with their dominant readings)" (Cherryholmes 1987, p. 154). The key task for the school leader, acting as a transformative intellectual, is to instill within the politicos and culture of the school social and moral processes that achieve social change. With this in mind, we now examine the implications of current leadership reform measures as to their potential to create transformative leaders with the capacity to exercise power morally.

IMPLICATIONS FOR SCHOOL LEADERSHIP REFORM

Recent proposals to reform school administration and leadership focus on related, but conceptually distinct, roles for the principal. These include the principal as instructional leader (Greenfield, 1987), the concept of school-based management/shared decision making (Berry & Ginsberg, 1990; also, see Cistone, 1989), and teacher empowerment (Glickman, 1990). The first measure, instructional leadership, owes its origins to the early work on school effectiveness (Edmonds, 1979; Brookover, 1982; Rutter, 1979) and focuses on the strong role of the principal in conducting frequent classroom observations, close monitoring of student achievement, and fostering a positive school climate. A structural shift in the role of the principal from administrator/manager to instructional leader is assumed.

While such structural assumptions may indeed lead to gains in student achievement in some cases, it is unlikely that this conceptualization will produce school leaders as tranformational agents, as Foster conceives of them. This role is heavily weighted to the principal as "leader" and others in the school as "followers." Although in theory there is no reason why such a leadership role could not fall on teachers (perhaps even students), little reference to these possibilities is found in the school effectiveness literature. Underlying this concept is the structural equating of leader with authority, even though the focus is on instructional authority as opposed to policy compliance (legal authority).

Our second illustration, school-based management/shared decision making, which has been popularized by school superintendents and school boards in districts in Dade County, Florida and New York City, decentralized decision-making authority from the school board and central office to the school site. Clearly, such a view conceptualizes power as an individual commodity that can be structurally shifted from one level within the school system downward to the next school level—the school site. Moreover, such structural assumptions of power ignore the power formations within the school as a social organization that have the potential to undermine the autonomy in school decision making favored by the reform movement. Empirical research on the dynamics of school site advisory councils, a central strategy used to implement school site management is constrained by the principal's exercise of power and the support and awareness level of central office (see Ferris, 1989).

Finally, calls for teacher and student empowerment are also flawed with structural assumptions with little potential to transform schools. Like measures aimed at school decision making and teacher and student empowerment assume that power is a commodity and individual possession, presently in the hands of school middle and senior managers and board members, which can be simply transferred to teachers and students. What is overlooked in such an analysis is the very real strategic exercise of power in the everyday life of teachers and principals (Blaise, 1989) that can be "proactively" or defensively employed in pursuit of individual or community goals. In both strategic and juridical use of power, little attention is paid to the needs of students whose empowerment (along with parents and community members) is deemed essential within a transformational model of leadership.

SUMMARY AND CONCLUSION

In this chapter, we have attempted to show how school administration theory and practice is fraught with flawed structural assumptions, assumptions that reinforce the status quo of schooling and undermine the potential transformational qualities of school leadership, advanced by Foster, Anderson, and others that embrace a poststructural analysis of the power formations within the school. We have articulated this approach as the moral exercise of power and argued here that the quest for meaning, purpose, and community is central to the role of school leader.

It is unlikely that, given the paucity of theoretical understanding underpinning the reform of school leadership and administration, reform measures will produce substantive changes in the way schools are run, despite the hopes of the school restructuring movement. On the other hand, such a pessimistic view of school change does not deny the fact, and the very real possibility, that school leaders, acting as moral agents, can make schools liberating sites through cultural resistance and struggle.

10
Reconceptualizing Higher Education Organizations

Barbara Curry

INTRODUCTION

Recent discussions about academic organizations have uncovered the need for significant changes in the way colleges and universities function and in the services they provide. Among the critics, there are those who seem to believe that the academy is incapable of changing or that it is changing *too* slowly. What appeared to be rapid change in corporations has been suggested as a standard that the academy must meet to remain vital in the coming decades. With a closer look and a more studious purpose, one might discern movement in the academy just as one might have discerned movement in corporations before their intention to change was made public. Whether or not the academy is moving forward or standing still can be discovered by a longer, more intense study by critics and by applying new paradigms for the conceptualization of life and activity within the academy by members of its various communities.

This chapter looks at the importance of constructions that govern the academic organization and are part of its collective consciousness. The discussion suggests that higher education organizations can and do change. However, they also need to be more responsive in order to meet the quickly changing needs of the people they serve. The discussion also suggests that in order to be more responsive the academy must reconstruct itself as an organization where innovation and change are ever present forces driving its movement. The discussion begins with Wells' treatise on the need for the academy to be adaptive, written decades ago but still relevant today. It continues with the consideration of developmental processes that influence constructions of life in organizations. Further, given those influences, the chapter considers reconceptualization of the academy as adaptive or innovative.

A VOICE FROM THE PAST

In 1953 Harper Brothers published a treatise by Harry L. Wells, then vice-president and business manager of Northwestern University, titled *Higher Education Is Serious Business: A Study of University Business Management in Relation to Higher Education*. In the volume, Wells entreated higher education organizations to be more adaptive in order to continue to provide services to their consumers. According to Wells, the academy needed to begin to be more responsive to the populations it served. Wells believed that his school and others were confused about their responsibility to the public. Wells believed in the academic enterprise. He also believed that the services provided by education organizations should be top quality and subject to redesign and refinement through innovative activity and good management. Business was influencing the academy, moving it to provide the best programs it could produce to its newest consumer group: men who were able to benefit from the G.I. Bill. Those men had families, needed careers, and needed an education to develop those careers. The academy was also being influenced by the influx of academics from other countries. Wells saw the forces imposing on the academy as possibly estranging it from the very people it would serve. How was a business based on providing services to survive if it estranged its publics? At the outset, Wells warned that his treatise "examin[ed] critically the creative function of management in educational policy and practice" (p. ix). He went on to say that as a result "precious pieces of the educational china are broken" (p. ix). In his treatise, Wells envisioned his university among those that needed to be adaptive in order to provide the best services to their consumers. Wells dedicated his treatise to his employer and his alma mater. In doing so he hoped to move his institution toward its second century "1951–2051."

Wells anticipated and wrote about the need for his organization to change. He also anticipated the need for Northwestern University to retain its sense of community as it experienced change. The importance of exploring Wells' concern for his organization lies in his vision of the adaptive organization. In part to be adaptive, the academy needed to perceive itself as changing or, at the very least, changeable. If it could not perceive itself as changing, it could not take the next step and become innovative. Perceptions shape responses and subsequently the ability of an organization to be adaptive. In the 1980s, Wells was joined by others who believed that the academy must become innovative or adaptive.

MOVING FORWARD OR STANDING STILL

Although many of its critics describe it as having the potential to be progressively innovative, they also claim that the academy has not changed significantly since the reforms of the 1960s and 1970s and that it is drifting into the twenty-first century rather than moving purposefully and innovatively into its future. At present it is not clear whether or not the curriculum issues that were so compelling during the last decade and during the more recent past, have been resolved. Critical incidents that are often assigned as catalysts for change emerge out of conflicts among individuals and groups and sometimes move through the campus like tidal waves. Mobilization begins and creative energy burns a course of action into the minds of debating factions. But for memory that allows us to recall months or years of planning and implementation, it is sometimes difficult to discern any appreciable differences in campus culture and physicality before and after motion. Are campuses now still? Or are they experiencing the imperceptible movement that is characteristic of beginning rhythms leading to the more visible and audible sounds of the academy's beating, changing heart? What does the quiet mean in higher education?

Quiet does not necessarily mean that organizational communities have been exhausted by the debates that were integral to the lives of their members or that their members returned quietly, aimlessly, unimaginatively to "tradition" regardless of what is impending. Innovation, change, and participation in those processes takes place within complex social structures where individuals and groups are engaged in and influenced by interrelated events. In a series of events and through reshaping parameters the academic context of colleges and universities changes. Yet notwithstanding an intuitive sense that change has occurred and is taking place in the academy, whether it is real, progressive, and significant is a matter of perception, a version or construction of reality. Consequently, the extent to which members of organizations perceive change as having taken place, as positive and successful, emerges out of social contexts where meaning is constructed (Schein, 1985; Tierney, 1987). Birnbaum (1988) illustrates the influence of context and positioning within the organization on the perception of members of the community.

In his discussion of "The Conflict of Roles and Authority in Governance," Birnbaum (1988) suggests that perceptions change depending on where one is positioned in organizations. Although the example offered here demonstrates the influence of positioning within organizations, perceptions from within and from outside the organization differ as well. Birnbaum's illustration follows.

I spent the first seventeen years of my professional career as an administrator in many university settings. My administrative colleagues and I never ceased to marvel at the indifference shown by faculty to institution-wide concerns, their appalling ignorance of the political, social, and economic realities facing their institutions, and their often single-minded pursuit of narrow self-interest. The usual response to proposed change was to arrange the wagons in a circle, so almost all the creative ideas for institutional improvement came from administrative initiatives. But those brave innovations that weren't attacked and willfully distorted one week by the senate executive committee would certainly be so next week by the union negotiating committee. The faculty I spoke with offered simplistic solutions to complex problems, often in terms as wrongheaded and impractical. . . . From where I sat in the executive offices, the issues were clear: the administration had the solutions, and the faculty was the problem. . . . Ten years ago, when I left administration to become a professor, there occurred, by the strangest of coincidences, a sudden and dramatic change in the governance patterns of higher education. Beginning at that time, and increasingly ever since, it has become clear to me and my faculty colleagues that administrators are responding inappropriately to political and social pressures. They are basing their decisions on fiscal rather than educational grounds, and in the mania for efficiency and accountability they have lost touch with the faculty, with traditional notions of quality, and with the real purposes of the institution. (pp. 29–30)

The example is long but it is also helpful for considering ways of reconceiving the academy and for addressing questions about the relationship of its members to its ability to be adaptive.

THE ACADEMY AS AN EVOLVING COMMUNITY

Wells' concern for the academy and his suggestions for its survival are as relevant today as they were in 1953. However, rather than becoming adaptive today he might suggest that higher education organizations become innovative and, in the language of his contemporaries, attempt to change in ways that fundamentally alter their structure and functioning (Beckhard & Pritchard, 1992). As such, the organization reconstructs itself as fluid or flexible and adaptive. This reconstruction changes the culture of the academy allowing for new and different realities to emerge. Becoming innovative requires an organization to reconceive itself as a systems-oriented, learning community (Senge, 1990; Argyris, 1982). As such its members perceive it as evolving toward some ideal or in the process of becoming (Senge, 1990; Argyris, 1982). Reconceiving the academy as a learning community will be taken up later in response to Wells. Before moving on to that reconceptualization, the layers of processes that represent organizational development should be considered. That consideration begins here with Cameron's and Whetten's (1984) description of organizations as evolving through life cycles taken from their "Models of the Organizational Life Cycle: Applications to Higher Education."

The authors have discerned four stages in a cycle: (1) where there is entrepreneurial activity, (2) where there is collective activity, (3) where there is formalization and control of structures and processes, and (4) where formalization and control are elaborated (Cameron & Whetten, 1984, pp. 31–61). The first stage of the cycle is characterized as a period when the organization is fluid, relying less on complicated, "bureaucratic methods of task assignment" with emphasis on "personal power" and creativity (Cameron & Whetten, 1984, p. 52). The second stage is characterized as a period where "teams are found," where the potential for systems identity is strong, "zeal and dedication to the organization" are "developed and high cohesion and interaction occur" (p. 52). The third stage is characterized by the development of formal and more rigid structures of control. The fourth stage is a continuation of the third and is characterized by attempts to consolidate formal structures. Because perceptions are influenced by positioning within the organization, individuals and groups within the community experience change differently as a temporal event. Each cycle can be conceptualized not only as layered but overlapping as well. New stages in the cycle are reached as problems encountered within previous stages are solved (Cameron & Whetten, 1984, p. 54). Although organizations evolve through the stages described here, issues having to do with life unfolding within its community are not necessarily resolved within those periods. Similarly, those issues are not necessarily resolved by moving on to the next stage (p. 54).

It happens that difficult periods sometimes stimulate "recycling" or regression. Rather than waiting for crises to stimulate responses or the development of issues that move the organization to begin a new cycle or regression, Wells and his contemporaries advocate retention of those features of earlier stages that stimulate creativity and innovative activity. An organization moves through successive developmental stages, retains those features that support innovative activity, and is increasingly ready to function in ways that are adaptive. It becomes a learning community, capable of self-study. In this developmental process organizations become what has been described as "prosocial" (Staw, 1984). Its members, for example, act in ways that are in the best interest of the organizational community rather than acting only in their individual interests (p. 79). The prosocial activity is similar to what Powers and Powers (1983) describe as consultive processes.

According to Powers and Powers, "Consultation must not be thought of as a fixed pattern of structural or functional relationships but as an ongoing process with constantly evolving participants and interconnections (1983, p. 14). The elements of the consultive process are included in the following:

1. Information exchange. The consultive process provides opportunities to involve representatives of various constituencies with different perspectives in examining problems and in proposing and evaluating alternative solutions.
2. Coalition building. Support generated by the consultive process for a policy or program change may lead to consensus on an issue.
3. Task orientation. Consultation focuses attention on outcomes, transcending problems of individual ego and territoriality.
4. Accommodation of conflicting needs. Otherwise irreconcilable institutional or structural needs can be accommodated through consultation by making necessary changes in functions or leadership.
5. Alteration of power distribution. Consultation fundamentally alters the distribution of power while not displacing legitimate authority.
6. Flexibility. A broad range of functions can be performed using the consultive process, including formulating goals, determining policies, planning, undertaking . . . elements of implementation and evaluation, and devising internal appellate procedures.
7. Institutionalization of group processes. Constituencies must be assured the right and the opportunity to participate in consultation.

8. Orchestration and coordination of consultive processes by leaders. Energetic leadership of consultive process prevents . . . slowing of decision process and duplication or contradiction among deliberative efforts. (p. 16)

The consultive approach helps to bring members of the organizational community into the innovative process and into the governance processes.

Cycles continue, new parts of the community evolve while other parts of the community disengage. As developmental processes, cycles are bound in the social, relational features of the community and help to fashion organizational consciousness. Change is perceived as continuous and related rather than a discrete noncontiguous event. Stability takes on new meaning, a stable organization is one that is engaged in self-study and is continually changing or evolving (Senge, 1990).

Leadership plays an important part in the growth and development of organizations and is especially relevant to this discussion. There are some distinctions within organizational leadership that are important to note here. The leadership role as a formal designation is bound by contractual arrangements. The leadership function is an informal designation where responsibilities or activities associated with leadership are shared among members of the organization. Both the leadership role and the leadership function are influential in producing change through organizational culture (James et al., 1990; Koestenbaum, 1991; Pettigrew, 1990; Rosen, 1984; Schein, 1985).

In large part, it is through leadership that an organization is likely to initiate reconceptualization as adaptive or innovative. Chaffee and Tierney (1988) point out the importance of leadership as it influences reality and constructs life in organizations. According to Chaffee and Tierney, the influence factors into three strategies that parallel three dimensions of culture: structure, environment, and values (p. 18). Those strategies can be "machine like linear systems, adaptive systems, and cultural systems" (p. 11). They are ways of "looking, listening, and thinking," "less a solution than a means of arriving at one" (p. 22). Accordingly, "the linear strategic approach is the formalized component of the structural dimension" (p. 11). This approach is represented by procedural structures in place in organizations. The second strategy is referred to as adaptive. "By perceiving the organization's environment as a complex, ever-changing set of consumer or constituency preferences, administrators can utilize adaptive strategies to align the institution with its environment through a process of organizational change. One might think of the adaptive strategy . . . in biological terms" (p. 23).

This treatment of the term "adaptive," as it functions with the other strategies, is in agreement with the approach to change and with the development of contextual relevance advocated by Wells. The third strategy is interpretive and "tends to emphasize the values dimension of organizational culture. Such strategies proceed from an understanding that the organizations can play a role in creating its structure and its environment. . . . Interpretive strategies enable constituencies to understand the organization and its environment and motivates them to support its mission" (p. 24). Chaffee and Tierney assert that "organizations need effective functioning in all three . . . ," the strategies are "interactive," and "hierarchical" (p. 24). They are ways of building structures and life within the organization. As these systems become integrated the prosocial, consultative approaches emerge.

The academy's consultative administrative style provides the open forum necessary for change to occur. Within that forum there is the reconciliation of divergent beliefs regarding the change process. Another significant part of this discussion has to do with the need for communities that want to be innovative to become learning organizations (Argyris & Schon, 1989). Learning organizations engage in self-study or a kind of reflective practice where learning and innovativeness are nearly synonymous. As such, issues contemplated as those organizations design innovations necessarily cover their identity, purpose, structures, processes, and activities. Within the conceptualization of the organization as evolving and becoming adaptive or innovative, there is also a point where it achieves maturation. However, this state, like the others described here, is not static, rather there are fluctuations within it. Maturation is fluid and a product of the organization's present and its historical contexts. The learning organization represents maturation.

CONSTRUCTING LEARNING ORGANIZATIONS

Much of the thinking about adaptive organizations includes conceptualizing them as learning organizations (Argyris & Schon, 1978; Argyris & Schon, 1989; Beckhard & Pritchard, 1992; Senge, 1990; Schon, 1983). What are the distinguishing features of the learning organization and what are the philosophical approaches that support them as such? Argyris and Schon (1978) laid the groundwork for conceptualizing organizational behavior as learning and innovative behavior with their study of interventions in for-profit organizations. In that study they worked with leaders and members of organizational communities and began to apply what they believed to be approaches to double-loop learning in organizations. Within their work the concept of the learning organization and the learning community took shape.

In his subsequent work on learning organizations published in 1982, Argyris referred to his collaboration with Schon and used their study to ground his discussion of the learning organization and learning community. He proposed that behavior in those organizations responds to or is based on "governing variables" also referred to as "governing values" (pp. 86–144):

1. Members of the organization must be provided valid information upon which they can base their actions and are thus in control of what happens to them as members of the community . . . The organizational community must then "[d]esign situations or encounters in which participants can be origins and experience high personal causation."

2. Members of the organization govern their actions through "free and informed choice." "Organizational tasks are controlled jointly."
3. There is "internal commitment to choice and constant monitoring of the implementation." "Protection of self is a joint enterprise and oriented toward growth." In addition, there is "[b]ilateral protection of others." (p. 103)

Argyris (1982) described experiences resulting from the foregoing in the following: (1) members of the organization experience each other as "minimally defensive," (2) there are "minimally defensive interpersonal relations and group dynamics," (3) "learning-oriented norms" emerge, and (4) there is "high freedom of choice, internal commitment, and risk taking" (p. 102). According to Argyris (1982), double-loop learning behavior is different from the behavior resulting from prior conditioning that commonly occurs throughout the lives of members of organizations. That prior conditioning is consistent with "variables or values" associated with what he labeled single-loop learning. Those "variables or values" include (1) "achieve[ment] of purpose as the actor defines it, (2) win do not lose, (3) suppress negative feelings, [and] (4) emphasize rationality" (p. 86). These items read much like a list of the single-mindedness, individualistic, and competitive practices that were at one time valued in entrepreneurial organization but have been criticized since. Although they may appear to be opposites, Argyris stated that the two sets of variables are not. Rather, the latter set emphasizes skillful articulation of purposes and goals and simultaneously controls others and environmental factors in order to ensure success (p. 101). The former set does not reject skillful articulation and precision regarding one's purpose; however, it does reject "the unilateral control that usually accompanies advocacy because the typical purpose of advocacy is to win" (p. 105).

Argyris (1982) described double-loop learning as "coupling articulation and advocacy with an invitation to . . . confront views, even to alter them, in order to produce action which is based on the most complete, valid information possible, and to which people can become internally committed" (p. 103). This means that members and particularly leaders of the organization are inviting and supporting double-loop learning (p. 103). The actor Argyris referred to here, in the present context, is the organizational leadership or the visionaries who are crucial to innovative processes. This invitation flattens the organizational hierarchy in ways that support exchanges of information and collaboration in the design and implementation of innovations.

Double-loop learning requires two-way communication where parties to the process encourage and facilitate development of heuristics in exploration of new meanings that support new organizational realities. There are paradoxes, which Argyris (1982) associated with double-loop learning, that provide useful insights into the nature of the human experience during the course of change. Moreover, those paradoxes are especially useful in directing the role and, thereby the experiences, of those who design and orchestrate creative activity as well. One of those paradoxes is that "in the interest of rationality, people act to produce consequences that [actually] inhibit rationality" (p. 10). Further, members of the organization are unaware that they are acting as such. Another paradox is that what should be discussed in order for learning to take place is not discussed (p. 10). That is to say, participants in the change experience theorize about what is taking place, moving from lower to higher levels of abstraction treating them as truths rather than points to be explored in dialogue with members of the organization. These paradoxes are related to the governing variables described as inhibiting double-loop learning. Although there are others, there is yet another paradox that is important to this discussion and should be mentioned here. Argyris called this the paradox of counter-productive control; that is to say, the "very competencies that keep [organizational leaders and managers] in control prevent double-loop learning" (p. 455). Drawing on his work with Schon (1978), Argyris (1982) suggested that by giving up control and becoming vulnerable or facing the possibility of failure, success is possible (p. 455).

Beckhard and Pritchard (1992) worked through Argyris' and Schon's (1978) conceptualizations to get to the same point in their discussion of learning organizations and organizational change. Beckhard and Pritchard demonstrated the alignment of learning and change in the following: "Learning and change processes are part of each other. Change is a learning process and learning is a change process. Ultimately underpinning these processes are changes in the way individuals think and act" (p. 14). They continue to draw on the similarities in the two processes in their description of each. Learning involves:

(a) "Unfreezing" oneself from currently held beliefs, knowledge, or attitudes
(b) "Absorbing" new or alternative attitudes and behavior
(c) "Refreezing" oneself in the new state and the necessity for change and support it accordingly.

In real organizations, commitment follows discussion and often follows debates that help create the setting for change by facilitating reconciliation of differences as well as further development of an innovation. The exchange of ideas, often done with much enthusiasm, conviction, and frequently with much acrimony, makes it more difficult for organizations to return to business as usual. This part of the change process has been described as chaotic in part because it is uncomfortable for some people and because it often leads to unpredictable outcomes. However, it may be that the catharsis, which also takes place during the debate, permits movement forward.

For all that it appears to be, the debate as part of the innovation process involves the application of standards of reasonableness. Leaders of the change process are able to provide information that facilitate development of those standards of reasonableness. Such information might include whether the innovation is compatible with the mission of the academy, whether the innovation can be supported financially, and whether the innovation will affect the way members of the organization function. The heuristics referred to earlier arise out of the need to satisfy the standards described here.

Innovations are sometimes seen as developing out of extreme viewpoints. Moreover, they often are not fully developed because they do not represent a range of perspectives from within the organizational community. Consequently, innovations that are not successful are often described as top-down initiatives that impose the will of upper levels of management on direct service providers. In the academy, for example, because of its governance structure and its collaborative approach to management, the expectation of its members is that at the very least, those who are likely to be affected by innovations ought to play a role in their design. The merit of an innovation is tied to issues of profitability. Levine (1980, pp. 11–25) makes the point well in his discussion of profitability.

Profitability takes two forms: self-interest profitability and general profitability (Levine, 1980, pp. 11–25). Self-interest motivates individuals and groups within the organization to adopt the innovation, and general profitability motivates the organization to select a particular innovation and to support its continuance (pp. 11–25). The two interests interact with a compatibility element (pp. 11–25). When compatibility is high then there is little complaining about the innovation, when compatibility is high and profitability is high as well, then the organization will seek to maintain the innovation (pp. 11–25).

The notion of profitability and compatibility that must be reconciled is another way of conceptualizing the need to discern and integrate organizational beliefs about the nature and extent of change. An agreement that has been negotiated and consequently bridges differences in understanding among organization members as to the nature and extent of change necessary to improve the organization is preferred to approaches that are solely top-down or bottom-up. However, in the learning organization self-interest is subordinated by the interests of the community, which is treated as a priority. Therefore, general rather than personal profitability directs the activity of the academy. In the paradigm of the learning organization, profitability and compatibility become systemic rather than individual concerns.

Returning to Birnbaum's point made earlier, members of the community look at change from where they are positioned within the organization. Although they may be at odds during the course of the process, those groups are potential contributors to the development of innovations that are integrative. Organizational change or innovation in the learning organization is a negotiated process that involves, at some point during its course, much if not all of the behaviors and managerial approaches that can be described as prosocial as well. For example, shared leadership is an important part of negotiating the change agreement, there ought to be open communication among parties in the change process, and prevailing beliefs held by members of the organization regarding the nature and extent of change ought to be discerned and addressed during the process.

The design for change in a negotiated agreement is one that is flexible, allowing for intervening factors, both internal and external to the organization, that affect its structure and the way it functions. It is the outcomes or goals that members of the organizational community agree on that remain constant. Within an innovative or adaptive organization, for example, its innovators openly communicate with members of the community their beliefs as to the need for change and the form it should take. That open communication invites further discussion and leads to a number of forums in which other points of view can be considered and even debated. The learning organization has in place several approaches to achieve its goals. And, in response to those several approaches, members of the community who might find it difficult to support or to involve themselves in one approach have others in which they can participate. The learning organization supports and encourages the development of new projects that facilitate achievement of its goal.

CONCLUSIONS

How do organizations become adaptive or innovative learning communities? Those that would be engaged as such involve their membership in systemic- and self-studies guided by the features Argyris and Schon (1989) and Senge (1990), in particular, suggested are common to learning organizations. Those features reflect a systems approach to organizational functioning and include

1. The organizational community is committed to systemic- and self-study.
2. Systemic- and self-study and development are supported by organizational leaders.
3. The leadership function is shared among organizational members.
4. Organizational functioning is relational.
5. Change is integral to the life of the organization.
6. The organization supports the personal and career growth of its membership.
7. The standards among members of the organization are personal best.

Although learning organizations are innovative, all innovative organizations are not necessarily learning organizations. To the extent that an organization's leaders and membership can commit themselves to its evolution, the organization is in position to become flexible in developing innovations. As suggested in the features describing it as such, the learning organization, as well as the evolving learning community, is mindful of the relational nature of a system approach.

In his treatise on the academy Wells (1953) described it as a business and urged that it must become adaptive and provide relevant services to its consumers in order to survive into the next century. Decades after Wells' treatise, there is some debate about whether or not the academy will be in position to handle new demands. The debate notwithstanding, it makes sense for organizations that want to be adaptive or innovative (the terms were treated as synonymous in the discussion) to engage in self-study or reflection and ultimately to reconstruct themselves as learning communities. Change is an integral part of the way such communities function. Rather than viewing change as a discrete and disruptive or a destabilizing event, it is viewed as an integral part of a continuously evolving organism. The organization remains malleable, able to respond to its public in ways that are creative because it strives deliberately to retain those features of its developmental stages that support it as such. The organization's development becomes an integrative process.

Afterword: Postmodern Directions in Educational Leadership

Spencer J. Maxcy

THEMES

The chapters in this book express in recurring fashion the elements of a postmodern response to contemporary crises in educational leadership and administration. The postmodern visions displayed here are pledged to an affirmative response to the question, "Is there a new paradigm in educational administration?" Scholars in the field of educational administration for decades have been plagued by this query, but, until as recently as 1988, Richard Bates concluded that the label of "intellectual turmoil" was something of an exaggeration where it was applied to educational administration scholarship. Few educational administration theorists were following the lead of Thomas Greenfield in developing a radically different theoretical position, thus leading Bates to conclude that the profession was gripped more by ennui than excitement and that unless the field of educational administration became informed by "a radically different paradigm" the field was in "a precarious and defenseless state" (Bates, 1988, pp. 20–21).

What has changed since 1988 is the emergence of strong indications that a postmodernism is possible. Cultural changes prompt our rethinking of the older modes of problem setting and solution. Leadership in the emerging postmodern culture has shifted in meaning and practice along a number of new lines.

We have seen the knowledge basis of educational leadership, as part of what postmodernism seems to mean for educational administration as a field of study as well as a domain of practice, take on new expression. Postmodernism has recast the virtues of pluralism and relativism in establishing truth. How we perceive educational administrative knowing is under critical scrutiny. The turn away from foundationalism is apparent in the new patterns of administration theorizing. No longer interested in the grounded theory of inquiry and meaning, a disavowal of any attachment to a metanarrative (such as science) is evident. On the further reaches of the movement, some postmodernists accede to a shift to an open-textured nonposition. Acceptance of the primacy of process over structure allows for this radical relativization, that in some theories, discredits truth-seeking entirely and relocates the agenda to "edifying discourse" and keeping the conversation going (Rorty, 1989; Bernstein, 1992).

Privileged views (primarily psychological and sociological) of educational leadership are being replaced by context-driven mosaics that highlight the transactional nature of leading and following. Owing to the redistribution of knowledge and power to those closest to the pedagogical event, administrative leadership as management and dictation finds substitutes in the form of collaborative and collegial leading in which the mantle of "leader" trades hands depending on the task and requisite skills needed.

Postmodernism has resurfaced the question of power and its relation to knowledge and organization. Postmodernists, often following Foucault, look at power with this reoriented viewpoint. How shall power (and empowerment) emancipate? In what ways shall the oppression some feel within educational structures currently in place be exorcised?

What is unique to postmodern thought is the openness to new processes whereby decisions and choices are to be made. Postmodernism has highlighted the importance of reflection in educational discourse and practice but without the need for metacriteria. The elevation of unique processes, stressing metaphor, analogy, and other devices, above that of scientific rationality mark the new postmodern school leadership. Gone is the commitment to a single mode of thinking, structuralist and positivist in nature.

Finally, postmodern views of organization take a departure from the model of organization as a predetermined structure. That the culture of the school shall experience dramatic changes in the future seems a foregone conclusion, if for no other reason than *something* will have to be done to address the dissatisfaction felt by all involved in mass education. What we should be on the alert for is refreshing conceptions of educational arrangement, different from the factory model that has dominated research and practice for so long. One such notion takes schools as moral communities with members joined through convenants (Sergiovanni, 1992). Other images place stress on organic, nondominating, psychic, and self-organizing creations (Morgan, 1986).

Hence the conditions of postmodern critical administration are tender outlines of things to come. Like any paradigm shift, postmodernism demonstrates some elements of the old along with vital elements of the novel and unique. In this afterword I wish to identify the key directions the new postmodernism is taking with reference to educational leadership, as well as some of the challenges that the movement may face as it takes form over the next few years.

NEW DIRECTIONS

Redefining School Leadership

It is singularly surprising that a text aimed at detailing "postmodern leadership" should have so little to say of leadership. Are we seeing these efforts resulting in a postmodern marginalization? The justification for such a lapse is found in postmodern intellectuals' penchant for moving the discourse/practice of leadership from a technical-rational "science of leadership" to a disseminated administration that relocates leading to the range of interactions and transactions of practicing teachers and learners, administrators and parents, and so on. This deflection is praiseworthy because we are able to rethink traditional theories of leadership in light of the new postmodern concern for disabling metanarratives and grand theories. Postmodern leadership as it is embedded in these chapters on epistemology, processes, and organization opens the discourse and relocates it in the methods used to establish truth claims, the means whereby we may challenge the trenchant and dogmatic procedures used to "handle" people and problems, and within constellations that counter the business/industry models of schools as organizations. Postmodernist views of educational governance and leadership are not constructed like the totalizing theories of traditional educational administration theory.

The New Communal Individualism

The postmodernist/poststructuralist effort to kill off the subject has meant the end of "entrepreneurial and inner-directed individualism." We also find "charisma" and "genius" are no longer appropriate labels (Jameson, 1991, p. 306). In the place of the charismatic leader we see democratically constituted groups using information in new ways. Society no longer requires prophets and seers in leadership positions: This conception of leadership and these types of leaders have lost their charm in the postmodern era Jameson tells us (1991, p. 306).

One of the barriers to leadership during the modernist and structuralist era has been the decentering of the individual. The self has been forced out of the picture as structuralists sought to explain how organizations developed in terms of the interrelations of their parts. Modernist painters performed surgery on our conventional understanding of the autonomous person, laying out the parts in disarray on the canvas. Social scientists further evacuated the task of purposeful human action when they began talking of human capital.

Substitutes for characterizations of historical experience as respondent to human willfulness and creativity emerged from Braudel's studies of the Mediterranean communities. Levi-Strauss redirected anthropological study of myth to bundles of linguistic-like expressions hanging in cultural space. Single creative expressions were redistributed through cultures in multiorigin accounts that successfully removed the individual creative architects of human thought/practice, transforming them into puppet-like respondents to cross-cultural universal themes. The consequence for education was to see such efforts in scholarship as the theory movement in educational administration. The latter moved individual agents further outside the discourse of educational phenomenon. The discourse/practice of free human beings engaging in creative effort was replaced by positivist efforts to relocate coherence regarding the interaction of "variables" in scholarly efforts to explain human failures and successes relative to terms of emic and etic forces.

The philosopher William James defined *self* as "a system of memories, purposes, strivings, fulfillments or disappointments." Postmodern conceptions of self have sought to reposition individuals within and as a part of the social. Theory has served to account for sentient beings in the maelstrom of poststructural/postmodern cultures. Whereas the structuralists had decentered the self, efforts are afoot to refocus the self in new ways relative to the problems and prospects facing our age.

The new individualism of the postmodern/poststructural theorists seeks to redistribute human agency. The self reenters the field. John Dewey in *Individualism Old and New* (1929) castigated the nineteenth-century liberals for embracing a version of individualism that reduced individuals to atomistic types or rugged individuals. Here man versus society took precedence over man in society. The romantic individual fighting against all odds to make a place on the frontier was no longer viable as explanation for how persons worked within social groups, Dewey reasoned. What was now required was a new individualism that joined people together rather than pitting them in eternal struggle, one against the other. Growth and progress could not continue following the modernist model, he asserted.

In the domain of leadership, and in particular educational leadership, the legacy of the modernist characterization of leading has produced a model that effectively posted the singular individual at the head of the organization. School leaders were (and in many ways this view continues despite changes) seen as effective or ineffective insofar as they were able to exercise control and direction over their organizations and charges. The effectiveness of the educational leader was measured by the productivity of the teachers and summarily the pupils. In the realm of educational administration, the theory movement, sought to retrofit educational explanations to the mounds of data flowing into data banks. Prescient regarding cybernetics, the theory movement, saw the orgy of data collection one day yielding up small range theories and rendering educational leadership as predictable. Contributing to this belief were the economists who embraced human capital theory as exhausting the explanation of how individuals within organizations were to be molded into productive units. By removing humanistic definitions of self and individual and replacing them with deterministic language of process/product the realm of educational management was redirected into the cul de sac of materialistic philosophy minus the Marxist dialectic.

Technology and Leadership

The postmodern/poststructural leadership will profit from the redefinition of educational value through the reduction of distance and time in instructional delivery. Computer driven technology provides a thousand flowers and sets them for bloom. Interactive computer-telephone connectivity, interactive television, talking books, and so forth promise to reduce the centrality of educator *qua* leader. Where technology provides knowledge, a leveling takes place. First the book competed with the dictated lecture, now the screen replaces the lecture. Instruction moves toward autonomy as knowledge becomes power.

While McLuhan first raised our sensitivity to the shift from media as the medium to medium as the message itself, Jean Baudrillard speaks of this shift and points up the new significance of the media in establishing belief autonomously. Hence, the myth of the single leader influencing his or her flock through television, for example, is demythologized through the recognition that mediated events frequently disable leaders. Presidential debates in the recent past have illustrated the power of media in this respect.

The New Leadership as Aesthetic

While the continental philosophers long understood it, Americans are only lately coming to realize that art directs life. The essential discovery, one may say, was begun by Dewey in his text *Art as Experience* (1934). While the preponderance of effort in educational administration research, as well as teaching, assumed the centrality and import of knowing, what was often overlooked was the significance of aesthetic understanding. This oversight was inherited, by and large, from the Kantian philosophers who separated knowledge from values. As a result, modernist administrators dealt with art, often reluctantly, only as non-rational.

Thus, where leadership has been characterized as the *design* of more appropriate social and cultural contexts within which school children, for example, are to live and create, modernism provides little support for the effort. With a deep fear of chaos and a penchant for order, retrograde administration theorists fail to see the opportunities offered by contemporary threatened structures for artistic reconstruction.

Composition and improvisation characterize the postmodern. Bateson (1989) speaks of "composing a life" through a grasp of the underlying esthetic. Postmodern administration illustrates both a balance and a diversity, a chaos and an order. Planning and taking risks through composition offers leaders a processual approach that yields far more than managed efficiency and effectiveness.

The New Philosophy of Postmodern Critical Leadership

In the *Handbook of Research in Educational Administration* (1988), Donald Willower concludes that of the six new trends in educational administration thinking, "there is still a great deal of philosophical innocence, even among leaders in the field [of educational administration]" (p. 742). And, Taylor (1989) tells us, "Much of what we live today consists of reactions to [modernism] and, more, of the dissociation and prolongation of the strands it united" (p. 482). Postmodernists, like those you have read in the present text, are attempting to inform this innocence and to break from the grip of modernism's hold.

What we have seen in the chapters of this text is a strong and sustained set of plural and new voices that both catalog a shift in administrative self-consciousness; progress toward a new administrative paradigm; and also, produce evidence and justification for further developments in postmodern and poststructural educational leadership.

DANGERS FACING POSTMODERN CRITICAL ADMINISTRATION

Ten dangers confront the postmodern response and the forward momentum of educational leadership conceived of as critique. These dangers range from singular alienation of teachers, students, and administrators to wholesale short-circuitry of any reform of education in America.

Postmodernity Sinking into Nihilism

As Baudrillard warns, postmodernity has signs of unraveling and rupturing. The death of the social seems likely and with it the end of social conceptions of schooling and leadership. If Baudrillard is correct, we face a further implosion that will turn every educative event, administrative, pedagogical, and so forth into mere simulacrum. Attached to Baudrillard's characterization of the postmodern is his belief that classical sociology must be refused through (1) a devalorization of the social; (2) a rejection of naturalistic discourse of the historical; (3) a refusal of dialectical reason; and, (4) a break with the normalizing, accumulative conception of power (Kroker & Cook, 1986, p. 171).

Exiling Moral Leadership

Efforts are afoot to redefine educational administration from a moral and ethical perspective. Certainly T. Greenfield, Bates, and others led the way in this regard. In the wings wait those who would have leadership in schools cast as a bit player. Moral/ethical features of community life are pervasive, but they are also messy. We lack the same kind of rigorous methods for dealing with such values. Nonetheless, commitment to the discourse/practice of value leadership has a Pygmalion effect: If we believe such values to be central, they can become so. Where we seek to marginalize morals and ethics, they will end up beyond our grasp.

Reducing the Postmodern Critique to Sloganeering

The assimilation of postmodernity into the world of educational praxis that is at once marked by trivial avant gardism and bourgeois, media-inspired, self-fulfillment runs the risk of disfiguring postmodernism and borderlining authenticity of self as well as the cultural and social. We can see traces of such a move in the deenergizing and dispersal of school crises into strategies of uplift and improvement underscored by the virtues of frenzy-induced fatigue over idleness, control/effectiveness over reflection, and test score changes over learning. Educational leadership in this swirl of postmodern positioning is subject to the pressures to materialize and concretize in measurable products what is essentially a relational state of affairs in which the chrysalis and the organism are one and the same. Leadership as an explanatory concept is thereby realigned with modernist motives and rational justifications of "the restructured school," and "the *highly* effective principal," and the virtues of "quality management" as applied to educational outcomes. In the desire to be "timely" and "relevant," administrative theory has lapsed into ad hoc, adjustment philosophies marked by "fix-it" literature and "Five-Minute Managers."

The Revival of Foundationalism

While poststructuralism and postmodernity have sought to disengage our commitment to foundational thinking, there are possibilities that point to a return to a new form of foundationalism. Postmodernity has wrestled with the ghost of Descartes by embracing Nietzsche, with the concomitant result that certain postmodernists (e.g., Baudrillard) lapse into states of nihilism and abject depression. Germanic-inspired French antimodernists such as Baudrillard, Deleuze, and Guatarri served as examples of the French penchant for anomy and alienating discourses linked with an Aryan mythos of ethnosuperiority.

Reacting to the emptiness of such a postmodernity, critical and reflective postmodernists and poststructuralists (see e.g., Cherryholmes, 1987) have sought to resurrect and revivify reasoning procedures, decision-making logics, and problem-solving strategies that more than unmask the earlier faith in abstract reason, but rather provide a new reasoned grounding for managerial and curricular theory and decision making. The path through the chaos of educational bureaucracy-induced unreason is marked by incomplete efforts to convince the yet unconverted to the postmodern through a kind of matching game involving intellectual weaponry.

The Return to Romanticism

The Romantic literature of hero-leader and the saga of the great quest (à la Joseph Campbell) has propelled postmodern culture theorists to resurrect the hunting and gathering tribes member, with talisman and shield facing the contemporary chaos of the schools. Efforts to depart from crises by managing fear trumps the suit of those who would have us employ creative intelligence in solving new postmodern problems in education. C. A. Bowers and other members of the new Romanticism offer a postmodern conservativism that conflates and contradicts the efforts to engage in an intelligent and well-formed discourse.

Postmodernity as neo-Romanticism is a real danger. Curriculum theorists engaging in the restoration of a 1960s neoprogressivism seek to convert postmodernity into a laissez-faire classroom in which teachers reassert their autonomy by adopting a Rousseauean child-centeredness. Cloaking their Freudian or Goodmanesque psychologistic reduction of education in the guise of postmodern contradictions of modernities' social functionalism, these efforts march us backwards.

The essential danger of this normative recalibration of Descartes' mechanistic world is to problematize the metaphysics of experience and to seize once again the dualistic views of mind and body, individual and social, sense and reference. Analyticity at the level of policy absorbs the mind of postmodernists of the new paradigm but at the sacrifice of analyticity at the level of theory. Theory becomes the handmaiden of the restructuring of schools, the decentralizing of educational bureaucracies, and demanaging messes the practical means for addressing chaos (Hess, 1991).

Postmodernity/Poststructuralism as Just Another Theory

Postmodern leadership faces the real possibility that it may be plateaued at a level of conflict and difference at the same time as we face the death of history. Fukuyama (1992) tells us that history is ending because the ideological battles are coming to an end. Democracy as a form of political and social life has won. We are led to believe that conflicts will continue, but these will be solely elaborations on a theme of democracy.

Irony produces a pluralism of belief systems and the postmodern gets relativized through at once an embrace of metanarratives (positivistic technique). Sarup (1989) points to the fragmentation of postmodern/poststructural theorizing. Already we are seeing postmodernity being fractured into subtheories with the result that conservative critics point out it has no cohesive core beliefs and flies under too many different flags (Willower, 1988).

Critics of poststructuralism and postmodernity tend to focus on the isolating influence of plural theoretical viewpoints. If each theoretician is not subject to some centralizing norms, the product is puny compared with typical positivistic research and needs to find a final, absolute truth regarding a text, no matter how we prize subjective takings (Ellis, 1989). The difficulty with such criticisms is that they fail to see the virtue of all research programs as often uneven and decentered, even within positivistic science. Evers and Lakomski (1991) propose a polytheoretical condition and a coherentist check for adequacy, thus moving the dialogue out of the Kuhnian paradigmatic commensurability versus incommensurability debates. They argue what is needed is better science, by which they mean a broader definition of science that rejects metanarratives.

Another feature of criticisms of poststructuralism and postmodernity attaches to the inherently antitheoretical stance taken in the movement (Ellis, 1989). This reading of postmodernism siphons off certain subsets of the movement, primarily the artistic, and incorrectly assumes all postmodernity to be antitheory. On the contrary, West (1989) reaffirms the theoretical role of postmodernity as a critical discourse and brings our attention to the dispossessed groups (African-Americans, Hispanic-Americans, etc.).

Postmodernity into Neostructuralism

Embedded in the quest for transformation, paradigm shift, reconstruction, and chaos/order debates is to be found a desire to psychologize the discourse of culture and society by smuggling in Piaget and followers. Transformation then becomes adjustment, and ontogeny undergoes subtle naturalistic shifts. Developmentalism provides a predictable pattern and postmodernity joins with structuralism to yield a witch's brew of security within the eye of the storm. Assertive postmodernism *qua* equilibrialization serves up accommodating mechanisms that posture as transcultural absolutes. Change is confused with innovation; living with life-adjustment; teaching with "throwing sand in their eyes."

Postmodernism as Babble

Postmodernism runs the risk of erecting barriers among groups such that continuous conversation relative to difference is marginalized. Ellsworth (1989) proposes a "pedagogy of the unknowable" in which it is assumed that groups cannot know the experiences of other groups nor can they know their own experiences fully. Coalitions of groups have not known that their actions would undercut the struggle of other groups or their own affinity groups. Thus, this set of assumptions allows us to build strengths and forces for change, but these are always relative to specific localized groups. Fearful of the single "master discourse" that represents white male coherent narrative of correctness, Ellsworth embraces plural and partial knowings and shies away from communications with other groups because they can only have partial knowledge of her.

Bernstein (1983) on the other hand, rejoices in dialogue and conversation as these lead to the postmodern move beyond objectivism of single metanarratives and the relativism of incoherent and nontranslatable utterances. Through the reclamation of "practical rationality," he finds local forms of community life may lead to solidarity and unity, participation and mutual recognition. Dialogue-laden communities would make every effort to communicate outside the group. Conversation and the breakdown of divisiveness is the practical task for Bernstein.

Linguistic Scientism

Another potential danger posed by postmodernism gone awry is the embrace of structuralist strategies that posit a metanarrative of linguistic scientism. A narrow refraction of postmodern trends through the lens of semiotical logical linguism is possible. Postmodernism, as culture critique, ought not to be reduced to simple epistemological categories. To posit a scientific and linguistic metalevel view of postmodern culture is to make such a view the *raison d'être* for antistructure while missing the richer dimension of postmodern *cultural criticism*. There is on the horizon of critique the tendency to narrow the sights to signposts and thereby miss the scenery. The neosignology becomes at once a strategy for dealing with the cacophonous postmodern experiences through a study of sign relation, while missing the referential beauty. And, so to construe the duty of critique in the postmodern educational era is to miss the moral and ethical dimensions of cultural participation and reconstruction.

Postmodernism as Apolitical Dalliance

Finally, it is important in the postmodern and poststructural era to maintain consciousness of the *political* nature of schooling. Postmodernism and poststructuralism in their antipathy to the political run the risk of slighting the study of politics as a power field in education. With any shift in history, freedom has been paramount in moving culture to newer thresholds: The political aspect of education must not be ignored.

CONCLUSIONS

The effort of this text has been one of opening up and keeping open the difficult critical administration discourse that at once focuses on the diseased assumptions and practices of modernist and structuralist educational leadership, as well as illustrates the modes of postmodern and poststructural critique of educational administration discourse/practice. Much of what has been said here is offered as ongoing and anticipatory of what the authors collectively view as a major new wave in educational administration theory and practice.

The dangers and the prospects are evident. There are no long-standing precedents for the ideas laid out here. However, unless new intelligent considerations are begun and maintained, school leadership and school organizations will continue to fibrilate and chaos will overcome us. The costs of barring the way to new inquiries is caught in the pained faces and the futures of our children and youth.

References

AASA Commission on the Preparation of Professional School Administrators (1971). *The American school superintendent: An AASA research study.* Washington, DC: AASA.
Abercrombie, N., Hill, S., & Turner, B. S. (1980). *The dominant ideology thesis.* Boston: George Allen and Unwin.
Alcoff, L. (1987). Justifying feminist social science. *Hypatia* 2(3), pp. 85–103.
———. (1988). Cultural feminism versus poststructuralism: The identity crisis in feminist theory. In Elizabeth Minnich, Jean O'Barr, & Rachel Rosenfeld (Eds.), *Reconstructing the academy: Women's education and women's studies.* Chicago: The University of Chicago Press, pp. 257–88.
Allison, G. T. (1971). *Essence of decision: Explaining the Cuban Missile Crisis.* Boston: Little Brown.
American Society for Training and Development. (1988). *Workplace basics: The skills employers want.* Washington, DC: U.S. Department of Labor, Employment and Training Administration.
Anderson, G. L. (1989a). *Invisibility, legitimation, and school administration: The study of non-events.* Paper presented at the annual meeting of the American Educational Research Association, San Francisco.
———. (1989b). *The management of meaning and the achievement of organizational legitimacy: A critical ethnography of the principalship.* Paper presented at the annual meeting of the American Educational Research Association, San Francisco.
Antonio, R. J. (1989). The normative foundations of emancipatory theory: Evolutionary versus pragmatic perspectives. *American Journal of Sociology* 94 (4), pp. 721–48.
Apple, M. (1971). The hidden curriculum and the nature of conflict. *Interchange,* 2(4).
———. (1979). *Ideology and the curriculum.* London: Routledge & Kegan Paul.

———. (1982). *Education and power.* Boston: Routledge and Kegan Paul.
———. (1991). Series Editor's Introduction. In P. Lather, *Getting smart: Feminist research and pedagogy with/in the postmodern.* New York: Routledge.
Argyris, C. (1982). *Reasoning, learning, and action: Individual and organizational.* San Francisco: Jossey-Bass.
Argyris, C., & Schon, D. A. (1978). *Organizational learning: A theory of action perspectives.* Boston: Addison-Wesley.
———. (1989). Participatory action research and action science compared: A commentary. *American Behavioral Scientist* 32 (5), May-June, pp. 612-23.
Bacharach, S. B. (Ed.). (1990). *Education reform: Making sense of it all.* Boston: Allyn and Bacon.
Bakhtin, M. M. (1986). In Caryl Emerson and Michael Holquist (Ed.), *Speech genres and other late essays.* Trans. Vern W. McGee. Austin: University of Texas Press.
Ball, S. (1987). *The micro-politics of the school: Towards a theory of school organization.* London: Melhuer.
Barnes, B. (1974). *Scientific knowledge and sociological theory.* London: Routledge & Kegan Paul.
Barnes, B., & Bloor, D. (1991). Relativism, rationalism and the sociology of knowledge. In M. Hollis and S. Lukes (Eds.), *Rationality and relativism* (5th ed.). Cambridge, MA: MIT Press, pp. 21-47.
Barone, T. E. (1990, April). *Subjectivity.* Paper presented at the Annual Meeting of the American Educational Research Association, Boston.
Barth, R. S. (1991). Restructuring schools: Some questions for teachers and principals. *Phi Delta Kappan* 73(2), pp. 123-28.
Barthes, R. (1972). *Mythologies.* London: Jonathan Cape.
———. (1976). *The pleasure of the text.* New York: Hill & Wang.
Bates, R. (1980). Educational administration, the sociology of science, and the management of knowledge. *Educational Administration Quarterly* 16(2), pp. 1-20.
———. (1984). Toward a critical practice of educational administration. In T. J. Sergiovanni & J. E. Corbally (Eds.), *Leadership and organizational culture.* Urbana: University of Illinois Press.
———. (1988, April 5-10). Is there a new paradigm in educational administration? Paper presented before the American Educational Research Association, New Orleans.
———. (1990, April). Leadership and the rationalization of society. Paper read before the American Educational Research Association. Boston.
Bateson, M. C. (1989). *Composing a life.* New York: Atlantic Monthly Press.
Beckhard, V. J., & Pritchard, W. (1992). *Changing the essence: The art of creating and leading fundamental change in organizations.* San Francisco: Jossey-Bass.
Belenky, M. F., Clinchy, B. M., Goldberger, N. R., & Tarule, J. M. (1986). *Women's ways of knowing: The development of self, voice, and mind.* New York: Basic Books.
Berger, P. L., & Luckmann, T. (1967). *The social construction of reality.* New York: Anchor Books.
Bernstein, R. J. (1978). *The restructuring of social and political theory.* Philadelphia: University of Pennsylvania Press.
———. (1983). *Beyond objectivism and relativism.* Philadelphia: University of Pennsylvania Press.
———. (1992). *The new constellation: The ethical-political horizons of modernity/postmodernity.* Cambridge, MA: MIT Press.

Berry, B., & Ginsberg, R. (1990). Creating lead teachers: From policy to implementation. *Kappan,* 71 (81), pp. 616–22.
Birnbaum, R. (1988). *How colleges work: The cybernetics of academic organization and leadership.* San Francisco: Jossey-Bass.
Blaise, J. (1989). The micropolitics of the school: The everyday political orientation of teachers towards open school principals. *Educational administration quarterly,* 25(4), 377–408.
———. (1991). The micropolitical perspective. In J. Blaise (Ed.), *The politics of life in schools: Power, conflict, and cooperation.* Newbury Park, CA: Sage.
Blount, J. (1993). "Women and the superintendency, 1900–1990: 'Destined to rule the schools in every city.' " Dissertation in progress at the University of North Carolina at Chapel Hill.
Boulding, E. (1988). *Building a global civic culture.* New York: Teachers College Press.
Bowers, C. A. (1977). Emergent ideological characteristics of educational policy. *Teachers College Record,* 79 (1).
———. (1987). *The promise of theory: Education and the politics of cultural change.* New York: Teachers College Press.
Bowles, S., & Gintis, H. (1976). *Schooling in capitalist America.* New York: Basic Books.
Braverman, H. (1974). *Labor and monopoly capitalism.* New York: Monthly Review Press.
Brookover, W. (1982). *Creating effective schools.* Holmes Beach, FL: Learning Publications.
Brookover, W. B., & Lezotte, L. (1979). *Schools can make a difference.* East Lansing: College of Urban Development, Michigan State University.
Brophy, J., & Good, T. L. (1986). Teacher behavior and student achievement. In Merlin C. Wittrock (Ed.), *Handbook of research on teaching* (3rd ed.). New York: Macmillan.
Brown, R. D. (1976). *Modernization: The transformation of American life 1600–1865.* New York: Hill and Wang.
Burns, J. M. (1978). *Leadership.* New York: Harper and Row.
Burrell, G., & Morgan, G. (1979). *Sociological paradigms and organizational analysis.* Portsmouth, NH: Heinemann.
Cahoone, L. E. (1988). *The dilemma of modernity: Philosophy, culture, and anticulture.* Albany: State University of New York Press.
Callahan, R. E. (1962). *Education and the cult of efficiency.* Chicago: University of Chicago Press.
Cameron, K. S., & Whetten, D. A. (1984). Models of the organizational life cycle: applications to higher education. In James L. Bess (Ed.), *College and university organization: Insights from the behavioral sciences.* New York: New York University Press, pp. 31–61.
Campbell, R. F., Cunningham, L. L., Nystrand, R. O., & Usdan, M. D. (1985). *The organization and control of American schools* (5th ed.). Columbus, OH: Merrill.
Campbell, R. F., Fleming, T., Newell, L. J., & Bennion, J. W. (1987). *A history of thought and practice in educational administration.* New York: Teachers College Press.
Carnegie Task Force on Teaching as a Profession. (1986). *A nation prepared: Teachers for the 21st century.* Hyattsville, MD: Carnegie Forum on Education and the Economy.

Carnoy, M., & Levin, H. M. (1976). *The limits of educational reform.* New York: David McKay.
———. (1985). *Schooling and work in the democratic state.* Stanford, CA: Stanford University Press.
Carnoy, M., & Shearer, D. (Eds). (1980). *Economic democracy.* Armonk, NY: E. Sharpe.
Chaffee, E. E., & Tierney, W. G. (1988). *Collegiate culture and leadership strategies.* New York: Macmillan.
Cherryholmes, C. B. (1988). *Power and criticism: Poststructural investigations in education.* New York: Teachers College Press.
Cistone, P. J. (1989). School-based management/shared decision making: Perestroika in educational governance. *Education and Urban Society* 20, 21(4), 363–66.
Clark, C. M. (1988). Teacher preparation: Contributions of research on teacher thinking. *Educational researcher,* 5–12.
Clark, C. M., & Elmore, J. L. (1979). *Teacher planning in the first weeks of school.* (Research Series No. 56). East Lansing: Michigan State University, Institute for Research on Teaching.
———. (1981). *Transforming curriculum in mathematics, science and writing: A case study of teacher yearly planning* (Research Series No. 99). East Lansing: Michigan State University, Institute for Research on Teaching.
Clark, C. M., & Lampert, M. (1986). The study of teacher thinking: implications for teacher education. *Journal of Teacher Education,* pp. 27–31.
Clark, C. M., & Peterson, P. L. (1986). In M. C. Wittrock (Ed.), *Handbook of research on teaching.* New York: Macmillan, pp. 255–96.
Clark, C. M., & Yinger, R. J. (1980). *The hidden world of teaching.* Eric Document, Ed. 191 844, pp. 1–35.
Clark, R. E. (1982). Antagonism between achievement and enjoyment in ATI studies. *Educational psychologist,* 17(2), pp. 92–101.
Clegg, S. (1979). *The theory of power and organizations.* London: Routledge and Kegan Paul.
———. (1989). *Frames of power.* London: Sage Publications.
Cohen, M. D., & March, J. G. (1974). *Leadership and ambiguity: The American college president.* New York: McGraw-Hill.
Cohen, M. D., March, J. G. & Olsen, J. P. (1972). A garbage can model of organizational choice, *Administrative science quarterly* (March), pp. 1–25.
College Board. (1983). *Academic preparation for college: What students need to know and be able to do.* New York: The College Board.
Cooper, D. J., Hayes, D., & Wolf, F. (1981). Accounting in organized anarchies: Understanding and designing accounting systems in ambiguous situations. *Accounting, organizations, and society* 6, pp. 175–91.
Corbett, H. D., & Wilson, B. L. (1992). *Testing, reform, and rebellion.* Philadelphia: RBS Publications.
Counts, G. S. (1927). *The social composition of boards of education: A study in the social control of public education.* Chicago: The University of Chicago.
CPRE. (1990). State education reform in the 1980's. *Policy briefs.* New Brunswick, NJ: Rutgers Center for Policy Research in Education.
Culbertson, J. A. (1988). A century's quest for a knowledge base. In Norman J. Boyan (Ed.), *Handbook of research on educational administration: A project of the Amer-*

ican Educational Research Association. New York: Longman, pp. 3–26.
Culler, J. D. (1982). *On deconstruction: Theory and criticism in the 1970s.* Ithaca, NY: Cornell.
Cunningham, G. M. (1990). *The role of management systems when the environment changes.* Unpublished manuscript.
Cyert, R. M., & March, J. G. (1963). *A behavioral theory of the firm.* Englewood Cliffs, NJ: Prentice-Hall.
Daft, R. L., & Wiginton, J. C. (1979). Language and organization, *The academy of management review,* pp. 179–91.
Deal, T. E. (1986). Educational change: Revival tant, tinkertoys, jungle, or carnival. In A. Leiberman (Ed.), *Rethinking school improvement: Research, craft, and concept.* New York: Teachers College Press, 115–28.
———. (1987). Effective school principals: Counselors, engineers, pawnbrokers, poets . . . or instructional leaders. In W. Greenfield (Ed.), *Instructional leadership.* Boston: Allyn and Bacon.
Derrida, J. (1974). *Of grammatology.* Baltimore: The Johns Hopkins University Press.
———. (1981). Semiology and grammatology: An interview with Julia Kristeva. In A. Bass (Trans.), *Positions.* Chicago: University of Chicago Press.
———. (1982). *Margins of philosophy.* Chicago: University of Chicago Press.
Dewey, J. (1929; 1962). *Individualism old and new.* New York: Capricorn.
———. (1934). *Art as experience.* New York: G. P. Putnam.
Doll, W. (1993). *A post-modern perspective on curriculum.* New York: Teachers College Press.
Donmoyer, R. (1985). The rescue from relativism: Two failed attempts and an alternative strategy. *Educational Researcher* 14 (10), pp. 13–20.
———. (1987). Beyond Thorndike/Beyond melodrama. *Curriculum Inquiry* 17(4), pp. 353–63.
———. (1991). Postpositivist evaluation: Give me a for instance. *Educational Administration Quarterly* 17(3), pp. 265–96.
Eaker, D., & Van Galen, J. (1992), *Reconnection rather than research.* Paper presented at the annual meeting of the American Educational Studies Association, Pittsburgh, PA.
Edmonds, R. (1979). Some schools work and more can. *Social policy,* 9, pp. 28–32.
———. (1986). Characteristics of effective schools. In Ulric Neisser (Ed.), *The school achievement of minority children.* Hillsdale, NJ: Erlbaum.
Edwards, R. (1979). *Contested terrain: The transformation of the workplace in the twentieth century.* New York: Basic Books.
Eisner, E. W. (1985). *The educational imagination.* New York: Macmillan.
———. (1988). The primacy of experience and the politics of method. *Educational Researcher* 17 (5), pp. 15–20.
Ellis, J. M. (1989). *Against deconstruction.* Princeton, NJ: Princeton University Press.
Ellsworth, E. (1989). "Why doesn't this feel empowering? Working through the repressive myths of critical pedagogy." *Harvard educational review* 59(3), pp. 297–324.
Eribon, D. (1991). In B. Wing (Trans.), *Michel Foucault.* Cambridge, MA: Harvard University Press.
Evers, C. W., & Lakomski, G. (1991). *Knowing educational administration.* Oxford: Pergamon.
Farran, D. (1990). Producing statistical information on young people's leisure. In L. Stan-

ley (Ed.), *Feminist praxis: Research, theory and epistemology.* London: Routledge, pp. 91–102.
Ferguson, K. E. (1984). *The feminist case against bureaucracy.* Philadelphia: Temple University Press.
Ferris, R. (1989). Principals' perceptions of their changed work life in implementing, in the initial stages, school-based management and schools of choice. Unpublished dissertation. Vanderbilt University.
Feyerabend, P. (1979). *Against method.* London: Verso.
Firestone, W. (1989). Using reform: Conceptualizing district initiative, *Educational evaluation and policy analysis* 11(2), pp. 151–64.
Fishel, L., & Pottker, J. (1975). Performance of women principals: A review of behavioral and attitudinal studied. In J. Pottker and Fishel (Eds.), *Sex bias in the schools: The research evidence.* London: Associated Universities Press, pp. 300–310.
Flax, J. (1990). *Thinking fragments: Psychoanalysis, feminism, and postmodernism in the contemporary West.* Berkeley: University of California Press.
Fleck, L. (1979). *Genesis and development of a scientific fact.* Chicago: University of Chicago Press.
Foster, H. (Ed.). (1983). *The anti-aesthetic: Essays on postmodern culture.* Port Townsend, WA: Bay Press.
Foster, W. (1986). *Paradigms and promises: New approaches to educational administration.* Buffalo, NY: Prometheus Books.
———. (1989). *School leaders as transformative intellectuals: A theoretical argument.* Paper presented to the Annual Meeting of the American Educational Research Association, San Francisco.
Foucault, M. (1969; 1972). In A. M. Sheridan Smith (Trans.), *The archaeology of knowledge and the discourse on language.* New York: Pantheon.
———. (1973). *The order of things.* New York: Vintage Books.
———. (1977; 1979). *Discipline and punish: The birth of the prison.* New York: Pantheon.
———. (1977). In D. F. Bouchard (Trans.), *Language, counter-memory, practice.* Ithaca, NY: Cornell University Press.
———. (1978). *The history of sexuality.* New York: Pantheon.
———. (1979). *Power, truth, strategy.* Sydney, Australia: Feral Publications.
———. (1980). In C. Gordon (Ed.), *Power and knowledge: Selected interviews and other writings.* New York: Pantheon.
———. (1991). Politics and the study of discourse. In G. Burchell, C. Gordon, & P. Miller (Eds.), C. Gordon (Trans.), *The Foucault effect: Studies in governmentality.* Chicago: University of Chicago Press.
Franklin, B. M. (1975). *George Herbert Mead, curriculum theorist: The curriculum field and social control.* Historical Studies within the Curriculum Field. Symposium conducted at the meeting of the American Educational Research Association, Washington, DC.
Fraser, N. (1989). *Unruly practices: Power, discourse, and gender in contemporary social theory.* Minneapolis: University of Minnesota Press.
Fraser, N., & Nicholson, L. J. (1990) Social criticism without philosophy: An encounter between feminism and postmodernism. In Linda Nicholson (Ed.), *Feminism/Postmodernism.* New York: Routledge, p. 21.

Frazier, R. R. (1926). The ideal principal, *Bulletin of the department of elementary school principals,* 5(4), pp. 205-6.
Fukuyama, F. (1992). *The end of history and the last man.* New York: The Free Press.
Fuller, S. (1988). *Social epistemology.* Bloomington: Indiana University Press.
Gadamer, Hans-Georg. (1985). *Truth and method.* New York: Crossroad.
Garrison, J. W., Parks, D. J., & Connelly, M. J. (1991). *Defining the "philosophical and cultural values" performance domain.* Report for The National Commission for the Principalship.
Gerth, H. H., & Mills, C. W. (eds). (1948). *From Max Weber.* London: Routledge and Kegan Paul.
Giddens, A. (1987). *Social theory and modern sociology.* Stanford, CA: Stanford University Press.
Gilligan, C. (1982). *In a different voice.* Cambridge, MA: Harvard University Press.
Giroux, H. A. (1983). *Theory and resistance in education: A pedagogy for the opposition.* Boston: Bergin & Garvey.
―――. (1988a). *Schooling and the struggle for public life.* Minneapolis: University of Minnesota Press.
―――. (1988b). *Teachers as intellectuals: Toward a critical pedagogy of learning.* New York: Bergin & Garvey.
Gitlin, A., Siegel, M., & Boru, K. (1988). The politics of method: From leftist ethnography to evaluative research. *International journal of qualitative studies in education* 2(3), pp. 235-253.
Glickman, C. D. (1990). School reform at the junction. *Educators forum.* 1(2), pp. 1-2.
Goodlad, J. I. (1984). *A place called school.* New York: McGraw-Hill.
Gordon, C. (1991). Governmental rationality: An introduction. In G. Burchell, C. Gordon & P. Miller (Eds.), C. Gordon (Trans.), *The Foucault effect: Studies in governmentality.* Chicago: University of Chicago Press, pp. 1-51.
Gordon, E. W., Miller, F., & Rollock, D. (1990). Coping with communicentric bias in knowledge production in the social sciences. *Educational researcher* 19(3), pp. 14-19.
Gouinlock, J. (1986). *Excellence in public discourse.* New York: Teachers College Press.
Greene, M. (1976). Challenging mystification: Educational foundations in dark times. *Educational studies,* 7, pp. 9-29.
―――. (1986). Reflection and passion in teaching. *Journal of curriculum and supervision,* 2(1), pp. 68-81.
Greenfield T. B. (1973). Organizations as social inventions: Rethinking assumptions about change. *Journal of applied behavioral sciences,* 9(5), pp. 551-74.
―――. (1975). Theory about organizations: A new perspective and its implications for the schools. In M. Hughes (Ed.). *Administering education: International challenge.* London: Athlone, pp. 71-99.
―――. (1978). Reflections on organization theory and the truths of irreconcilable realities. *Educational administration quarterly* 14(2), pp. 1-23.
―――. (1991). Re-forming and revaluing educational administration: Whence and when cometh the phoenix? *Organizational theory dialogue.* April, pp. 1-17.
Greenfield, W. (1987). *Instructional leadership.* Boston: Allyn and Bacon.
Griffiths, D. E. (1988). Administrative theory. In N. J. Boyan (Ed.), *Handbook of research on educational administration.* New York: Longman, pp. 27-51.

Gutting, G. (1989). *Michel Foucault's archaeology of scientific reason.* Cambridge: Cambridge University Press.

Habermas, J. (1971;1972). *Knowledge and human interest.* Boston: Beacon Press.

———. (1975). *Legitimation crisis.* Boston: Beacon Press.

———. (1979). *Communication and the evolution of society.* Boston: Beacon Press.

———. (1981). Modernity vs. postmodernity. *New German critique* 22, pp. 3–14.

———. (1987). In F. Lawrence (Trans.), *The philosophical discourse of modernity.* Cambridge, MA: MIT Press.

Hanson, E. M. (1979). *Educational administration and organizational behavior.* Boston: Allyn & Bacon.

Hansot, E., & Tyack, D. (1981). "The dream deferred: A Golden Age for women school administrators." Policy Paper No. 81-C2, May.

Haraway, D. (1988). Situated knowledges: The science question in feminism and the privilege of partial perspective. *Feminist studies* 14(3), pp. 575–99.

Harding, S. (1986). *The science question in feminism.* Ithaca, NY: Cornell University Press.

———. (1991). *Whose science? Whose knowledge?* Ithaca, NY: Cornell University Press.

Hawley, W. D. (1988). "Missing pieces of the educational reform agenda: Or why the first and second waves may miss the boat," *Educational administration quarterly* 24(4), pp. 416–37.

Hess, G. A., Jr. (1991). *School restructuring, Chicago style.* Newbury Park, CA: Sage.

Hess, M. (1978). Theory and value in the social sciences. In C. Hookway and P. Pettit (Eds.), *Action and interpretation: Studies in the philosophy of the social sciences.* Cambridge: Cambridge University Press, pp. 1–16.

———. (1980). *Revolutions and reconstructions in the philosophy of science.* Brighton, U.K.: The Harvester Press.

Holmes Group (1986). *Tomorrow's teachers.* East Lansing, MI: Holmes Group.

Horrigan, M. W., & Haugen, S. E. (1988). The declining middle-class thesis: A sensitivity analysis. *Monthly labor review* 111, pp. 3–43.

House, E. R. (1978). Evaluation as scientific management in U.S. school reform. *Comparative education review.* 22(3), pp. 388–401.

———. (1991). Realism in research. *Educational researcher* 20(6), pp. 2–9, 25.

Hoy, W. K., & Miskel, C. G. (1982). *Educational administration: Theory, research, and practice* (2nd ed.). New York: Random House.

Hutcheon, L. (1989). *The politics of postmodernism.* London: Routledge.

Huyssen, A. (1986). *After the great divide: Modernism, mass culture, postmodernism.* Bloomington: Indiana University Press.

Jacoby, H. (1973). *The bureaucratization of the world.* Berkeley: University of California Press.

James, L. R., James, L. A., & Ashe, D. K. (1990). The meaning of organizations: The role of cognition and values. In Benjamin Schneider (Ed.), *Organizational Climate and Culture.* San Francisco: Jossey-Bass, pp. 479–504.

Jameson, F. (1991). *Postmodernism, or, the cultural logic of late capitalism.* Durham, NC: Duke University Press.

Jauss, H. R. (1988-89). *Cultural critique,* 4(11), pp. 23–61.

Johnston, B. J. (1991). Narratives of empowerment in school restructuring. *Review journal of philosophy and social science.* 16(1, 2), pp. 43–58.

Joncich, G. (1968). *The sane positivist.* Middletown, CT: Wesleyan University Press.

Jones, J. A., & Rosenfeld, R. A. (1989). Women's occupations and local labor markets: 1950-1980. *Social forces* 67:666-92.

Kaufmann, W. (Ed.). (1969)."*On the genealogy of morals*" *by Friedrich Nietzsche.* New York: Random House.

Keller, E. F. (1985). *Reflections on gender and science.* New Haven, CT: Yale University Press.

Kellner, D. (1989). *Jean Baudrillard: From Marxism to postmodernism and beyond.* Stanford, CA: Stanford University Press.

Kerlinger, F. N. (1986). *Foundations of behavioral research* (3rd ed.). New York: Holt, Rinehart & Winston.

Kirst, M. W. (1988). Recent state education reform in the United States: Looking backward and forward. *Educational administration quarterly* 24(3), pp. 319-28.

Knezevich, S. J. (1984). *Administration of public education: A sourcebook for the leadership and management of educational institutions* (4th ed.). New York: Harper & Row.

Koestenbaum, P. (1991). *Leadership: The inner side of greatness.* San Francisco: Jossey-Bass.

Kroker, A., & Cook, D. (1986). *The postmodern scene.* New York: St. Martin's Press.

Kuhn, T. (1962). *The structures of scientific revolutions.* Chicago: University of Chicago Press.

———. (1970). *The structures of scientific revolutions* (2nd ed.). Chicago: University of Chicago Press.

Kutscher, R. E., & Personick, V. E. (1986). Deindustrialization and the shift to services. *Monthly labor review.* 109, pp. 3-13.

Kyle, W. C. (1980). Curriculum decisions: Who decides what. *The elementary school journal,* 81(2), pp. 77-85.

Lacan, J. (1977). In Alan Sheridan (Trans.), *Ecrits: A selection.* New York: W. W. Norton.

Langer, S. (1971). *Philosophy in a new key* (3rd ed.). Cambridge, MA: Harvard University Press.

Lather, P. (1986a). Issues of validity in openly ideological research: Between a rock and a soft place. *Interchange* 17(4), pp. 63-84.

———. (1986b). Research as praxis. *Harvard educational review* 56(2), pp. 257-77.

———. (1988). Feminist perspectives on empowering research methodologies. *Women's studies international forum* 11(6), pp. 569-81.

———. (1991a). Deconstructing/Deconstructive inquiry: The politics of knowing and being known. *Educational theory* 41 (2), pp. 24-35.

———. (1991b). *Getting smart: Feminist research and pedagogy with/in the postmodern.* New York: Routledge.

———. (in press). Critical frames in educational research: Feminist and poststructural perspectives. *Theory into practice.*

Latour, B., & Woolgar, S. (1979; 1986). *Laboratory life: The construction of scientific facts.* Princeton, NJ: Princeton University Press.

Levi-Strauss, C. (1964). *Le cru et le cuit, mythologiques.* Paris: Librairie Plon.

Levin, H. M. (1990). Economic trends shaping the future of teacher education, *Educational policy* 4(1), pp. 1-15.

Levine, A. (1980). *Why innovation fails.* Albany: State University of New York Press.
Lincoln, Y. S., & Guba, E. G. (1985). *Naturalistic inquiry.* Beverly Hills, CA: Sage Publications.
Lubiano, W. (1991). Shuckin' off the African-American native other: What's "po-mo" got to do with it? *Cultural critique* 20 (Winter), pp. 149–86.
Luke, C., and Gore, J., eds. (1992). *Feminisms and critical pedagogy.* New York: Routledge.
Lukes, S. (1974). *Power—A radical view.* London: Macmillan.
Lyotard, J. F. (1979; 1984). In G. Bennington and B. Massumi (Trans.), *The postmodern condition: A report on knowledge.* Minneapolis: University of Minnesota Press.
Major-Poetzl, P. (1983). *Michel Foucault's archaeology of western culture: Toward a new science of history.* Chapel Hill: University of North Carolina.
March, J. G., and Olsen, J. P. (1976). *Ambiguity and choice in organizations.* Bergen, Norway: Universitetsforlaget.
———. (1986). Garbage Can Models of Decision Making in Organizations. In James G. March and Roger Weissinger-Baylor (Eds.), *Ambiguity and command.* Marshfield, MA: Pitman Publishing, pp. 11–35.
March, J. G., & Simon, H. A. (1958). *Organizations.* New York: Wiley.
Marcuse, H. (1960). *Reason and revolution.* Boston: Beacon Press.
Martin, J. R. (1985). *Reclaiming a conversation: The ideal of the educated woman.* New Haven, CT: Yale University Press.
Martin, W. J., & Willower, D. J. (1981). The managerial behavior of high school principals. *Educational administration quarterly,* pp. 69–90.
Maxcy, S. J. (1991). *Educational leadership: A criticial pragmatic perspective.* New York: Bergin & Garvey.
Maxcy, S. J., Crow, G. M., Roy, S., & Cormier, S. (1992). Leadership as design in school restructuring. *International journal of educational management* 6(6), pp. 20–28.
Maxcy, S. J., & Maxcy, D. O. (1992). Design, leadership and higher education. In *Academic Profiles in Higher Education.* Ed. J. J. Van Patten. Lewiston, NY: Edwin Mellen Press, pp. 329–351.
May, W. T., & Zimpher, N. L. (1986). An examination of three theoretical perspectives on supervision: Perceptions of preservice field supervision. *Journal of curriculum and supervision* 1(2), pp. 83–99.
McCutcheon, G. (1980). How do elementary teachers plan? The nature of planning and influences on it. *Elementary school journal* 81, pp. 4–23.
———. (1981). Elementary school teacher's planning for social studies and other subjects. *Theory and research in social education* 9(1), pp. 45–66.
———. (1982). What in the world is curriculum theory? *Theory into practice* 21(1), pp. 18–25.
———. (1988). Curriculum and the work of teachers. In M. Apple & L. Beyer (Eds.). *The curriculum: Problems, politics and possibilities.* Albany: State University of New York Press.
McLaren, P. (1988). Schooling the postmodern body: Critical pedagogy and the politics of enfleshment. *Journal of education* 170(3), pp. 53–83.
McMahon, P. J., & Tschetter, J. H. (1986). The declining middle class: A further analysis. *Monthly labor review* 109, pp. 22–27.

McNeil, L. M. (1988). Contradictions of Reform. *Phi delta kappan* 69(5), pp. 478-85.
——. (1990). Reclaiming a voice: American curriculum scholars and the politics of what is taught in schools, *Phi delta kappan* 71(7), pp. 517-18.
Merquior, J. G. (1985). *Foucault.* Berkeley: University of California Press.
Michels, R. (1949). *Political parties.* Glencoe, IL: The Free Press.
Miller, D. L. (1973). *George Herbert Mead, self, language, and the world.* Chicago: University of Chicago Press.
Miller, J. H. (1989). In J. D. Culler (Ed.), *On deconstruction: Theory and criticism in the 1970s.* Ithaca, NY: Cornell University Press.
Minh-ha, T. T. (1989). *Woman native other.* Bloomington: Indiana University Press.
Miron, L. (1991, Fall). The dialectics of school leadership: Post structural implications (newsletter). *Organizational theory dialogue.* San Diego: University of San Diego.
Mishler, E. G. (1990). Validation in inquiry-guided research: The role of exemplars in narrative studies. *Harvard educational review* 60(4), pp. 415-41.
——. (1991). Representing discourse: The rhetoric of transcription. *Journal of narrative and life history* 1(4), pp. 255-80.
Morgan, G. (1986). *Images of organization.* Newbury Park, CA: Sage.
National Commission on Excellence in Education. (1983). *A nation at risk.* Washington, DC: U.S. Department of Education.
Neurath, O. (1962). *Foundations of the social sciences.* Chicago: University of Chicago Press.
Neville, R. C. (1992). *The highroad around modernism.* Albany: State University of New York Press.
Nicolaides, N., & Gaynor, A. (1989, December). *The knowledge base informing the teaching of administrative and organizational theory in UCEA universities: Empirical and interpretive perspectives.* Charlottesville, VA: The National Policy Board for Educational Administration.
Nielsen, J. M. (Ed.) (1990). Introduction. In *Feminist research methods: Exemplary readings in the social sciences.* Boulder, CO: Westview Press.
Noddings, N. (1984). *Caring: A feminine approach to ethics and moral education.* Berkeley: University of California Press.
Norris, C. (1987). *Derrida.* Cambridge, MA: Harvard University Press.
——. (1990). *What's wrong with postmodernism: Critical theory and the ends of philosophy.* Baltimore, MD: Johns Hopkins University Press.
Ortiz, F. I., & Marshall, C. (1988). Women in educational administration. In Norman J. Boyan (Ed.), *Handbook of research on educational administration: A project of the American Educational Research Association.* New York: Longman.
Pape, S. L. (1988). *Student teacher thinking: The development and content of practical theories.* Columbus, OH: Unpublished doctoral dissertation.
Perrow, C. (1970). *Organizational analysis: A sociological view.* Belmont, CA: Wadsworth Publishing.
Personick, V. A. (1987). Industry output and employment through the end of the century. *Monthly labor review* 110, pp. 30-45.
Peters, M. (1989). Techno-science, rationality, and the university: Lyotard on the postmodern condition. *Educational theory* 39(2), pp. 93-105.
Peters, T. J., & Waterman, R. H. (1982). *In search of excellence.* New York: Harper and Row.

Pettigrew, A. M. (1990). "Organizational climate and culture: Two constructs in search of a role." In Benjamin Schneider (Ed.), *Organizational climate and culture.* San Francisco: Jossey-Bass, pp. 413-33.

Phillips, D. C. (1983). After the wake: Postpositivistic educational thought. *Educational researcher* 12 (5), pp. 4-12.

Polanyi, M. (1958). *Personal knowledge.* Chicago: University of Chicago Press.

Polkinghorne, D. (1983). *Methodology for the human sciences: Systems of inquiry.* Albany: State University of New York Press.

Powers, D. R., & Powers, M. F. (1983). *Making participatory management work: Leadership of consultive decision making in academic administration.* San Francisco: Jossey-Bass.

Presseisen, B. Z. (1986). *Thinking skills: Research and practice.* Washington, DC: National Education Association.

Ratner, J. (1939). *John Dewey's philosophy.* New York: Random House.

Reed, M. (1992). Introduction. In M. Reed. & M. Hughes (Eds.), *Rethinking organization: New directions in organization theory and analysis.* Newbury Park, CA: Sage.

Reid, W. (1978). *Thinking about the curriculum.* London: Routledge & Kegan Paul.

———. (1979). Practical reasoning and curriculum theory: In search of a new paradigm. *Curriculum inquiry* 9(3), pp. 187-207.

Richardson, L. (1988). The collective story: Postmodernism and the writing of sociology. *Sociological focus* 21(3), pp. 199-208.

Rorty, R. (1979). *Philosophy and the mirror of nature.* Princeton, NJ: Princeton University Press.

———. (1982). *Consequences of pragmatism.* Minneapolis: University of Minnesota Press.

———. (1989). *Contingency, irony, and solidarity.* New York: Cambridge University Press.

———. (1991). Objectivity, relativism, and truth. *Philosophical papers.* Volume 1. Cambridge: Cambridge University Press.

Rosen, D. M. (1984). Leadership systems in world cultures. In B. Kellerman (Ed.), *Leadership: Multidisciplinary perspectives.* Englewood Cliffs, NJ: Prentice Hall, pp. 39-62.

Rouse, J. (1987). *Knowledge and power: Toward a political philosophy of science.* Ithaca, NY: Cornell University Press.

Rubin, G. (1975). "The traffic in women." In Rayna R. Reiter (Ed.), *Toward an anthropology of women.* New York: Monthly Review Press.

Rutter, M. (1979). *Fifteen thousand hours: Secondary school and their effects on children.* Cambridge, MA: Harvard University Press.

Sanders, D. P., & McCutcheon, G. (1986). The development of practical theories of teaching. *Journal of curriculum and supervision* 2(1), pp. 50-67.

Sarup, M. (1989). *An introductory guide to postmodernism and poststructuralism.* Athens: University of Georgia Press.

Saussure, F. (1916; 1966). *Course in general linguistics.* New York: McGraw-Hill.

Schein, E. H. (1985). *Organizational culture and leadership.* San Francisco: Jossey-Bass.

Scheurich, J. J., & Lather, P. (1991). Paradigmatic compulsions: A response to Hill's issues in research on instructional supervision. *Journal of curriculum and supervision* 7(1), pp. 26-30.

Schon, D. A. (1983). *The reflective practitioner.* New York: Basic Books.

Schubert, W. H. (1988, April). *Teacher lore: A basis for understanding praxis.* Paper presented at the meeting of the American Educational Research Association, New Orleans.

Senge, P. M. (1990). *The fifth discipline: The art and practice of the learning organization.* New York: Doubleday Currency.

Sergiovanni, T. J. (1984). Leadership as cultural expression. In T. J. Sergiovanni and J. E. Corbally (Eds.), *Leadership and organizational culture: New perspectives on administrative theory and practice.* Urbana: University of Illinois.

———. (1992). *Moral leadership.* San Francisco: Jossey-Bass.

Shakeshaft, C. (1989). *Women in educational administration* (updated ed.). Newbury Park, CA: Sage.

Shakeshaft, C., & Hanson, M. (1986). Androcentric bias in the educational administration quarterly. *Educational administration quarterly,* 22(1), pp. 68-92.

Shank, S. E. (1988). Women and the labor market: The link grows stronger. *Monthly labor review* 111, pp. 3-17.

Shor, I. (1986). *Culture wars: School and society in the conservative restoration 1969-1984.* Boston: Routledge and Kegan Paul.

Simon, H. A. (1947). *Administrative behavior.* New York: Macmillan.

———. (1955, February). "The behavioural model of rational choice." *Quarterly journal of economics* 69(1), pp. 99-118.

Smart, B. (1983). *Foucault, marxism and critique.* Boston: Routledge and Kegan Paul.

Smith, M. P. (1984). Cities in transformation: Class, capital, and the state. *Urban affairs annual review,* 26.

Smith, R. E., & Vavrichek, B. (1987). The minimum wage: Its relation to incomes and poverty. *Monthly labor review* 110, pp. 24-43.

Solomon, B. M. (1985). *In the company of educated women.* New Haven, CT: Yale University Press.

Spivak, G. C. (1967; 1976). Translator's preface. In J. Derrida, *Of grammatology.* Baltimore, MD: Johns Hopkins University Press.

———. (1988). *In other worlds: Essays in cultural politics.* New York: Routledge.

Spring, J. (1993). *Conflicts of interest: The politics of American education* (2d ed.). New York: Longman.

Stallings, J. (1980). Allocated academic learning. Time revisited, or beyond time on task. *Educational researcher* 9(11), pp. 11-16.

Stanfield, J. (1985). The ethnocentric basis of social science knowledge production. *Review of research in education* 12, pp. 287-415.

Stanley, W. (1991). *Curriculum for utopia.* Albany: State University of New York Press.

Staw, B. M. (1984). Motivation research versus the art of faculty management. In James L. Bess (Ed.), *College and university organization: Insights from the behavioral sciences.* New York: New York University Press, pp. 31-61.

Stone, C. N. (1989). *Regime politics: Governing Atlanta, 1946-1988.* Lawrence: University Press of Kansas.

Task Force on Education for Economic Growth. (1983). *Action for excellence.* Washington, DC: Education Commission of the States.

Taylor, C. (1989). *Sources of the self: The making of the modern identity.* Cambridge, MA: Harvard University Press.

Taylor, F. (1911). *The principles of scientific management.* New York: Harper.

Taylor, M. C. (1986). Introduction: System . . . structure . . . difference . . . other. In

M. C. Taylor (Ed.), *Deconstruction in context: Literature and philosophy.* Chicago: University of Chicago Press.
Taylor, W. D., & Johnsen, J. B. (1986). *On reducing teachers and students to components.* Unpublished manuscript.
Teddlie, C. (1984). *Louisiana school effectiveness study: Phase two, 1982-84.* Baton Rouge: Louisiana State Department of Education.
Tierney, W. G. (1987). Facts and constructs: Defining reality in higher education organizations. *The review of higher education* 11(1), pp. 61-73.
Toulmin, S. (1990). *Cosmopolis: The hidden agenda of modernity.* New York: The Free Press.
Turner, J. H., & Starnes, C. E. (1976). *Inequality: Privilege and poverty in America.* Pacific Palisades, CA: Goodyear Publishing.
Twentieth Century Fund. (1983). *Making the grade: Report of the Twentieth Century Fund Task force on federal elementary and secondary educational policy.* New York: The Twentieth Century Fund.
Tyack, D. (1974). *The one best system: A history of American urban education.* Cambridge, MA: Harvard University Press.
———. (1990). "Restructuring in historical perspectives: Tinkering toward utopia." *Teachers college record* 92(2), pp. 481-508.
University Council on Educational Administration, National Commission on Excellence in Educational Administration. (1987). *Leaders for America's schools: The report of the National Commission on Excellence in Educational Administration.* Tempe, AZ: University Council on Educational Administration.
University Council on Educational Administration, National Policy Board for Educational Administration. (1989). *Improving the preparation of school administrators: An agenda for reform.* Tempe, AZ: University Council on Educational Administration.
Van Manen, M. (1977). Linking ways of knowing with ways of being practical. *Curriculum inquiry* 6(3), pp. 205-28.
von Neuman, J., & Morgenstern, O. (1947). *Theory of games and economic behaviour.* Princeton, NJ: Princeton University Press.
Weick, K. E. (1976). Educational organizations as loosely coupled systems. *Administrative science quarterly* 21, pp. 1-19.
Weiler, K. (1988). *Women teaching for change: Gender, class & power.* New York: Bergin & Garvey.
Wells, H. L. (1953). *Higher education is serious business.* New York: Harper & Brothers.
West, C. (1989). *The American evasion of philosophy: A genealogy of pragmatism.* Madison: University of Wisconsin Press.
Wexler, P. (1987). *Social analysis of education: After the new sociology.* New York: Routledge and Kegan Paul.
Williamson, O. E. (1975). *Market and hierarchies: Analysis and anti-trust Implications.* New York: Free Press.
Willower, D. (1988). "Synthesis and projection." In Norman J. Boyan (Ed.), *Handbook of research on educational administration. Postmodern Educational Leadership and Beyond.* New York: Longman, pp. 729-47.
Wirth, A. G. (1983). *Productive work—In industry and schools.* New York: University Press of America.

Wise, A. E. (1979). *Legislated learning: The bureaucratization of the American classroom.* Berkeley: University of California Press.
Wise, A. (1988). "The Two Conflicting Trends in School Reform." *Phi delta kappan* 69(5), pp. 328-33.
Wolin, S. S. (1988). On the theory and practice of power. In J. Alao (Ed.), *After Foucault.* New Brunswick, NJ: Rutgers University Press.
Woody, T. (1929). *A history of women's education in the United States* (vol. 2). New York: The Science Press.
Wrong, D. H. (1979). *Power: Its forms, bases and uses.* Oxford: Basil Blackwell.
Yinger, R. J. (1977). Research on teacher thinking. *Curriculum inquiry* 7(4), pp. 279-304.
———. (1979). Routines in teacher planning. *Theory into practice* 28(3), pp. 163-69.
———. (1980). A study of teacher planning. *Elementary school journal* 80, pp. 107-25.
Yinger, R. J., & Clark, C. M. (1982). *Understanding teachers' judgements about instruction.* Eric Document (Ed. 228 194), pp. 1-40.
Young, R. (1990). *White mythologies: Writing history and the West.* London: Routledge.

Index

academy: consultative process in, 145–47; and G.I. bill, 142; as learning organization, 142, 144, 146–52; perception of change in, 142–43; women in, 55
accountability, versus responsibility, 106–8
accounting systems, in organizational community, 74–76
Action for Excellence, 71, 115
adaptive organization, 142–47
administrator training reforms, 2, 71–72, 116
Animal Intelligence, 79
Art as Experience, 98, 157
authority/domination concept, and nature of organizations, 128

Barthes, Roland, 5
Bates, Richard, 9
Baudrillard, Jean, 157, 158
Bentham, Jeremy, 11, 77
Bernstein, Richard, 9
Bobbitt, Franklin, 90
bricolage, 33, 44 n.25

Carnegie Task Force, 71, 115
Cassirer, Ernst, 5, 31

causation, conception of, 20
Cherryholmes, Cleo, 9, 65, 89, 136
competency based education, 80, 81
concept of solidarity (Rorty), 102, 105
credentialing programs, gender bias in, 51–52
criticism, educational, 98–99
cultural feminism, 48
curriculum: alignment, 81–82, 117; hidden, 86; postmodern, 92–94; and qualitative criticism, 99, 110; technical knowledge in, 93

Danforth Foundation, 71–72, 116
data, definition of, 36–38
decision making: bounded rationality model, 73; economic rationality models, 72–73; school-based management shared, 139
deconstruction, 8; and binary logic, 27–28; as essentialist critique, 49; and transcendent meaning, 65–66, 126
Derrida, Jacques, 8, 27, 65–66, 126
de Saussure, Ferdinand, 5, 8
Descartes, Rene, 3
Dewey, John, 9, 98, 156, 157
discourse: and discourse-practice, 88,

92-94, 96 n.25; and exercise of power, 128-29; and text, 65-68
doctoral programs, women's enrollment in, 55

Educational Administration Quarterly, androcentric bias in, 55
educational administration training, 2, 51, 62-64
Educational Imagination, The, 98
educational leadership: academic researchers in, 53-55; accountability of, 53-57; business sector in, 53; cultural conceptions of, 50-53; discourse, control of, 52-58; discrimination in, 50-52, 56; principal's role in, 134-35, 137-39; transformational models of, 138-39. *See also* Teacher(s)
educational practice: and administrative praxis, 106-7, 111; behavioral science approach in, 51, 62; discourse-practices in, 92-94; empowerment in, 12, 71, 128-31, 139; examinations and power in, 78-79; gender bias in, 11, 32; legitimacy and power in, 66-68; as moral practice, 91-94; outcomes-based, 92; performativity of process in, 87; policy domains in, 86; power/knowledge discourse in, 128-30; and problematic of education, 91-92; role of theory and research in, 62; scientific management in, 90-91, 134-36
Educational Psychology, 79
educational reform: of administrative leadership, 116-17, 138-39; of administrator training, 2, 71-72, 116; of curricula, 81-82, 117; and economic conditions, 115-16, 118-19; effective teaching rhetoric in, 115; first wave, 71, 79, 82, 115, 124; Panopticon model in, 11-12, 77-80; and school text, 129-31; second wave, 71, 82, 115-17, 124; site-based management model, 82-83; structuralist-functionalist, 115-16, 134-36; technocratic management models of, 80-81; third wave, 11, 71, 82-83, 116
educational research: aesthetic understanding in, 157; closed system in, 54-55; conventional science dominance in, 25, 38; effective schools, 72; and epistemology, choice of, 38-39; feminist, 11, 32, 38; and naive realism, 18-19, 40 n.7; qualitative versus quantitative, 127; scientific method in, 18; terminology in, 36-37
educational theory: essentialist approach to, 61-64; foundationalist base in, 62-64, 66; modernist, 2, 6, 61-68; postmodernist, 9-10, 61-68, 127-31; scientific management approach, 12, 13, 34-35, 80-82, 90-91; structuralist, 2, 6, 134-36; and Theory Movement, 1-2, 40 n.7, 43 n.18, 156
Eisner, Elliot, 98
Enlightenment ideals, 3, 117-18, 122; and feminism, 25-26; and postmodernism, 25-26, 76-77, 117-18; and poststructuralism, 23; of rational decision making, 74, 76; and relativism, criticism of, 25-26
epistemology, 17, 39 n.1; and ontology, 17, 39 n.2; and politics, 35-39; and positivism, 17-18; and truth game, 22-25, 42 n.17; value-free, 38-39
expert system analysis management model, 81

females, in education leadership, 55
feminism: cultural, 48; essentialist, 48-49; foundationalist, 25-26; postmodernist, 48-49; and social relativism, critique of, 25-29
Foster, William P., 9
Foucault, Michel, 5-6, 10, 11, 17, 21, 22, 41 n.11, 42 n.17, 65, 76-80, 136-37
foundationalism: feminist revision of, 25-26; foundationalism/relativism binary in, 26-27; revival of, 159; as strong objectivity, 27, 29
framework of solidarity (Rorty), 97
Frazier, Raymond, 50
functionalism, 4, 23

Gadamer, Hans-Georg, 8
garbage-can models of organizational management, 72-76

generalized other (Mead), 97, 104–6
Greenfield, Thomas B., 9, 153

Habermas, Jürgen, 4, 23, 125, 138
Handbook of Research in Educational Administration, 157
hermeneutics, 8, 9, 21
Holmes Group, 71, 116
humanism, and poststructuralism, 8
Hume, David, 20
Hunterism, 87

Kellogg Foundation, 51
Knowing Educational Administration, 20, 21
knowledge domain, versus recommending domain, 86
knowledge production: legitimation, 122–24; as political process, 30, 44 n.23; and positionality, 21–22, 41 n.10; and power, 23, 41 n.11, 128–29, 136–37; socially constructed, 136–37
Kuhn, Thomas, 8, 32

Lacan, Jacques, 5
language game(s): of educational reform, 129; in school setting, 137; of science, 122–23; technical, 12, 89–90, 92; theory of (Lyotard), 89–90
learning organization: consultive process in, 145–47; double-loop learning behavior in, 148–49; governing values in, 147–48; negotiating change in, 150–51; prosocial activity in, 145
Levi-Strauss, Claude, 5, 8, 88
Lyotard, Jean-François, 7, 80, 89–90, 122, 125

McNamera, Robert, 81, 82
Mead, George Herbert, 12, 97, 102–3
meaning, in discourse-practices of schooling, 93
metanarrative, 88–89, 123
Mill, John Stuart, 20
modernism, 3–6, 7, 76; discourse in, 64–66; postmodern analysis of, 64–68; and technical-rationality, 119–21
modernization, concept of, 4

moral practice, and educational practice, 13, 91–94

naive realism: and causation, 19–20; criticism of, 18–21; and theory movement, 40 n.7
narrative: and legitimation, 122–23; and metanarrative, 88–89, 123; school, 129–31; totalizing, 126
National Education Association (NEA), 50
Nation at Risk, A, 49, 71, 115
Naturalistic Inquiry, 100
naturalistic inquiry, axioms of, 100–102, 106–7
Neurath, Otto, 40 n.5
Nietzsche, Friedrich Wilhelm, 21, 42 n.13, 77
Northwestern University, 142

ontology, and epistemology, 17, 39 n.2
organization(s): language view of, 88; life cycle stages of, 144–45; power as authority/domination in, 128; as social agency, 87
organizational management: adaptive approach to, 146; garbage-can models of, 72–76; interpretive strategies, 146–47; linear strategic approach to, 146; prosocial activity in, 145; systems of accounting, 74–75
output oriented educational legislation, 81

Panopticon model, 11–12, 77–80
performance-based education, 81
performativity of procedures, and legitimation, 87, 89–90
Phenix, Philip, 92–93
pluralism theory, 108–9
positionality, and relativity, 21–23, 41 n.10
positivism: as enhancement of democracy, 40 n.5; epistemological position of, 17–18, 120; failure of, 17–18, 40 n.4; and theory movement, 40 n.7; as value free, 23
postfoundationalism, 30–31
postmodernism, 3–4, 6–8, 9–13, 121–22, 153–54, 162; and feminism, 47–59;

fragmentation of, 160–61; linguistic scientism as, 162; as methodology for criticism, 65; as neo-Romanticism, 159–60; as neostructuralism, 161; postpositivist contributions to, 122–24; poststructural contributions to, 124; power and agency concepts in, 125–26; social and intellectual context of, 117–18; textualism in, 126
postmodernist relativism. *See* social relativism
postpositivism, 122–24
poststructuralism, 6–10; and concept of totality, 88; power and structure in, 136–38; and structuralism, 4–5, 88–89; and Symbolic Order, 124, 126; as truth game, 23
power: and action, 134, 137–38; and discourse, 124, 128–29; and knowledge, 23, 41 n.11, 81, 128–29, 136–37; and language games, 125, 136, 137; and legitimacy, 66–68; moral use of, 129–30, 138; and structure, 136–38; and tests and examinations, 78–79. *See also* empowerment
Power and Criticism, 9
practical theories of teaching, 110–11
praxis, and qualitative criticism, 106–7, 111
principal, school, 134–35, 137–39
Principles of Scientific Management, The, 80
problematic of education, 91–92, 95 n.30
professors, as privileged class, 65
public school(s): administrator, transformative role of, 13, 130–31, 137–39; boards, 56, 139; loose coupling in, 73; as organized anarchy, 72–76; power hierarchy in, 24–25; principal in, 134–35, 137–39; restructuring, and economic competitiveness, 71, 115–19, 127; school site management in, 139; school story in, 130–31; student empowerment in, 56, 139; tight coupling in, 135; value domains in, 85–86, 158. *See also* Teacher(s)

qualitative criticism, 97–100; and community standards, establishment of, 103–6; critic role in, 101; data gathering in, 100–102; and naturalistic inquiry, 100–102, 106–7; solidarity framework for, 102–6; and teacher planning, 110

rational decision making, 72–76, 116–17, 119–20
rationality procedures, 30–32, 44 n.23
realism. *See* naive realism; scientific realism
reality, social construction of, 27, 43 nn.20, 21
reification of concepts, 67, 68
relativism: foundationalism/relativism binary, 26–27; "might makes right" in, 23–25, 44 n.23; modernist definition of, 28; self-refuting character of, 42 n.14
responsibility, versus accountability, 106–8
Rivlin, Alice, 81
Rorty, Richard, 9, 12, 18, 45 n.28, 102, 105, 111
Russell, Bertrand, 20

school suffrage, and suffrage movement, 56
schools. *See* public schools
scientific management, in educational practice, 2, 12, 13, 80–82, 90–91, 134–35
scientific realism: and causation, 20; coherency standards in, 33–34; theoretical mediation in, 19; and truth games, 35–36
self: Mead's social idea of, 102–5; postmodern conceptions of, 155–56
semiology, 5, 8
sex discrimination, in public education, 50
shared exemplars concept, 32–33
Simon, Herbert, 51, 73
site-based management, 82–83
social interaction framework (Mead), 102–5
social relativism, 10, 21–23; and critique of scientific realism, 33–35; and emancipatory concerns, 25–26; feminist

critique of, 25–29; "might makes right" criticism of, 23–25; postfoundational alternatives to, 29–33; and truth games, 22–25, 28–29
social sciences: political nature of, 162; presiding exemplars in, 32–33; gender-biased research in, 51; historical positionality of, 21–22; language game in, 122–23
solidarity, Rorty's conception of, 97, 102, 105–7, 111
strong objectivity, as foundationalism, 27–29
structuralism: educational application of, 2, 6, 90–91; group as social agency in, 87; history of, 5–6; human agency in, 87, 91, 129; myth in, 5–6; narrative and metanarrative in, 5, 88–89; and structural linguistics, 88; techno-language of, 12, 89–90; and transformative purposes, 124
student empowerment, 56, 139
symbolic interaction theory (Mead), 102–4
synnoetics, 12, 93–94
synoptics, 12, 93–94

Taylor, Frederick, 12, 71, 80, 125
teacher(s): accountability, 80, 115; and effective teaching rhetoric, 81, 115, 135; empowerment, 71, 128, 129, 139; evaluation, and approved behaviors, 81; planning, and qualitative criticism, 110; and practical theories of teaching, 110–11; and school story, 129–31; and transformative administration, 130–31

technical language game, 90, 92
technical-rationalism, 119–21, 129
technocratic education, 12, 80–82, 115
terminology, contextual relativity of, 36–37
tests and examinations: as exercise of power, 78–79; language-based, 109; as measure of accountability, 82, 115
text: in modernist perspective, 65–66; in postmodernism, 126–27
Theory Movement, 2, 40 n.7, 43 n.18, 156
Thorndike, E. L., 12, 79
time-motion studies (Taylor), 80
time on task, 135
Title IX, 55
top down management, 100, 109–10, 115, 150
totality, concept of, 88
transformational model of leadership, 13, 130–31, 137–39
truth games: as politics, 38–39; and positionality, 21–22, 28–29; poststructuralism as, 23; as power, 22–25; and scientific realism, 35–36; in social sciences, 22–23

Unified Science movement, 40 n.5
University Council on Educational Administration (UCEA), 41, 71–72, 116

value domains, in public schools, 85–86, 158

Weber, Max, 4
Wells, Harry L., 142, 144, 146, 151

Contributors

JACKIE M. BLOUNT is Assistant Professor at Iowa State University, Ames, Iowa, in the Department of Curriculum and Instruction in the College of Education. She teaches in the area of Educational Foundations.

BARBARA CURRY is Assistant Professor of Education at the University of Delaware in Newark, Delaware. Her field of specialization is Higher Education Administration.

JON S. DAVIES is Assistant Professor of Education at Hofstra University in Hempstead, New York. He received his doctorate from the University of San Diego. His research interests focus on leadership and school reform.

RICHARD J. ELLIOTT is Professor of Educational Foundations in the Department of Educational Leadership and Foundations at the University of New Orleans. His research and writing on Phenomenology and Existentialism as applied to educational research and administration stretches over nearly three decades.

CHARLES J. FAZZARO is Associate Professor of Education in the Department of Educational Studies at the University of Missouri–St. Louis. His undergraduate preparation was in the fields of physics and mathematics, and he holds the doctorate in Educational Administration. Dr. Fazzaro's research emphasis has been on the work of Michel Foucault as it may be applied to questions in educational administration.

WILLIAM FOSTER is Professor of Educational Administration at Indiana University in Bloomington, Indiana. His book *Paradigms and Promises* (1986) has had wide-ranging impact on the postmodern/poststructural reform of education in the United States.

JAMES W. GARRISON is Professor of Education in the College of Education at Virginia Polytechnic Institute and State University, Blacksburg, Virginia. Dr. Garrison is widely published in the areas of philosophy of science and education. He has a special interest in the area of educational administration and governance.

BILL J. JOHNSTON of the University of North Carolina at Wilmington has the position of Associate Professor of Educational Administration. He is recognized as an outstanding young scholar in the field of Sociology of Education.

SPENCER J. MAXCY is Professor of Education in the Department of Administrative and Foundational Services, Louisiana State University, Baton Rouge, Louisiana. He has authored *Educational Leadership: A Critical Pragmatic Perspective* (Bergin & Garvey, 1991), and numerous articles and book chapters dealing with education and leadership.

K. KELLY McKERROW is Assistant Professor of Education at the University of Missouri–St. Louis. He has published in the field of Educational Leadership and teaches in the Department of Educational Studies.

JOSEPH R. McKINNEY is Assistant Professor of Education in the Department of Educational Leadership at Ball State University in Muncie, Indiana. He has been a frequent collaborator in publishing ventures with Dr. James Garrison of Virginia Tech.

LOUIS F. MIRON is Associate Professor of Educational Leadership in the Department of Educational Leadership and Foundations at the University of New Orleans. Dr. Miron has been active in social reform and is an expert on urban school policy.

JAMES JOSEPH SCHEURICH is Assistant Professor of Educational Administration at the University of Texas at Austin. Dr. Scheurich has been active as a grants-person and has an interest in the knowledge bases of educational leadership.

JAMES D. SWARTZ is an Assistant Professor in the Department of Educational Technology at the University of Arkansas, Fayetteville, Arkansas. His writings focus on techology and culture.

JAMES E. WALTER is an Associate Professor of Education in the Department of Educational Studies at the University of Missouri–St. Louis. He has published in the area of Educational Leadership.